Cinema Verite in America

The MIT Press
Cambridge, Massachusetts, and London, England

Cinema Verite in America:
Studies in Uncontrolled Documentary

Stephen Mamber

This book was set in Claro Light
by University Graphics, Inc.,
printed on Decision Offset
and bound in G.S.B. Silver Grey
by The Maple Press Company
in the United States of America.

Library of Congress Cataloging in Publication Data

Mamber, Stephen.
  Cinema verite in America.

  Bibliography: p.
  1. Moving-pictures—United States. I. Title.
PN1993.5.U6M24   791.43'53   73-13706
ISBN 0-262-13092-0

Contents

Contents

Acknowledgments

I wish to express most grateful appreciation to Howard Suber for his encouragement and friendship at all stages of my work and for offering many valuable suggestions. Arthur Knight, Colin Young, Mary Kiersch, Diana Dreiman, Hubert Smith, Robert Mundy, and Richard Hawkins also offered helpful assistance. Of course, I am particularly indebted to Robert Drew, Richard Leacock, D. A. Pennebaker, David and Albert Maysles, Frederick Wiseman, and many of their associates too numerous to list here by name for so patiently tolerating my many hours in their offices, graciously answering my questions, screening films, and assisting with film credits and photos. Without their cooperation, this book would not have been possible.

The University Film Association awarded me a scholarship during the middle stages of this study, and I continue to be grateful for that timely aid. I would also like to thank Jan Kerwin for her first-rate typing. I owe a debt as well to James Blue and Louis Marcorelles, whose early writings and interviews did much to stimulate my interest in this subject.

This book is dedicated with love to my parents.

Stephen Mamber

Cinema Verite in America

Cinema Verite: Definitions and Background

At its very simplest, cinema verite might be defined as a filming method employing hand-held cameras and live, synchronous sound. This description is incomplete, however, in that it emphasizes technology at the expense of filmmaking philosophy. Beyond recording means, cinema verite indicates a position the filmmaker takes in regard to the world he films.

The term has been debased through loose critical usage, and the necessary distinction between cinema-verite films and cinema-verite techniques is often lost. The techniques are surely applicable in many filming situations, but our exclusive concern here is for cinema-verite documentaries, as will become clear through further definition. Even granting the many film types within the cinema-verite spectrum (where, for instance, most Warhol films would be placed), it is still possible to speak of cinema verite as an approach divorced from fictional elements. The influence of fictional devices upon cinema-verite documentaries is an important issue, but the two can be spoken of as separate entities.

Cinema verite in many forms has been practiced throughout the world, most notably in America, France, and Canada. The term first gained popular currency in the early sixties as a description of Jean Rouch's *Chronique d'un Eté.* To embrace the disparate output of Rouch, Marker, Ruspoli, Perrault, Brault, Koenig, Kroitor, Jersey, Leacock, and all the others under one banner is to obscure the wide variance in outlook and method that separates American cinema verite from the French or Canadian variety and further to fail to take into account differences within the work of one country or even one filmmaker. Just as Rouch and Marker have distinct approaches, the Marker of *Lettre de Sibérie* is not the Marker of *Le Joli Mai.*

Because cinema verite in all its forms is so varied, we shall concentrate on one relatively distinct branch. The work of Americans Robert Drew, Richard Leacock, D. A. Pennebaker, the Maysles Brothers, and Frederick Wiseman presents a sufficiently consistent filmmaking philosophy to allow for independent discussion.

Happily, for critical purposes, enough diversity is also present to allow exploration of a range of responses to key cinema-verite questions. But in all ensuing discussion, it should be clear that *cinema verite* is being employed under deliberately arbitrary circumstances, more in the context of what the American outlook expresses and as I envision a certain ideal for this kind of filming than as a universally applicable term.

The problem is further confused by terminology. *Cinema verite* is a pretentious label that few filmmakers and critics have much use for. In America, and to some extent in France, the term *direct cinema* is preferred, although that too with some reservation. I prefer the French designation if only for its now traditional association with the nonfiction film. Any use of *direct cinema* in the chapters that follow is intended to be synonymous. Most important, cinema verite is not to be translated literally, for claims to higher truth by proponents of these films will not concern us.

The essential element in cinema verite is the act of filming real people in uncontrolled situations. *Uncontrolled* means that the filmmaker does not function as a "director" nor, for that matter, as a screenwriter. In a cinema-verite film, no one is told what to say or how to act. A prepared script, however skimpy, is not permissible, nor are verbal suggestions, gestures, or any form of direct communication from the filmmaker to his subject. The filmmaker should in no way indicate that any action is preferred by him over any other. The filmmaker acts as an observer, attempting not to alter the situations he witnesses any more than he must simply by being there (along with, usually, another person recording sound). Cinema verite has a faith in the spontaneous; the unwillingness to assert control goes so far as to refuse to recreate events, to have people repeat actions for the sake of being filmed. Interviews are also not employed, since their use, in effect, is a form of directed behavior.

The meaning of the term *real people* develops from the commitment to uncontrolled shooting. *Real* indicates not only avoiding the use of professional actors (unless, of course, we see them as actors) but also not placing nonactors into roles selected by the filmmaker, even to "play" themselves. Cinema verite asks nothing of people beyond their permission to be filmed.

The need for portable equipment is a result of the desire to shoot in uncontrolled situations. Instead of having people come to the camera, the camera goes to them. The filmmaker must be free to follow action without dominating it through sheer mechanical presence. Tripods, heavy lights, cables, and the rest of the paraphernalia of studio shooting are eliminated. The filmmaker is a reporter with a camera instead of a notebook.

Editing of footage shot in this fashion attempts to re-create events as the filmmaker witnessed them. An outcome of the cinema-verite approach is that it integrates the filmmaking process: selecting a subject, filming it, and editing the raw footage become continuous steps in a single effort and not discretely assignable tasks. The connection between the uncontrolled event and the finished film is enforced by the filmmaker's functioning as his own editor. The footage shot can then be judged while editing as much by what is missing as by what is present. The idea is that the film will not contradict the events themselves through an ordering of shots, juxtaposition of sequences, or use of other manipulative devices at variance with the filmmaker's own response as an actual witness. When editing is viewed as an independent function, left to people who did not participate in the filming, a whole new set of priorities and biases, based solely on the footage, can conflict with the commitment not to distort the event itself.

Editing, of course, is a selective process and inevitably implies at least some shaping of the material. Use of the word *re-create* allows for a variety of responses in editing, and a cinema-verite film does bear the selective influence of its creator. However, the respect in shooting for noninterference carries over as the determining force in the form of the final film. Even though reality is filtered through one sensibility, the filmmaker tries not to shape his material on the basis of limiting preconceptions.

In line with this commitment, some of the standard devices of fiction film and traditional documentaries fall by the wayside, especially music and narration. The former is never added (one of the few generalities about these films that nearly always applies), and the latter, if necessary at all, should do no more than provide facts essential to following events on the screen. Whatever the filmmaker's initial interest in the subject, the final film does not try to make the material seem as if it was included for the purpose of proving one specific point. The lack of "mood" music and guiding narration are part of a general outlook that does not try to push the viewer in one direction and one direction only. Room is left for responses as individual and complex as the situation itself.

Cinema verite as we are speaking of it, then, is an attempt to strip away the accumulated conventions of traditional cinema in the hope of rediscovering a reality that eludes other forms of filmmaking and reporting. Cinema verite is a strict discipline only because it is in many ways so simple, so "direct." The filmmaker attempts to eliminate as much as possible the barriers between subject and audience. These barriers are technical (large crews, studio sets, tripod-mounted equipment, special lights, costumes, and makeup), procedural (scripting, acting, directing), and structural (standard editing devices, traditional forms of melodrama, suspense, etc.). Cinema verite is a practical working method based upon a faith in unmanipulated reality, a refusal to tamper with life as it presents itself. Any kind of cinema is a process of selection, but there is (or should be) all the difference in the world between the cinema-verite aesthetic and the methods of fictional and traditional documentary film.

Unfortunately, some writers have claimed that cinema verite practically makes other film methods obsolete.[1] We should view such claims in a dialectical spirit, for while this kind of filming questions many assumptions of fiction films (as well as providing fiction filming with new devices to exploit), it will certainly never displace fiction film any more than photography has replaced

painting. Still, cinema verite is more than a mutant offspring of
documentary techniques. It deserves a place of its own as an
alternative kind of cinema—neither documentary (as usually practiced) nor fiction (though often telling a story). Its relative newness (primarily due to the recent development of the necessary
equipment) does not necessarily mean it is the wave of the future
that will drown all past efforts. Nevertheless, it must be reckoned
with as an extension of the present limits of cinema, an independent form raising its own critical questions.

Cinema verite did not sprout full-grown in the early sixties. A
broad historical approach could locate traces of similar concerns
from the beginnings of cinema, and such an approach would
give the misleading impression that cinema verite is the culmina-
tion of a sixty-year search for a new cinematic form. However,
the supposed influences generally depart from cinema verite in
crucial areas, and the links are often rather tenuous. Instead of
undertaking this sort of comparative survey in this chapter, we
shall explore the work of selected filmmakers and theoreticians
who anticipate key cinema-verite concerns. This will be done primarily to discuss ideas still relevant to cinema-verite practices today, not to provide a full examination of cinema-verite prehistory.

Dziga Vertov
The writings of Dziga Vertov, the Russian filmmaker and theoreti-
cian, are replete with statements that reflect a deep awareness of
issues related to cinema verite. Vertov coined the term *Kino-Pravda,* which was applied to a series of 23 films he made between
1922 and 1925, each organized around a specific theme or
idea.[2] Georges Sadoul claims that his translation of *Kino-Pravda*
into *Cinéma Vérité* in his 1948 *Histoire du Cinéma* is the first use
of the term.[3] The origin of the label, however, is not so important
as what it has come to mean. The Kino-Pravda of Vertov is not
the cinema verite of the sixties. It anticipates many key ideas of
modern cinema verite, but no more than that is claimed here.

In the strongest possible terms, Vertov denounced all forms of theatrical, fictional cinema, calling for an end to the dependence of cinema upon literature, drama, and music, in other words, the characteristics of nearly all films made to that point[4] (and, I might add, most since then). He wrote of his cinema as being a branch of science[5] and of each film as an experiment.[6] He set for himself and his fellow filmmakers this task: "To combine science with cinematic depiction in the struggle to reveal truth . . . to decipher reality."[7] With characteristic boldness, Vertov spoke of the goal of "observing and recording *life as it is* (italics in original)."[8]

Vertov insisted upon exploring the real world and the actual objects in it. He wrote, "If a fake apple and a real apple are filmed so that one cannot be distinguished from the other on the screen, this is not ability, but incompetence—inability to photograph. The real apple has to be filmed in such a way that no counterfeit can be possible. . . ."[9] He was also opposed to the use of actors, except when they are presented as real people in a film that attempts to study the relationship between their feelings and the roles they must play.[10] An idea quite common in cinema verite was expressed in 1929 by a Russian writer describing Vertov's method: "The director ordinarily *invents* the plot for the scenario—Dziga Vertov *detects* it. He does not, with the aid of authors, actors, and scenery-carpenters, build an illusion of life; he thrusts the lens of his camera straight into the crowded centers of life (italics in original)."[11]

These sentiments are commendable but now seem somewhat platitudinous. Vertov's most important contribution was his realization of the crucial role of editing. He wrote that each "Kino-Eye" film (a name he applied to a broad part of his work[12]) "is in the act of being edited from the moment the subject is chosen until the finished film comes out, that is to say, it is being edited during the whole film-making process."[13] In a fitting metaphor, Vertov saw the bits of film as bricks. With these bricks, he said, one could build a chimney, the wall of a fort, or many other things. And just as good bricks are needed to build a house, in order to make good films one needs good bits of filmed material.[14] He also recognized that there was no one truth, that editing could serve to support any truths (or lies) that one wished.[15]

Vertov even went so far as to note three key "periods" in the filmmaking process and the different activities during each: the selection of the subject and the period after it is chosen when a shooting plan is developed, the period of shooting itself (which he realized was a selective period), and the "central editing" period when the film is assembled.[16] Although he saw each of these periods in a very different light from the cinema-verite goals discussed earlier, the recognition of these steps as closely related parts of a continuous process was, and is, very important.

Vertov was not opposed to scripts or some kind of scenario, reluctantly feeling that they were necessary in order that there be "a continuity and correspondence of scenes to result in an irresistible movement forward."[17] He does, though, speak of making the script as brief and condensed as possible. Interestingly, he said that the cameramen themselves should try to set up preliminary schemes, but since not every cameraman may be sufficiently knowledgeable about his subject, they should be assisted by "specialists," that is, scenario writers, who would work "arm in arm with the cameramen."[18] With admirable tentativeness, he admitted that his thoughts on this matter were not very clear, and he invited further dialogue. In an empirical spirit that is very much a part of cinema verite, he asked only that his idea of the small scenario be tried, as "practice is the criterion of truth."[19]

Almost as important as Vertov's idea of editing was his recognition of the importance of sound and, even more crucial, the need for synchronous sound.[20] Along with his "Kino-Eye" theory he developed the "Radio-Ear," and he considered the two inseparable.[21] This was another outstanding observation on his part, for cinema verite as we speak of it has come about only since the need for synch sound was again realized and the technical battle was won. Vertov's recognition of the technical goals went even further, for he spoke of the need for a camera that could go anywhere under all conditions. He wanted the "Kino-Eye" to be as mobile as the human eye.[22] As happened with sound, we will see how filmmakers forty years later came to discover the same need.

Vertov also suggests yet another important cinema-verite concept—that it tries to capture life as it happens and is not a re-enactment of past events. He brings this up in the context of a discussion of the "Kino-Eye" as a means to study the lives of individual people, an idea at the very heart of the films we will be talking about:

I do not write on paper, but on film. . . . Many writers took their heroes from real life. For instance, *Anna Karenina* was based on the life of one of Pushkin's daughters. I thought about recording on film the history of Marya Demchenko from the life of Marya Demchenko. The difference was that I could not write on film events that had already occurred. I can only write simultaneously as the events are occurring. I cannot write about the meeting of the Komsomol after it has taken place. And I cannot, like some correspondents, write an article on events, on spectacles, on carnivals several days after they have taken place. I do not demand that the cameraman be at the scene of a fire two hours before it breaks out. But I cannot permit that he go to film a fire a week after the fire has gone out. . . .
Now I am working on films about the Woman. . . . They will be about a schoolgirl, about a girl at home, about a mother and a child . . . [and so on through ten or more examples].
I will also write about specific people, living and working. . . . I will film the development of man from diapers to old age. . . . The endless process of taking creative notes on film. The endless process of observation with camera in hand.[23]

The final entries on the bulging credit side of Vertov's ledger relate closely to a key cinema-verite issue—camera awareness. In speaking of the filming of Vertov's *The Man With a Movie Camera,* Sadoul says: "They chose people who were sufficiently absorbed in some spectacle or violent emotion so that they would forget the presence of a camera."[24] Sadoul also speaks of their filming at a party filled with drinking and jazz, where those being filmed became more used to the presence of the cameras as the

evening wore on (as a result of both their increased ease in front
of the equipment and the effects of the dancing and alcohol)
until they were behaving in the same manner as if they were not
being filmed. Sadoul compares this to Richard Leacock's ideas
on needing the confidence of the subject for this kind of filming.[25]
    In this section, I have selected only those aspects of Vertovian
thought that correspond to present cinema-verite ideas. A detailed
account of the substantial differences between Vertov and
cinema verite will not be rendered, but it should be emphasized
that an equally lengthy outline of these aspects is possible.
Vertov's interest in hidden camera and telephoto and infrared
lenses, his use of slow and fast motion, his extensive preplanning
of filming according to a particular theme, and especially his
emphasis on strong editing control in many ways correspond
more closely to other forms of documentary than to cinema
verite. Still, he was phenomenally prescient in this area, even if
the direct path of influence goes off in a different direction.

Robert Flaherty

Robert Flaherty, like Vertov, is not strictly a precursor of cinema
verite, but again he prefigures important central elements. Also,
the links between Flaherty (who was American by birth, though
he traveled extensively) and American cinema verite are more
clearly established, primarily through Richard Leacock's association with Flaherty during the making of *Louisiana Story.*
    The term that has come to be associated with Flaherty's method
is "non-preconception," through its use by Mrs. Flaherty in lectures and writings about her husband.[26] To quote her: "Non-preconception, a method of discovery as a process of film-making,
was Robert Flaherty's contribution to the motion picture. From
that method everything there is in his films flows."[27] The difference
between what the word itself suggests and what Mrs. Flaherty
means by it is somewhat misleading. Nonpreconception, I would
think, should imply an idea no more complicated than the absence of preformed opinions, biases, or attitudes concerning the

subject to be filmed. As such, it is a method very much in keeping with cinema verite. But Mrs. Flaherty uses the term in another way, to differentiate between the purpose her husband had in making documentaries and the goals of the English documentary school and also Hollywood films. Films like John Grierson's, she says, "have been preconceived for political purposes, for propaganda," while, to her, Hollywood "preconceives" its films "for the box office."[28] Robert Flaherty's films, however, "do not argue. . . . What they celebrate, freely and spontaneously, simply and purely, is the thing itself for its own sake."[29] Nonpreconception, then, is used as a term to describe goals rather than methods.

The problem of terminology aside, Mrs. Flaherty does have a point. Flaherty's films are different from Grierson's and Hollywood's. And, as I hope will become clear, cinema verite has strong affinities with Flaherty's way of making films.

The major Flaherty contribution, in terms of cinema verite, begins with his interest in studying real people in their actual surroundings. Beginning with his 1922 *Nanook of the North*, he made films that explored cultures through the activities of a small number of people. In effect, Flaherty found stories about individuals that served as means to structure his films in a way that would show what he felt to be important about the people (in a cultural sense) he was observing. (Said Flaherty on this point: "A story must come out of the life of a people, not from the actions of individuals.")[30] And, quite significantly, the films only took shape in the arduous process of shooting and editing, out of observation of life as it presents itself and not as the result of a prepared script. (". . . You cannot superimpose studio-fabricated plots on an actual setting without finding that the reality of the background will show up the artificiality of the story.")[31]

The Flaherty method of filmmaking was as intuitive as it was complex. A fascinating analogy between Flaherty's work and certain Eskimo attitudes reveals a concept very much akin to cinema verite. Basically (although the passage this is quoted from should be read in full), the idea is that the form of an object is an expression of its purpose. The carver of ivory, for example, seeks to bring out that which is already hidden within the unworked piece. Through a "ritual of discovery," turning it in his hand this way and that, carving aimlessly if the result is not immediately apparent, he finds, say, a seal within the ivory. "Then he brings it out; seal, hidden, emerges. It was always there: he didn't create it; he released it; he helped it step forth." Or, a found piece of an antler is examined, as always, only in terms of its intended use: "Form and function, revealed together, are inseparable. Add a few dots or tiny rings or just incisions, rhythmically arranged to bring out the form, and it's finished."[32] According to Arthur Calder-Marshall, "This attitude is implicit in all Flaherty's work, though he never stated it more fully than 'First I was an explorer; then I was an artist.'"[33]

In terms of his method, this "ritual of discovery" meant shooting a tremendous amount of footage, often with no idea of how it was to be used in the finished film. (In *Louisiana Story*, for example, 200,000 feet of material was shot to make an 8,000-foot film,[34] a 25 to 1 ratio.) Calder-Marshall notes elsewhere in his book that the end of a Flaherty film usually came only when the money ran out.[35] In reference to *Nanook of the North*, he says, "Perhaps if he had been given an annuity by Revillon Frères (sponsors of the film), he might have gone on shooting in Hudson Bay until he died, because the camera eye had become to him more perceptible than his own."[36] If nonpreconception is to be taken as a working method, this is its basis in Flaherty's work —the notion that filming should flow from the filmmaker's boundless interest in his subject and that shooting should not be overly selective.

This kind of shooting, of course, places a great burden on editing. The idea that the camera eye is more perceptive than the human eye is a bold concept and one that, if accepted, must call into question the nature of the editing process itself. Richard

Griffith places even stronger emphasis on this point than Calder-Marshall, connecting this view of the camera eye and Flaherty's shooting methods as follows:

He was the first film director to understand that the eye of the camera does not behave like the human eye, which selects from a field of vision only what interests its owner. The camera's eye unselectively records everything before it. . . . Robert Flaherty trust[ed] the camera before himself. He wanted what the camera's eye could show that his own eye could not see. Because of this, he shot everything, and only afterward, in the projection room, did he really "make" his films, looking at all he photographed again and again until the underlying pattern emerged for him. His was first of all an art of observation and afterward of selection.[37]

It becomes a simple but important matter then (though neither Calder-Marshall nor Griffith do it) to connect the faith in the camera eye as a superior recording instrument and the influence of Eskimo attitudes on Flaherty. The connection comes about because of what, I believe, the actual advantage of the camera is (which is not the advantage Calder-Marshall and Griffith see), the opportunity for repeating the event as many times as necessary to assist in the "ritual of discovery." It is because repeated projection can yield new facets of reality that editing could be a creative process for Flaherty. It is a step comparable to the Eskimo carver's holding his work up to the light and twisting it about. Without the possibilities for seeing the material in a different light with each viewing, Flaherty would have had no urge to edit (although it does seem that editing was of less interest to him than filming).

The relation between shooting and editing is basic in cinema verite. Flaherty wrote (close to the end of his life) that his first thought in connection with the use of a movie camera on one of his expeditions was as a means "to compile visual notes."[38] This attitude of tentativeness toward the raw footage is not characteristic of other kinds of filming but is certainly so of cinema verite.

Flaherty's way of editing, as described by Griffith, is precisely analogous to cinema verite. The selection process seeks to determine "the underlying pattern" (Griffith's term) in the material. (This is not to be found in Vertov, who saw editing as the step that wedded the original theme to the footage shot in service of that theme.) That "pattern," if it evolves out of the material, might not conform to traditional notions of film structure. In most films, of course, whether documentary or fiction, the editing stage is not the time when such basic structural decisions are made.

Flaherty's *The Land* comes closest of all his films to following a cinema-verite approach. Flaherty traveled around the United States beginning in 1939, shooting material relating to soil erosion, the plight of migrant farmers, and new mechanized farming techniques. *The Land*, to quote Calder-Marshall, "was not a film in the sense that it had an argument or a constructed pattern. It was a record of a personal journey. . . ."[39] Flaherty shot without a script, and the film does not have a continuing "cast of characters" to provide dramatic continuity (unlike his previous work). While Calder-Marshall sees in the film "an epic theme he [Flaherty] could not resolve,"[40] this lack of resolution is indicative of an unwillingness to wrap problems in a neat package. Flaherty was torn between sympathy for the migrant workers' plight and fascination for advances in agricultural technology. To be a unified work, *The Land* would require an allegiance to one side or the other. But Flaherty took no stand, and the film reflects the complexity of the situation.

Observations by Richard Leacock, who was Flaherty's cameraman on *Louisiana Story* (1948), his last film, point to the technical impasse that had been reached. Most of *Louisiana Story* was shot silent with two Arriflex cameras, a relatively light piece of equipment.[41] At the end, a sound crew with a Mitchell camera (much heavier than the Arriflex) came in for the sequences where synchronized dialogue was needed.[42] Over ten years later, Leacock was to recall these difficulties:

... I saw that when we were using small cameras, we had tremendous flexibility, we could do anything we wanted, and get a
wonderful sense of cinema. The moment we had to shoot dialogue, lip-synch—everything had to be locked down, the whole
nature of the film changed. The whole thing seemed to stop. We
had heavy disk recorders, and the camera that, instead of weigh-
ing six pounds, weighed two hundred pounds, a sort of monster.
As a result of this, the whole nature of what we were doing
changed. We could no longer watch things as they developed,
we had to impose ourselves to such an extent upon everything
that happened before us, that everything sort of died.[43]

Leacock has said in several other interviews that this was the
time when it became clear to him that the next step in developing
these techniques of filming was a technical one, the need for having portable equipment that could also record synch sound.[44]
(As I have already noted, Vertov anticipated this necessity some
time earlier.)

We can think of Flaherty as the man who best expressed the
faith in open observation that is at the heart of cinema verite. Like
Vertov, his methods extend beyond cinema verite's (and sometimes contradict them, especially in the matter of restaging
events), but the consistent homage paid to Flaherty by the major
practitioners of this kind of cinema throughout the world is certainly merited. Flaherty could say, "First I was an explorer; then I
was an artist," but rarely has film art dealt so reverentially with the
real world.

Cesare Zavattini

Italian neorealism is often cited as a forerunner of cinema verite,
but the relationship is marginal at best, and discussion of the
question would shed more light on neorealism than upon cinema
verite. Instead, we shall consider briefly a "position paper" by
Cesare Zavattini, neorealism's foremost proponent, which in spirit
is very close to our present concerns.[45]

Zavattini calls for "a direct approach to everyday reality . . . without the intervention of fantasy or artifice."[46] The force of Zavat-

tini's argument is distinguished throughout by an emphasis on
the possibility of making films without the contrived drama of
most fiction films, basing them instead on the simplest of incidents. Theoretically at least, Zavattini argues for a faith in real
time with more zeal than has been demonstrated by any cinema-
verite advocate: "No other medium of expression has the cinema's original and innate capacity for showing things, that we believe worth showing, as they happen by day—in what we call their
'dailyness,' their longest and truest duration."[47] Elsewhere, Zavattini has also claimed that the supreme act of faith for a neorealist
would be to present, in the middle of a film, ninety consecutive
minutes in the life of a man.[48] (A more drastic application of the
same notion, suggested by Fernand Léger, is described by Kracauer: "Léger dreamed of a monster film which would have to
record painstakingly the life of a man and a woman during twen-
ty-four consecutive hours: their work, their silence, their intimacy.
Nothing should be omitted; nor should they ever be aware of
the presence of the camera.")[49]

Zavattini is equally adamant on the matter of technical equipment and the general way that films are made. This paragraph,
indeed, makes a good deal more sense in relation to cinema
verite than to neorealism:

The term neo-realism—in a very Latin sense—implies, too, elimination of technical-professional apparatus, screenwriter included.
Handbooks, formulas, grammars, have no more application.
There will be no more technical terms. Everybody has his personal shooting script. Neo-realism breaks all the rules, rejects all
those canons which, in fact, only exist to codify limitations. Reality breaks all the rules, as can be discovered if you walk out with
a camera to meet it.[50]

His feelings about screenwriting are especially surprising, considering that it has been his major capacity in filmmaking. He
goes so far as to say, "The screenwriter as such should disap-
pear, and we should arrive at the sole author of a film."[51] Like
Vertov in his writings and Flaherty in his practice, Zavattini also

emphasizes the importance of the individual filmmaker: "Everything becomes flexible when only one person is making a film, everything possible. . . ."[52] And on one last point he further concurs with these two earlier filmmakers: "The actor . . . has no more right to exist than the story."[53]

Zavattini has to be cited as part of the aesthetic foundation of cinema verite, regardless of the failure of neorealism to fulfull this stated commitment to undirected reality. There has to be room here for a man who can say: "However great a faith I might have in imagination, in solitude, I have a greater one in reality, in people. I am interested in the drama of things we happen to encounter, not those we plan."[54] Here, he beautifully articulates a cinema-verite outlook.

Georges Rouquier

Georges Rouquier's 1946 *Farrebique* is cited in A. William Bluem's *Documentary in American Television* as an example of cinema verite, and Bluem then uses it as a means to castigate this kind of filmmaking for seeking, he says, to hide the fact that events have been reconstructed for the film.[55] While Bluem is mistaken, *Farrebique* is a step between Flaherty and cinema verite, although it is closer to the former.

Rouquier lived on a French farm for one year to record the life of one family during that time. (This is a goal analogous to Flaherty's in *Nanook of the North,* which he said began with the thought, "Why not take . . . a typical Eskimo family and make a biography of their lives through a year?")[56] Like Flaherty, Rouquier does not content himself with undirected reality, preferring instead to reconstruct events for the camera, but the point is, the film does not pretend to be otherwise. There is a moment in Flaherty's film when Nanook smiles briefly at the camera; Rouquier's film has many similar moments of unhidden complicity. When Bluem says we can see "that these people are aware that they are performing,"[57] he errs in assuming that the rest of the audience doesn't see it too and that the filmmaker is making a special effort to hide this situation.

Farrebique is a step toward cinema verite for the faith it shows in its people. Its success on this score is reflected in a comment like that of James Agee, when he says the film makes one "real-ize with fuller contempt than ever before how consistently in our time so-called simple people, fictional and non-fictional, are con-sciously insulted and betrayed by artists and audiences. . . . this is the finest and strongest record of actual people that I have seen."[58] Agee also saw, and liked, Rouquier's interest in the sim-ple details of their life, what he calls "the small casual scraps of existence."[59] The film's interest in routine chores, the milking of cows, the slicing of bread, is indeed indicative of a concern for nonplot elements that is still exemplary.

We are also indebted to Agee for taking issue with what would become a common cinema-verite criticism; he quotes Bosley Crowther's remark that *Farrebique* is "lacking in strong dramatic punch . . . not even a plain folk triangle."[60] Agee correctly saw that the absence of "punch" was very much to Rouquier's credit.

Jean Renoir and the Camera

Jean Renoir, in an interview with André Bazin that first appeared in *France Observateur* and later, translated, in *Sight and Sound,* indicates a new view of the role of the camera, partly inspired by television, that has become typical of cinema-verite attitudes.[61] Leacock has said that he is certain this article influenced him,[62] but whether this is so or not, Renoir does make a crucial dis-tinction that is at the heart of cinema verite—essentially, that the camera should be looked upon as a recording device and no more, subordinate to what is being filmed:

. . . In the cinema at present, the camera has become a sort of god. You have a camera, fixed on its tripod or crane, which is just like a heathen altar; about it are the high priests—the director, cameraman, assistants—who bring victims before the camera, like burnt offerings, and cast them into the flames. And the camera is there, immobile—or almost so—and when it does move it follows patterns ordained by the high priests, not by the victims.

Now, I am trying to extend my old ideas, and to establish that the camera finally has only one right—that of recording what happens. That's all. I don't want the movements of the actors to be determined by the camera, but the movements of the camera to be determined by the actor. This means working rather like a newsreel cameraman. . . . It is the cameraman's duty to make it possible for us to see the spectacle, rather than the duty of the spectacle to take place for the benefit of the camera.[63]

Renoir means this standard to apply to all forms of cinema, but when considered in conjunction with comments he makes later in the same interview about the power of reality as sometimes seen on television, his observations become very much to the point. In speaking of televised political hearings, presumably the Army-McCarthy hearings, he says, "I found this tremendously exciting . . . and somehow an indecent spectacle to watch (ellipsis in original). Yet this indecency came nearer the knowledge of man than many films."[64] The idea of the camera in service of the subject is more suited to unstaged reality, for in fiction the subject matter exists solely for the purpose of being filmed. In cinema verite, the subject is of interest whether the filmmaker is there to record it or not. In other kinds of films, the way the material is shot and edited is usually a prime determining factor in whether the finished work is of interest. Cinema verite adopts Renoir's idea of the camera and uses it as a recording tool, so that the events themselves, "the knowledge of man," become the standard we use to judge the film.

Siegfried Kracauer

Throughout this study so far, we have noted a continuing dissatisfaction with the artifices of traditional storytelling techniques as they have been employed in cinema. The objection has generally been to the preparation of stories prior to filming instead of allowing stories to grow out of the events themselves.

To recount this thread, here are several examples previously noted:
1. "The director ordinarily *invents* the plot for the scenario—Dziga Vertov *detects* it." (italics in original)
2. "A story must come out of the life of a people, not from the actions of individuals." (Flaherty)
3. "I am interested in the drama of things we happen to encounter, not those we plan." (Zavattini)
  The relationship between planned and encountered drama is the subject of extended consideration in Siegfried Kracauer's *Theory of Film: The Redemption of Physical Reality.* Kracauer's book is based upon his belief that "films come into their own when they record and reveal physical reality. . . . this reality includes many phenomena which could hardly be perceived were it not for the motion picture camera's ability to catch them on the wing."[65] His feeling that film "gravitates toward unstaged reality" is strong enough for him to assert that "staging is aesthetically legitimate to the extent that it evokes the illusion of actuality,"[66] but he limits his argument almost exclusively to the domain of prescripted fiction films. Nevertheless, many of his arguments are applicable to cinema verite and reflect a faith in the real world that is shared by these films. The appearance of Kracauer's book in 1960, just prior to the wide-scale blossoming of this movement, marks it as an important step in the aesthetic battle on behalf of reality in cinema that in many ways justifies the goals of cinema verite. Kracauer has been properly rebuked for his intolerance toward many kinds of films, but, without assuming that he speaks for the whole of cinema, there is still a good deal of merit in his argument.
  Kracauer does touch briefly on the nonfiction film, and it is primarily in connection with the notion now under discussion, the relationship between realistic and formative tendencies. He quite correctly locates the heart of the conflict: "On the one hand, the documentary maker eliminates the intrigue so as to be able to

open his lens on the world; on the other, he feels urged to re-introduce dramatic action in the very same interest."[67] As Kracauer observes, the faith in reality without plot has never been very strong: "In fact, the body of existing documentaries testifies to a persistent tendency towards dramatization."[68] To this seemingly insoluble dilemma, Kracauer proposes a solution. Assuming that stories will creep in one way or another, he suggests that some are more suitable than others.

It is here that we are back to the quotations listed at the beginning of this section, for Kracauer, too, is a proponent of "discovered" drama. His term is the "found story," which, he says, "covers all stories found in the material of actual physical reality."[69] His description of this finding process sounds like Flaherty's Eskimo influence: "When you have watched for long enough the surface of a river or a lake you will detect certain patterns in the water which may have been produced by a breeze or some eddy. Found stories are in the nature of such patterns." And, further, on a point of such importance that a good deal more substantiation would have been desirable, Kracauer considers found stories to be entirely unlike their fictional counterparts: "Since the found story is part and parcel of the raw material in which it lies dormant, it cannot possibly develop into a self-contained whole—which means that it is almost the opposite of the theatrical story." Also, the found story "tends to render incidents typical of the world around us."

Kracauer is very much taken with Flaherty's storytelling methods, especially his avoidance of strict linear narrative. While Kracauer believes Flaherty took it for granted that a story is desirable in documentary (a point with which he agrees), Flaherty depended upon a succession of typical incidents for structure rather than upon a story growing "from the actions of individuals." That is, Flaherty avoided situations too closely tied to unique personalities in order to lessen the strictures of forced interpretation through dramatic form. We should feel, for instance, that Nanook is one Eskimo of many, that because his

"story" is freed from tight plot through the universality of his
constant struggle for survival, it has a significance beyond his
actual circumstance. According to Kracauer, Flaherty's lessened
reliance on plot was due to his being "afraid lest fully developed,
rounded-out stories, which often have pronounced patterns of
meaning, [would] prevent the camera from having its say."[70]

Kracauer's wariness toward fully fleshed-out drama is difficult to reconcile with his refusal to abandon narrative entirely.
His preference for the "found story" and the "slight narrative"
(the latter a description of Flaherty's storytelling methods taken
from Rotha)[71] still indicates a firm commitment to dramatic structure in documentary film. While Kracauer emphasizes that stories
should be elicited from "the raw material of life rather than sub-
jecting the raw material to pre-established demands,"[72] this distinction is rather vague. "Raw material," as we shall see, may itself be highly dramatic, so the very selection of subject matter
may be a marked element of preconceived structure. In practice,
we have little way of knowing whether a story does indeed come
out of the material or whether it is forcibly extracted.

While Kracauer's arguments concerning the found story and
the slight narrative may provide some justification for the persistent dependence upon story in cinema verite, his most valuable
contribution for our purposes is his delineation of the problem
rather than his overly conservative conclusion. That a possible
conflict exists between uncontrolled events and the varieties of
meanings permitted by imposed structures is a complex, crucial
issue in cinema verite.

The attempt in this chapter has been to shed some light on the
intent behind cinema-verite filmmaking through discussion of
some ideas that anticipated it. Influences from fields other than
filmmaking, however, have scarcely been considered. A compre-
hensive analysis of the development of cinema verite would include, among other topics, influences of written journalism,
photography, photojournalism, and television, as well as a clearer

picture of the traditional forms of documentary (including types popular on television). Such an analysis is not within the scope of this volume. It is hoped, however, that even such a brief background as the one given in this chapter will refute the suggestion, too prevalent in studies of this nature, that the methods of filmmaking under discussion popped up spontaneously and without precedent in the 1960s.

Drew Associates

Robert Drew and Richard Leacock are together primarily responsible for putting cinema-verite methods into practice on a grand scale. For three years, from *Primary* to *Crisis: Behind a Presidential Commitment,* they were the guiding force for what is still the most substantial body of work employing these techniques. Their films demonstrated the possibilities in spontaneous, uncontrolled shooting and first came to grips with major aesthetic questions growing out of that commitment. In effect, Drew Associates defined American cinema verite, establishing so strong an approach that its influence continues to dominate.

Drew came from photojournalism—once an assistant picture editor and reporter for *Life.* He became interested in applying the techniques of candid photography in the *Life* style to motion pictures. In 1953 NBC asked him to develop a half-hour television news show produced in this manner.[1] He made a pilot film called *Key Picture,* and the result was, to use his word, "catastrophic."[2] Drew now feels that the problem with *Key Picture* resulted from the use of an unwieldy eight-man crew and his own confusion as to how a candid film had to be structured, the difference between cutting on picture logic as opposed to word logic.[3] At any rate, *Key Picture* has gone the way of all unsold pilots, and no print presently seems to be in existence.

In 1954 Drew took a year leave from *Life* to study these problems and went to Harvard on a Nieman fellowship. It was during this time that he saw Leacock's *Toby* on television, and he went to New York to meet the film's creator. "Leacock's ideas and mine coincided almost perfectly," Drew later said, and from there, with Time Inc. backing, their association began.[4]

The man responsible for *Toby* was deeply rooted in documentary cinema. Richard Leacock spent his childhood on his father's banana plantation in the Canary Islands, making his first film, a 16-millimeter silent film about the growing and packing of bananas, at the age of thirteen. In England he attended school with Robert Flaherty's daughter Monica and met Flaherty after someone showed young Leacock's banana film to him. Leacock

Robert Drew

helped to found a film group at his school and made educational
films about geography. At seventeen he served as film man on
an expedition to the Galapagos Islands led by his school biology
teacher. Leacock came to the United States in 1938 to attend
Harvard, where he studied physics for three and a half years
before leaving school to engage in more film work. Prior to being
drafted into the Army in World War II, he assisted in the editing
of *Native Land,* made by Paul Strand and Leo Hurwitz, worked
in varied capacities on Charles Corvin's Frontier Films, and did
a film about folk music. As a Signal Corps cameraman in Burma
and China during the war, he shot battle footage for weekly Army
newsreels.[5]

  After the war he visited his old acquaintance Flaherty, who
asked him if he was free for a while. Leacock replied in the affir-
mative, and Flaherty said, "OK, let's drive to Louisiana." So, on
the basis of a film about bananas made by a child many years

before, Flaherty selected his cameraman for *Louisiana Story.* Leacock worked awhile as a cameraman on a series called *Geography,* films produced by Louis de Rochemont for Universal Pictures, which included work on a film about a nomadic tribe of Berbers in the Sahara Desert. His description of this project sounds particularly Flaherty-like: "Our purpose in making a film of the life of such people is never to condemn them; it is rather to depict how, by leading an incredibly hard and frugal life, the Berber Nomads of the western Sahara are able to live in a land that we, with our rich natural resources, would dismiss as a total loss."[6] Leacock also shared another Flaherty trait at this point—but one he would soon abandon—his willingness to re-create events for filming purposes.

Early Leacock Films—*Toby and the Tall Corn* and Others
Toby and the Tall Corn (1954) was made for the television series "Omnibus." Television at that time provided a freedom Leacock had not known previously in commercial film work, since this Sunday afternoon cultural exercise did not need to press a sponsor's viewpoint (even a subdued one, as in *Louisiana Story*) or serve a specific educational purpose. *Toby* is interesting now for its struggle to overcome the limitations of its equipment and for the verite spirit that nearly managed to subdue this formidable problem.

   Toby affects a story device that has since been used in other direct cinema films: a magazine writer out getting his story. The narrator, who says he is a writer from *Harper's,* is first shown on a rainy night in his stopped car, peering at a road map. He is supposed to do a story about a traveling tent show, but he's lost in the Midwestern wilderness. This slightly quizzical beginning is the first indication of a standard concession the Drew-Leacock team made for television, the "teaser" opening. Leacock often mentions the need for this type of beginning, an affectation he feels is not necessary in films made specifically for theaters.[7] *Toby* is about "America's only living folk theater" and the man

who runs it. The film was shot with heavy 35-millimeter cameras
and a tape recorder that weighed over 200 pounds.[8] Leacock
compensated for the lack of equipment mobility by taking advantage of the opportunity to shoot a little bit each day of the presentation, which could eventually be put together to give a full idea of
the tent show performance.[9] In between excerpts from the show
are sequences of members of the troupe traveling, setting up the
tent, putting up photos, and selling tickets.

  Toby is a fairly talky film, with an element absent from Leacock's
later work: on-camera interviewing. The narration, also, is unlike
that in most direct cinema films, since the writer-narrator offers
an "outsider's" view of the proceedings, including interpretations
of the show's humor, the motives of the people in it, and the
tastes of the small-town audiences they play to. The narrator, in
effect, describes an alien culture.

  The camerawork and editing are generally uninspired. Due to
the heavy equipment, the succession of unmoving tripod shots
gives *Toby* a restrained, conventional look. Because of the piece-
meal shooting procedures, the performance scenes are abundantly interspersed with unconvincing cut-away audience reaction
shots. The only sequence of particular visual interest is a nonsynch episode of the tent being erected in a stiff wind, a brief but
energetic man-against-nature scene.

  Despite equipment shortcomings, *Toby* is an engaging piece
of work clearly several cuts above the usual treatment given to
obscure, almost exotic subject matter of this nature. Leacock,
working in complete freedom for the first time,[10] was surely out
to show his stuff. The title character is a fascinating, colorful fellow very much at ease in front of the camera, a human interest
story come to life. Not coincidentally, he is the first of a succession of performers who have been subjects for direct-cinema
films. In *Toby* we learn about a man and his way of life, again
a Flaherty-like objective that has remained the primary goal of
Leacock's work and most of direct cinema.

  After *Toby,* Leacock made two more films for "Omnibus," *How the F-100 Got Its Tail* (1956) and *Bernstein in Israel* (1956). The former was completely scripted, and again shot with a heavy 35-mm Mitchell.[11] The film suggests another direction direct cinema was to take, trying to impart a "you are there" feeling to the audience. A good deal of footage shot from jets is used to suggest what it feels like to actually fly a plane. (Test pilots and car drivers were another group of personalities that would be drawn upon several times for later films.) The beginning is again a Leacock made-especially-for-TV device, a routine interview at an airfield that is interrupted by an enormous jet whooshing by at about twenty feet off the ground. It is a well-made but undistinguished documentary, limited by the necessity of having to adhere to a prepared script.

The film about conductor Leonard Bernstein was shot with 16-mm equipment, but it was a clumsy type of sound camera that required a connecting cable to the recording device in order to maintain synchronization. Leacock has often recalled his frustration on this film with the equipment problems and has said that it was during this film that he realized the crucial necessity of mobile, quiet cameras that could operate independently of the recorders and yet remain in synch.[12]

A second Bernstein film was made later in Moscow, but it was shot entirely with 35-mm equipment again. If it is noteworthy at all, it is because it was the first time that Leacock, Albert Maysles, and D. A. Pennebaker worked together. The film is quite conventional, most of it taken up with the playing of the first movement of a Shostakovich symphony. The few shots in the film that were made outside the concert hall, like a meeting of Bernstein and Boris Pasternak, do not have live sound.

Drew and Leacock Together—The Early Years

The professional teaming of Drew and Leacock began about 1957. The two were agreed upon the need for better equipment in order to shoot more flexibly in a wider variety of circumstances. Both Drew's *Key Picture* and Leacock's films had been badly hampered by these limitations. Drew's interest in "creating a new form of journalism which would take documentary into the street"[13] and Leacock's approach as exemplified by *Toby* were not widely separated at this time. Drew obtained the sponsorship of the Time-Life Broadcast Division, and they set out to develop the equipment they needed and to put it into use making films.

The collaboration did not result in any instantly acclaimed successes, and it was three years before the landmark *Primary.* Most of these early films appeared on network TV shows in conjunction with the appearance of a *Life* photo-article on the same subject. There was a film about a Navy balloon ascent into the stratosphere for the purpose of getting a clear telescope view of Mars to see if there was any water on the planet. It was shown on the "Today" program, and another film about weightless astronauts reached the public on the "Ed Sullivan Show." The most interesting film of this period never made it to television; it was about a football game between the Air Force Academy and the University of Colorado (not to be confused with the 1961 *Mooney vs. Fowle,* also called *Football*).[14]

Typical of this group is *Bullfight at Malaga* (1958), part of which appeared on the "Tonight" show. It is a transitional work, still hindered by poor live sound but suggesting elements that were to become familiar in the later films, especially the heroic nature of the central characters. The story of the bullfight is presented in personal terms, as the duel between two bullfighters. *Bullfight at Malaga* shows, however, that mere conflict is not enough to sustain these films, that there had to be a close look at how protagonists live and work in order to lessen the sense of dramatic contrivance. The language barrier keeps Dominguin and Ordonez, the bullfighters, too distant for us to maintain much interest in the outcome of their conflict. The language problem, though, is probably not so important as the synch sound difficulties, since a later film, *Yanki, No!,* has some very effective scenes that transcend language barriers. The Drew-Leacock films rarely display this lack of emotional contact with the subject, and the difference that synch sound later made in effecting this kind of character identification gives the bullfight film an antiquated feeling, a problem further compounded by the artificial framing device, again, of a *Life* photo team out on assignment.

Authorship—A Preliminary Qualification

Some explanation is necessary in regard to the term "Drew-Leacock films," the label used to describe their work in this period. Drew Associates employed and often trained a great many cameramen, reporters, and editors. Important names during this period include D. A. Pennebaker, Albert Maysles, James Lipscomb, Gregory Shuker, Hope Ryden, along with many others. As James Lipscomb has pointed out, referring to the key *Living Camera* series of ten films, Pennebaker was cameraman on more films than Leacock, Shuker produced more, and others edited larger portions.[15] It is incorrect to call any single work a Drew-Leacock film or to refer to the films as a group in this fashion, but the convenience of this appellation is difficult to resist.

Louis Marcorelles, who has written extensively on American direct-cinema films, even went so far as to differentiate between a "Drew line" and a "Leacock line." He characterized the Leacock group (which he says includes Pennebaker and Albert Maysles) as "more cognizant of personal expression than the journalistic efficacy" of the Drew group (where he places Lipscomb and Shuker).[16] It would be very convenient to leave the matter there, but this is at least a simplification.

Primary responsibility for all films up to and including *Crisis* must go to Robert Drew. Drew did far more than form the organization that bears his name and secure the funds for its operation. His interest in the films went beyond the supervisory; he took an active part (although never in the crucial role of cameraman). While Drew's central role should not be forgotten, these films are, at the same time, team efforts. They were usually shot with multiple crews and in many cases edited by people other than those who did the shooting. It has been reported that Drew Associates at one time had as many as 75 employees.[17]

Still, there should be no dispute concerning Leacock's half of the title. Although no single film of this period can be justly labeled Leacock's alone, his profound influence on all Drew Associates work as well as his own remarkable shooting deserves substantial recognition. The term "Drew-Leacock" seems most appropriate because it was the initial collaboration of the two that appears to have sparked the whole movement, despite the complexity of the authorship question. There is nothing to be gained through further speculation as to how to slice the pie. The films exist, and all contributed; the labels are simply for convenience.

Primary
Nearly everyone involved with the making of *Primary* feels that it marked the real breakthrough in their filming. Drew, Leacock, Pennebaker, and Albert Maysles all recognize it as the turning point, and generally by reason of the equipment. Leacock, for instance, has said of the film: "For the first time we were able to walk in and out of buildings, up and down stairs, film in taxi cabs, all over the place, and get synchronous sound."[18] Drew makes a point of the equipment as well: "*Primary* was the first place where I was able to get the new camera equipment, the new editing equipment, and the new ideas all working at the same time."[19] There is much more to *Primary* than equipment improvement, however; and actually the improvement is not felt so much here as it is in a film made soon after, *The Children Were Watching. Primary,* though, remains a fine example of their work and is as exciting to watch now as it must have been when first shown.

Primary is an hour film (the same length as nearly all the films, including the fifty-five or so minutes of a TV "hour" remaining after allowances for commercial breaks) on the Kennedy-Humphrey battle in the Wisconsin Democratic Primary election in 1960. The film is about evenly divided between episodes of each candidate (cutting back and forth between them, rather than splitting the show into separate full segments on each). We see them giving speeches, hustling on the street for votes, speaking on television, and waiting in their rooms on election night for the results. Kennedy wins, but not decisively, and they now must push on to West Virginia to start the struggle all over.

Drew originally had the idea for *Primary* and with Leacock sought out Senator Kennedy to persuade him to yield to this new technique of being followed everywhere in the course of the campaign. (It is interesting that Drew and Leacock felt the necessity of being able to shoot in private situations as well as public ones, for some of the most effective scenes in the film are views of the thoroughly fatigued candidates when they are out of the public eye.) Kennedy relented and Humphrey later agreed, so the film was set. Drew arrived in Wisconsin two days in advance and

Primary. Kennedy in the streets.

Primary. Humphrey talking to farmers.

Primary. Kennedys at a Madison, Wisconsin, rally. (Just after the long tracking shot.)

Primary. Kennedy poses for a portrait.

Primary. Shot after Kennedy pose is Humphrey's photo on front of campaign bus. A typical transition.

Primary. Humphrey in a private moment.

Primary. John Kennedy on night of Wisconsin Democratic Primary election (photographed by Leacock).

hastily made up a working plan, deciding which team would go where and how long filming would last. It was only at the last moment that the camera crews came in.[20] As we shall see, this minimal preparation was typical and quite unlike the planning behind most documentary films.

Leacock, Pennebaker, Al Maysles, and Terence Macartney-Filgate all did a good deal of shooting. Macartney-Filgate was a major figure in the National Film Board of Canada, especially for the *Candid Eye* series in the late fifties. He worked on this film and *X-Pilot,* but he took a dim view of the New York school of direct cinema, feeling that it was doing things then (around 1960) that the N.F.B. had done several years earlier.[21] Drew, Leacock, and Maysles all acknowledge that he shot a good deal of *Primary,* although his name is often overlooked in references to the film.

For a breakthrough in cinema verite, it is surprising what a small portion of *Primary* was shot with synchronized sound. Leacock has said that he was the only one to make extensive use of synch sound equipment, that Pennebaker and Maysles were shooting with silent Arriflexes.[22] At this time, it was still necessary for him to use a wire connecting the recorder to the camera (though the cameras were much lighter than they were several years earlier when he faced this restriction while filming *Bernstein in Israel*). However, his ingenuity was abundant, and the technical bravura of his work is certainly a major reason for *Primary's* success.

The two most intimate glimpses of the candidates were accomplished under particularly difficult circumstances. In both cases, Leacock shot synch sound entirely on his own, with no sound man or other technical assistance. The first comes early in the film, a scene shot inside Humphrey's car as he travels from one small town to another. He talks a bit about the countryside and then leans back to catch a few minutes of sleep, as the windshield wipers tap out a monotonous rhythm on a rainy day. George Bluestone stated his case strongly, but in the proper spirit, when he wrote, "That one sequence gives us more insight into the bone-crushing fatigue of a primary campaign than a thousand narrative assertions."[23]

Leacock was sitting in the back during this journey; a microphone was attached to the seat, and shooting was done with a small, amateur 16-mm camera. Leacock believes Humphrey didn't even know who he was that day, probably thinking he was just a friend of someone in his entourage. Leacock was equally inconspicuous in filming Kennedy in his hotel room on the evening of the election. Since the Senator was sitting in the same place the whole time (clearly exhausted by the campaigning experience), Leacock hid a microphone in an ashtray (remembering to change reels on the portable tape recorder at the required intervals) and had another attached to his camera to catch other voices in the room.[24] Then, to quote Leacock, "I retired into the corner and got lost, sitting in a big comfortable arm-chair with the camera on my lap. I'm quite sure he hadn't the foggiest notion I was shooting."[25]

There is much more to this scene than mere technical trickery. It demonstrates the special brilliance of a first-rate cameraman like Leacock (or, later, Al Maysles), the ability to transcend passive observation through a series of selections within single shots, but without losing the sense of actuality. Leacock pans quickly, from Jackie Kennedy whispering hello to a friend over to the Senator talking on the phone, to Kennedy later dragging himself out of his seat to shake hands, and all the time we have a full sense of the room and the activities of the many people in it. The sound quality is poor; there is hardly any light; there are many quick pans and zooms, but it is still an astounding revelation. Leacock is being overmodest when he says that he just sat there "with the camera on my lap."

There is one shot in *Primary* that no writer fails to mention, a long tracking shot behind Kennedy. The shot begins outside a door to a building, where a small crowd is waiting. Jackie walks by and into the door, and then the Senator comes into the frame and heads for the door. The camera stays right behind him as he walks down a long corridor, shaking hands quickly as he moves through the mass of people. We go through a door, up a small set of stairs, and onto a stage, the shot ending with a view of the loudly applauding crowd. It is exuberant and exciting, that wide-angle lens sticking to Kennedy through thick and thin. (There is, though, a cut about one minute into the four-minute scene that makes the sequence slightly less spectacular than it might have been.)

The shot's punch is also partially weakened by the use of a portion of it earlier in the film (an editing gaffe that occurred again in *The Chair,* when a similar long tracking shot down a hall to the electric chair is used twice). It also indicates a mixed view of what the film should be, either a re-creation of the feeling of what it's like to be a primary candidate (the same way you'd re-create a jet pilot's experience by aiming a camera out a cockpit window) or a study of two personalities locked in conflict. There is a confusion of purpose in *Primary,* coupled with an energetic sense of trying to do everything and be everywhere at once.

Albert Maysles, who executed this famous shot, is also responsible for a particular device, used shortly after, of a type that soon became outmoded in direct cinema, a cut-away close-up of a small action. The shot in question is a close-up of Jackie Kennedy's fidgeting hands as she says a few words to the audience. The problem with the shot is that this detail doesn't first become noticeable within a larger context; it needs to be zoomed in on instead of cut to. The distinction may sound trivial, but it is visually clear. Subjective details are fine, but we need to share in a sense of their discovery. Maysles understands this and said recently that if he were to be shooting this now, he would try to integrate it into a lengthier shot to make the gesture more meaningful.[26] This is an editing as well as a shooting problem, for the way the shot appears in the film, it could actually have been photographed days apart from the rest of the scene and simply inserted for dramatic effect. It is cases like this shot and the general need for the filmmaker to understand the power of the tools at his disposal that make direct cinema a more delicate exercise than it might seem.

Besides the standout scenes, *Primary* is divided between fine, insightful moments and some crude, ineffective ones. This wouldn't be worth noting, except that the good footage is all in synch, and most of the rest was not shot with live sound. In the latter category are several long handshaking scenes, a clumsy montage of feet in voting booths, and a lengthy speech by Humphrey shown primarily in long-shot and in the faces of the audience so as to hide the obvious lack of synch sound. The former group includes an excellent scene of Kennedy posing for a studio photo (which cuts to a shot of the Humphrey photo on the front of his bus), Humphrey being interviewed on a local radio station, and good scenes with both candidates talking to people on the street. The contrasts between the two kinds of shooting suggest once more the absolute superiority of synch sound, for non synch material becomes agonizingly artificial when placed in juxtaposition.

Seeing that many of the technical difficulties that hampered Drew Associates' earlier work are still present in this film, one has to conclude that the real breakthrough was a creative one: they began to comprehend the special strengths of their methods of filming. They realized the value of little moments that do not necessarily advance a story, and at the same time they saw the potential drama in a situation they did not create. If our final judgment of *Primary* is favorable, it must be for the energy behind it, the unpretentiousness of its approach, and the suggestion of later possibilities for these techniques. *Primary* humanizes an impersonal process. It shows us a side of elections we rarely see, as opposed to giving us a "more truthful" view. As Leacock admits, "*Primary* was a breakthrough, but in no way, manner, or form did *Primary* achieve what we set out to do, which was to show what really goes on in an election."[27] Regardless of the initial intentions, *Primary* fills in some gaps that aren't (and couldn't be) filled by more traditonal documentary forms or journalistic reporting.

On that last point, there has been a good deal of argument as to the relative merits of *Primary* and Theordore H. White's book *The Making of the President 1960.* (Incidentally, White is clearly visible but never identified in the scene in Kennedy's room on election night, stalking about with a small pad in his hand.) The general opinion was that perhaps *Primary* was superior as a vehicle to show the noise and fatigue of campaigning (like the Humphrey scene that Bluestone thought was better than anything that could be written), but that on the whole the White book fills in more details and gives some necessary information that the camera can't convey. A not overly extreme case was advanced by one French critic, who took *Primary* to task for not pointing out the intricacies of Wisconsin voter registration (which permitted Republicans to cross over in primaries to vote for Democratic candidates), as White's book had done.[28] (This is alluded to in the film, though, when Kennedy refers to the Nixon people who may have voted for Humphrey to hurt JFK's chances. This aside might not have been translated in the French subtitles.) Jean-Luc Godard, in a stinging rebuke of Leacock in particular and direct cinema in general, also denigrated *Primary* because it told us less about Kennedy than we could find in White.[29]

The book versus movie argument is one side of the cinema-verite squeeze, the other being cinema verite versus fiction films. The temptation to compare the films with both written journalism and filmed fiction reveals something of the mixed qualities of cinema verite, but the arguments usually find cinema verite on the lesser side of either comparison. In the particular case of *Primary,* the only problem is one of intention. Whether or not Drew, Leacock, and the rest wanted "to show what really goes on in an election," their failure to do so by no means implies that the film is a failure. Just as *Primary* is not *Making of the President,* the reverse is equally true. There is no reason to assume that the two are in competition, that their respective creators must achieve the same ends. Part of *Primary's* appeal is that it seems resolutely to avoid the more mundane electoral matters that fill up so much television and newspaper space during those periods. Rather than supplanting White, it supplements him considerably.

It is interesting that negative critics had to cite a book in their argument—that there is no film, documentary or fiction, they could name that approaches *Primary's* degree of revelation on the workings of American politics. Surely David Wolper's television version of *The Making of the President* (scripted by White) is precisely the type of documentary Drew and Leacock resolutely oppose: heavily narrated history lessons. Even here, though, it is possible to see *Primary* as an alternative, equally accurate and not necessarily contradictory. Unfortunately, *The Best Man* and *Advise and Consent,* the best fictional films on recent American politics, are further away from any feeling for reality than even Wolper's film. Both fiction films are hopelessly burdened at crucial moments with contrived melodrama. In both films, for instance, a homosexual accusation is sprung as a key dramatic point. By pretending to give us the inside story, which they expect people to believe is sordid and perverse, they lose considerable claim to veracity. Despite common source material, then, the final products of each of the three genres (direct cinema, journalism, and fiction films) are hardly comparable.

Primary was shown on the four Time Inc. television stations; their next film, *On the Pole,* was to receive the same limited circulation. ABC became interested in the work of Drew Associates after these first two programs demonstrated that this type of film had commercial possibilities, and Drew signed a contract along with Time Inc. to coproduce four one-hour documentaries for the ABC "Close-up" series. John Daly, who was then in charge of ABC News, objected to the ABC-Drew arrangement, claiming that his authority as head of news and public affairs

shows was being violated. Daly subsequently resigned.[30] This
kind of infighting is indicative of the network politics that later
kept most of the Drew-Leacock films from reaching a large audience, no doubt causing from this very beginning a dilution of
quality in an attempt to avoid network disfavor.

The "Close-up" films

Yanki, No!
The initial Drew production for "Close-up," Yanki, No! (1960),
deals with an immense subject for this kind of filming: anti-Ameri-
can feeling in Latin America. Yanki, No! sought to convey complex issues on a personal level, through the presentation of brief
episodes in the lives of certain key or representative Latin American personalities. While not wholly successful, Yanki, No! remains
one of the most ambitious Drew-Leacock films, a rare attempt for
them to stretch the new techniques to cover material that might
not be ideally suited to these methods.

   Drew was at first reluctant to tackle this subject, feeling that to
do an hour program about a whole continent was precisely
the kind of idea they were against. (CBS and NBC had already
done reports on Latin America, but they were just that, reports
and not films.) He was asked to study the matter for a week.
While reading about Latin America during this period, he came
to feel that the story of the continent was quite simple, a conflict
between a small ruling oligarchy and the mass of poor people
who were seeking other ways of living, one of which was represented by Castro. There was a showdown about to take place at
a meeting of the Organization of American States, and Drew felt
that this would bring out the reactions all over the continent that
they wanted to observe. So, on the basis of his feelings about
the nature of the problems in Latin America and the upcoming
events that he anticipated would be of a dramatic nature, he
agreed to do the film. Without these conditions, Drew feels he
probably would not have consented to make the film.[31]

The primary difference between *Yanki, No!* and most of the Drew-Leacock films is a basic structural shift: The sharpest conflict comes at the beginning, in order to engage our interest, and the remainder of the film is an elucidation of the forces seething beneath the visual confrontation. The starting point is the OAS meeting, where the issue under discussion is a resolution condemning Cuba's cooperation with Russia and Sino-Soviet intervention in Latin America. When the resolution is passed, Cuba's delegation walks out in protest. Following an ostensible story line from the OAS meeting to its repercussions in Venezuela and then to Cuba's response, *Yanki, No!* is actually more a filmmaker's view of life in Latin America than a narrated analysis of political viewpoints. Freeing itself of the necessity to relate each sequence to the others (beyond the common goal of each to show a relevant facet of Latin American life), the film suggests possibilities for direct cinema outside of conventional dramatic expectations. Today a good deal of the narration, despite its worthy intention of encouraging U.S. concern for Latin America, sounds jejune. The power of the images, however, stands.

The two best scenes, one in Venezuela and the other in Cuba, depict simple family life. Leacock shot the first, a sequence that begins with two long tracking shots through narrow slum passageways (quite similar to certain shots in Chris Marker's *Le Joli Mai,* made two years later), giving a sense of the oppressive closeness of slum dwellings. The Gabriel family is very poor. At one point in the film, the father, an unemployed electrician's helper, talks with a friend about his job problems; and the look in his eyes, the gestures of his hands, reach us more firmly than his translated words. Leacock's camera, certainly an alien instrument to these people, is once more above passive observation, instead registering a sensitivity to its subject that is exemplary.

The scene with the Cuban family, like all the Cuban footage, was shot by Albert Maysles. Jesus Morero, a fisherman, and his family are moving into a government-built house, part of a fishing cooperative that has been set up since the revolution. Morero

Yanki, No! Fidel Castro.

Yanki, No! Cuban soldier-peasants.

Yanki, No! Castro rally.

talks about the effects of the revolution on their lives (all good), and his family is seen in their new quarters. Again, the opportunity just to observe how other men live is sufficient to sustain our interest. Ethnographic content is dominant over possible political ramifications. Either of these two scenes could have been the basis for a full-length film.

   Except for a few other brief segments on Cuban life, the rest of the film is more directly political: the Venezuelan representative to OAS being fired, an interview with a Russian seaman on a tanker that has brought oil to Cuba, university students talking about revolution, and long portions of a Castro speech (freely paraphrased and interpreted by the narrator). There is also a fair amount of obvious sound and image juxtaposition. At one point, a student talks about the need for revolution while the visuals show members of the wealthy oligarchy playing in a swimming pool. Elsewhere, the film cuts from a rainy view in front of a peasant's muddy hut to a sun-filled shot in front of the Presidential palace, and we even find the obligatory cliché, a pan from high-rise apartments by a modern highway to nearby slum dwellings. Leacock once said at a Flaherty seminar that he feels *Yanki, No!* was the Drew film best suited to television because it was a "screaming, yelling picture." One certainly has to admit that its point, that Latin America is in the midst of tremendous change and we had better care about it, is not lost on anyone.

   A good deal of the narration in the Cuban sequences seeks to slant audience attitudes to an unpardonable degree. During shots of people walking to a rally, the narrator says, "Now the revolution is going to stage a show," implying that the rally to come could not be a true expression of support for Castro by the Cuban people. Likewise, little need be said about these twisting words: "Fidel Castro, who looks like a raving madman to North Americans, is seen by Latin Americans as a sort of messiah. Now you will see him at his messianic best." This kind of narration is either superfluous or misleading, and in both cases, highly undesirable. Furthermore, there is a free interpretation of events beyond the goal of the film to awaken us to the problems of Latin America. *Yanki, No!*'s ultimate argument is that unless we provide more assistance (mainly financial, but also spoken of generally as "concern") to Latin America, the whole continent will fall into violent, Communist-supported revolution that will do great harm. This type of theorizing is sometimes contradicted by the film's own evidence (the Cuban family in a new house is clearly much better off because of their revolution), and the power of the visuals is surely more persuasive than the narration.

The attempts at political assessment are worth noting because *Yanki, No!* was the first Drew-Leacock film to elicit what was to become a familiar brand of criticism, that direct cinema opts for emotion over reason. Robert Lewis Shayon, long one of television's most respected critics, faulted Drew for not explaining "*just how* we could go about 'caring' for our Latin American neighbors" (his italics). He continued, "*Yanki, No!* drew tight the emotional bow, but never discharged the arrow." Shayon felt that the narration should have gone into more detail about the nature of the problem, to its "withinness" instead of its "withoutness." Quoting him further: "It is nonsense that the camera 'replaces' the commentator in a documentary. The fervent narrative . . . was the essential anatomy of *Yanki, No!*." He calls the film redundant, saying that it had made its point by the thirty-minute mark. In short, Shayon argues for more words and fewer pictures: "Emotion . . . is but one half of the pure gold coin of documentary creativity. Intellect is the other half."[32] (It might be worth noting further that Shayon had a distinguished career writing radio documentaries and has written narration for many television documentaries as well.)

To be opposed to such a conclusion sounds like championing anti-intellectualism, but that is precisely Shayon's error. Leading viewers to specific conclusions and persuading them of the rightness of future courses of action is not necessarily a superior operation of intellect. Shayon calls for a blend of emotion and intellect, a misleading request for compromise because it equates unnarrated direct cinema with "emotion" and narration with "intellect."

A concise reply to this charge was made some years before by Cesare Zavattini in reply to similar criticism leveled against neorealism (that the films do not offer solutions and that the end of a neorealist film is often inconclusive) when he wrote, "Every moment of the film is, in itself, a continuous answer to some question. It is not the concern of the artist to propound solutions. It is enough, and quite a lot, I should say, to make an audience feel the need, the urgency for them."[33] Zavattini went on to note correctly that if the reality of the film is properly complex, solutions by their very nature are superficial. In fact, subjects of great interest (as in *Yanki, No!*) are often worth investigating precisely because they do *not* offer easy solutions. If anything, *Yanki, No!* isn't quite as good as it might be because its tacit suggestion of solution (by simply speaking of "caring") gives the audience an easy out. The film does not quite settle for presenting its view of the problem. But Shayon's criticism, old when he wrote it and still with us, wants issues wrapped in little bundles and neatly dispatched. *Yanki, No!* at least refuses to strip issues of their essential complexity, which in itself is a more sophisticated intellectual process than "finding answers."

X-Pilot

X-Pilot, second of the "Close-up" films, is a rather undistinguished offering. Its subject is the final test flight of the X-15 and the activities of its pilot, Scott Crossfield. The film is moderately dull, not because its material is necessarily uninteresting, but as a result of the constant conflict between a narration telling of the monumental import of this flight and its apparent routine nature. Having taken on the twin goals of telling the story of the flight and attempting a personality study of its pilot, *X-Pilot* ends up doing neither very well.

Crossfield's reticence is an unconquerable obstacle, and the film might have been more successful if the attempt at examining his personal qualities had been abandoned in favor of simply showing him in action. "I'm a pilot, not an actor," Crossfield says in one scene when he abruptly departs, but what he should have said was that he is something of an impersonal automaton and not much of a talker. Direct cinema, when it aims at character revelation, requires at least a minimum level of volubility. Interestingly, the narration acknowledges Crossfield's reserve, explaining that he's "too busy" to talk any more and that we will learn about him by watching his activities. These activities, however, are decidedly impersonal in nature, and the added personality assessments by Crossfield's secretary and other associates are merely desperate attempts at making the machine human. The footage of the flight is good, but interest in the pilot's danger is scarcely sufficient to support the supposedly tense nature of the flight.

The relevant comparison to *X-Pilot* will be *Eddie,* most of which had already been filmed (and shown as *On the Pole*) before *X-Pilot.* If we are to be led up to a moment of dramatic crisis (as *X-Pilot* would have us), some feeling toward the people involved beyond indifference is essential. On this standard (which it sets for itself through suggesting that Crossfield is more interesting than he appears), *X-Pilot* is a disappointment.

The Children Were Watching

The Children Were Watching, third of the four "Close-up" films (made before *X-Pilot* but shown after it), was shot in New Orleans during one week of a school integration crisis. Completed the same year as *Primary,* the improvement in technique and story construction is considerable. *The Children Were Watching* is the first of the Drew-Leacock films to emerge fully formed, where no apologies have to be made for equipment problems or unsuitability of subject matter.

A good summary of the film's events is available,[34] though it is hardly a substitute, of course, for seeing the film. (Another measure of the success of a direct cinema work appears to be the extent to which telling "what it's about" comes close to reporting the events themselves, that is, the degree to which the film cannot be broken down into an easily repeated story or quickly outlined arguments.) Briefly, the film is an exploration of white segregationist attitudes as they manifest themselves in situations surrounding an attempt to integrate a local public school and of their effects upon a black family (the Gabriels) whose daughter is supposed to be one of the first to attend a previously all-white school.

The Children Were Watching is a suitable test case at this point for the omnipresent question of objectivity. Since the film divides its time between white segregationists and a black family, can it be said that both sides are treated fairly? One test for this would be to ask whether the people involved would object to the way they are shown. While the nature of the filmmaker's commitment is apparent in the film, the scales are not unduly tipped. White segregationists would presumably not find fault in the portrayal of their actions or convictions. Amidst the flurry of activity, *The Children Were Watching* allows them a lengthy opportunity to air their views. Arnold Dubrow, a white PTA leader, discusses in detail his feelings that blacks are essentially inferior and that integration is a Communist movement. Leander Perez, a well-known white segregationist leader in Louisiana, adds his agreement in a later scene. The film certainly treats white segregationists more squarely and openly than those supposedly more rational documentaries that try to soften the deep feelings behind their beliefs in order to suggest that objections to integration can be easily overcome. These whites are actually more interesting than the blacks in the film, since the rightness of the latter's cause makes their own activities and comments more predictable.

If there is a point in *The Children Were Watching* where over-emotionalism becomes objectionable, it is in the title conception, the rather obvious assertion that prejudice is passed on from parents to children. This is translated three or four times into visual terms by pans and/or zooms to children looking on as their parents yell "nigger" or other heated epithets. It is too conspicuous a device, too much a play on our sympathies through deliberate visual manipulation. The nature of prejudice is too complex for this facile connection to carry sufficient weight.

A. William Bluem in *Documentary in American Television* is prepared to use *The Children Were Watching* as a test case, too. Through it, he brands direct cinema of this kind "a negation of that virtue which underlies the documentary idea," of failing to "explain the meaning of events in order to invoke the sobriety of reason."[35] Leacock, Bluem says, "was predisposed to show only hate and fear at its most tumultuous level, leaving no room, no avenue, for thoughtful action." He feels that emotional involvement here becomes an end in itself, rather than a means to lead people to intellectual involvement. He goes on to conclude that direct cinema's "significant niche" is to be found in stories outside situations of social concern, that it "must, in the final analysis, be removed from the contemporary disputes which men must resolve in the name of reason if they are to survive . . . but New Orleans, the places where great national decisions are made, and all the other pressure points of a civilization cannot be the foci of application."[36]

Though his argument is more fully expounded, his essential point is the same as Shayon's in relation to *Yanki, No!,* that judicious narration is required to analyze events and that a positive course of action must be outlined. This view misunderstands the intentions of direct cinema as badly as it misinterprets the possibilities for reasoned discourse by television. It is clearly no accident that Bluem, like Shayon, has won laurels for documentary writing, for their attitude thinly veils a belief in the supremacy of the narrated word ("reason") over the word spoken by a participant in a real event ("emotion"), of the explanation for why something happens over the power of an event to be its own

The Children Were Watching. Angry parents.

The Children Were Watching. One of the "watchers."

The Children Were Watching. The Gabriel child on her way to school.

evidence. Bluem and Shayon imply that the visual image (and even the synchronized word) should be no more than a lesser adjunct to the voice of narrative wisdom.

Any reasoned proposal for ways to effect integration has to answer the challenge of *The Children Were Watching*. Traditional documentaries are founded upon the assumption that there are answers to all issues, that solutions can be found. The past ten years have not seen segregation problems solved, and the fault for that cannot be laid at the door of verite. Furthermore, "reason" can be put forth in printed form, and if the only purpose for its use in news documentary is that it can reach more people, then there is no need for these efforts to be considered anything more than photographed essays, which, alas, is what most of them are.

Bluem specifically calls for detachment, and the crux of his error is that he sees detachment as prerequisite to reason. When Bluem says that in *The Children Were Watching* "no room is left for thoughtful action," he means either that there is always room for thoughtful action and Leacock has closed it off or, possibly, that if the events themselves do not reveal room for thoughtful action then it is the filmmaker's task to tone down their innate emotionalism by distorting the event. The issues of *Yanki, No!* and *The Children Were Watching,* revolution in Latin America and integration in the United States, are two fine examples of problems that are discussed by a citizenry so far removed from actual experience that their rational discourse lacks a firm foothold in reality. To pass judgment on any proposed solutions to the integration problem in the South, one must first realize the formidable opposition that exists there toward *all* solutions.

But in any case, *The Children Were Watching* contradicts no plans for integration and does not deny the possibility for later change. It simply shows what happened the first time it was tried in New Orleans. It is the task of each viewer to consider the events, not for a narrator to indicate how to react. The emotional-

ism of *The Children Were Watching* is, in fact, its fundamental
strength. There is a scene on the street in front of the school
when an irate woman, after talking about her willingness to "die
for her cause" of keeping the schools white, turns in anger upon
the camera and starts to smash it. The screen goes black for
about ten seconds, as the yelling and noise continues. At this
moment the camera communicates a truly subjective experience, making the viewer feel like an actual participant. When the
woman lashes out at the camera (at us), we know more about
the pressures against integration than any verbal presentation
(narrated or in print) could convey. Rather than assuming, as
Bluem does, that Leacock was predisposed to show hate and
fear (since Leacock's predispositions are entirely a speculative
matter), it is more natural to assume that he was faced with the
task of reporting what he witnessed. Further, as Bluem chooses
to ignore but as we have already noted, the scenes of anger are
not the whole film. Those who overreact to the emotional moments are voicing their distaste for the event as much as for its
depiction in the film.

If *The Children Were Watching* were all sound and fury, it would
be easy to dismiss it as a cursory examination of an extremist
event. But we are also shown what's behind the anger and what
its effects (on the black family) can be, and the connections
among these elements (the anger, its motives, its results) are
convincingly made. That it is powerful dramatically is almost beside the point.

Adventures on the New Frontier
Until February 1961 Drew was still a salaried employee of Time
Inc. At that time he formed his own production company, Robert
Drew Associates. For all intents and purposes, however, the pro-
duction arrangements remained the same as they had been be-
fore the new company was set up. Time Inc. continued to finance
Drew Associates as they had Drew's earlier efforts and still acted

as selling agent for the films while retaining future rights.[37] Though free from Time Inc. by name, Drew Associates remained bound on both sides (financing and distribution) by the parent company.

The last of the "Close-up" programs was shown one month after the formation of the new company. *Adventures on the New Frontier* is "a day in the life" of John F. Kennedy in the White House. It is a film that should be mercifully passed over. Beyond a structural interest and its value for comparison with more successful projects, *Adventures on the New Frontier* has little to merit attention. It is usually best to ignore the overinflated opening and closing narrations of these films, but the beginning of this one points up the unrealized possibilities that are at the heart of the problem: "Now you will begin to move with the President, seeing and hearing for yourself in a new kind of report, not a filmed version of a summary or opinion you could find in print, but a personal adventure with the President as he confronts the great problems of the U.S. and the world. . . ." The idea is admirable, but its execution leaves much to be desired.

The first part of the film suggests that it has been assembled from old snippets too choice to be discarded. We see about ten minutes of footage from *Primary* (without being told it is part of the earlier film), a brief scene with John Kenneth Galbraith and John Steinbeck on the way to the Inauguration, and a slight segment from the Inaugural Ball. From here *Adventures on the New Frontier* is organized by themes, and the device is too artificial and limiting. The trick used is to play a line from Kennedy's Inaugural Address (over a shot of the White House) to introduce the subject of the following segment. This is done five or six times. The separate parts are a nice introduction to some of the responsibilities the President has to bear, but it plays like a classroom lesson.

After an interminable succession of theme segments (which include conferences about unemployment, the economy, the Peace Corps, Africa, the military), there is a final glimmer of hope

when a segment is introduced by a shot of the White House at
night and a narrative promise that "Now you will see and hear
Kennedy at more intimate moments." While we see him, though,
we aren't permitted to hear him. Overaggressive narration is
again called into service to substitute for film deficiencies, as we
are told what is happening instead of being left alone to hear
(and see) for ourselves. One must assume either that extensive
synch shooting of private conversations was not permitted or that
they were later excised. In either case, there is nothing so frustrating as being promised a peek in a keyhole and then having
the light inside turned off. Despite its own claims to the contrary,
Adventures on the New Frontier dotes on the JFK charisma without getting beyond it.

Kenya, Africa

Kenya, Africa (it is often called *Kenya,* but the longer title appears
in the film and is also the more proper label, as Kenya is to be
taken as a typical African nation) was a venture in the *Yanki, No!*
genre, a political analysis through a combination of individual
personality studies and more general segments about conditions
in the country. The film is nominally divided into two parts, *Land
of the White Ghost* and *Land of the Black Ghost.* Opening narration says that the first half will show Africa from the point of view
of the white settlers, and the second will deal with "what it's like
to be in an African country about to become independent." The
conception and its realization are again two different things, and
this is another case of certain parts being superior to the whole.

The best segment of the film is the only one that sticks to the
original intentions, that tries to show Africa through one man's
point of view. That man is Jim Hughes, a British colonist who
owns a large farm in Kenya. Hughes talks freely as he leads a
tour of his farm, telling of the difficulties he had in settling in Africa and the struggle to establish a good life for his family. He
proudly shows off the village he built for his native workers and
tells how civilized he has made them. He is asked if he knows

Kenya, Africa

Kenya, Africa

Kenya, Africa

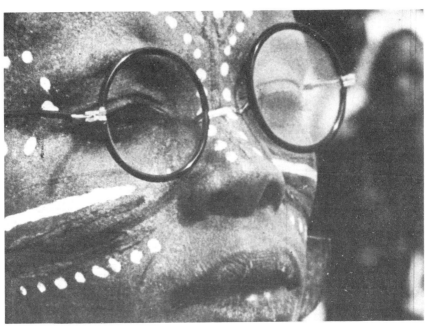

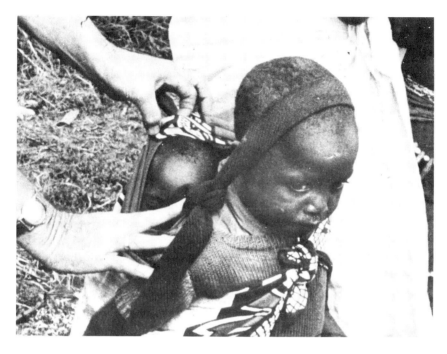

what the word *uhuru* (freedom) means, and he replies that he
does not. Talking about the state of his country, Hughes asks,
"What's going to happen to law and order?"

Like the white segregationists in *The Children Were Watching,*
but on a quieter, more refined level, Hughes damns himself with
his own words (that is, if the viewer is opposed to colonialism).
The possibility of his "acting" for the camera is irrelevant, as
Hughes is clearly putting on a show for its benefit. It is his colonialist assumptions, the core of his very nature, that leave him
exposed. As Paul-Louis Thirard has observed, even though
Hughes has carefully prepared his presentation, it is no less revealing. As in a court of law, "everything you say may be held
against you."[38]

Louis Marcorelles says of the Hughes segment: "Politically, the
brief portrait of the Kenyan colonist, who will appear infamous to
some and touching to others, according to what you think of
whites and blacks, defines most precisely the words 'filmed journalism.'"[39] Thirard and Marcorelles are making the same point,
that it is possible with direct cinema to let a person reveal his
thoughts and way of living and still allow the film to stand as evidence to support different conclusions. Ideally, and it is so here,
there is even room for mixed feelings. Hughes is a very friendly
sort, well meaning, and hardly violent. He just doesn't question
his role as a colonialist. A viewer with different assumptions is
free to leave with different conclusions. Neither biased narration,
argumentative interview questions, deliberate attempts to make
the subject look foolish, nor garish camera angles intrude on the
film portrait. Leacock, again, was responsible for this difficult feat
of treating an unpopular subject openly. He has spoken of his
view of "the fundamental equality of all the people we film,"[40] and
this is a fine example of the result of openness to a subject's
views.

Sadly, the Hughes segment comprises less than half of Part I
of *Kenya, Africa,* and the rest of the film is quite a muddle.

Hughes is introduced at the start, but, with the narrated excuse
that "to understand Jim Hughes you have to understand . . . ,"
the film goes off on a number of tangents. This portion is standard travelogue material, with rather bad narration. For instance,
over shots of an ordinary city scene, the narrator tries to pep
things up by reporting, "This sunlit calm is deceptive. Underneath
is fear." There are even brief shots of wildlife so clichéd they
could be stock footage (narrator: "This is a hard land"). The only
bright spot in this first half of *Land of the White Ghost* is a scene
of some rich Californians on safari, dining on lobster and aspara-
gus in the middle of the wilderness and chatting about baboons.
Shortly after, the Hughes material begins and is interrupted several times by other interviews.

Part Two, *Land of the Black Ghost,* is a disappointment, failing
to get as close to any black as the first part got to Jim Hughes.
There is much talk of the "ghost" of Jomo Kenyatta, a native
leader still in jail seven years after Mau Mau uprisings he helped
instigate. A theatrical gimmick is used several times, Kenyatta's
face superimposed (like a ghost, apparently) over different
scenes of the country. The narration constantly attempts to build
a tension between the promise of emerging independence and
the threat of tribal uprising. The natives, however, hardly look
threatening, and, after all, the Mau Mau revolt was a good time
earlier. There are some scenes with election candidates (a feeble
attempt to make this an African *Primary*), and the Kenyatta ghost
continually pops up. It is even used as the final shot, where the
narrator says his release from prison is still the key issue. This
seems, though, little more than a lame excuse for failing to provide a fuller examination of the black condition in Kenya.

A couple of years later, Drew and Leacock expressed dissatisfaction with *Kenya, Africa.* Drew felt that the documentary genre
(presumably referring to this film and *Yanki, No!*) was less satisfying than the single-person dramas. He went on to say that the
very fact of its lengthy narration made it inferior to a film like

Eddie, which has much less external commentary.[41] At any rate, it will be interesting to see that with *Nehru,* they studiously avoided a broad show-the-whole-country approach. Although the outcome is still less than satisfactory, their willingness to risk different mistakes on ambitious projects, rather than always repeating easy formulas, contributed importantly to the high level of accomplishment in their films.

"Living Camera"—An Aside

Over the next couple of years, from mid-1961 to the end of 1963, Drew Associates (which no longer included Albert Maysles) made an even dozen one-hour films. Of the twelve, only two were shown on network television. The other ten films were eventually tied together as a series called the "Living Camera" (a name often mistakenly applied to all the Drew-Leacock films). They made these films in the hope of enticing a buyer for a TV series that would continue,[42] but this plan didn't work out, mainly because the networks considered the films to be documentaries, and they chose to produce their own. The "Living Camera" series was eventually shown on RKO General stations. Prior to the time they were shown on American television, several of the films were shown at European festivals, and some even had a few commercial showings there, so the work of Drew Associates was known and discussed in Europe well before it had any impact here.

The films were all financed by Time Inc., at a reputed total cost of about two million dollars.[43] It remains to that organization's credit that they so richly supported such a pioneering experiment. In terms of both technique and subject matter, it was quite a gamble. In view of the network feelings about independently produced documentaries (recall the conflict at ABC that led to John Daly's resignation), it is simply incredible that Drew Associates was given sufficient freedom to make these relatively expensive films on subjects as unnewsworthy as a retiring airline pilot, a high school football game, and a young pianist's competition. For whatever compromises made to network tastes, the adventurousness of the whole enterprise is still formidable in retrospect. The irony is that although the films conformed to prime-time network conditions, they were rarely shown over that medium.

On the Road to Button Bay

The one Drew Associates film that *was* shown on network television in 1962, a year they were at work on six other films that would eventually become a part of the "Living Camera" series, is a piece of completely uncondescending Americana. *On the Road to Button Bay* slips easily into its story of three girls from Topeka, Kansas, and their trip to a Fiftieth Anniversary Girl Scout celebration in Vermont. The structure is simply defined (preparations for the trip, the Jamboree, the return), and the small moments of drama and fun are plentiful. The only "crisis" is not a dominant element of the story, a minor trauma as one of the girls cries over the problems of being a patrol leader. For the most part, the film is carried by the light banter of the kids and their wide-eyed innocence while coping with a series of unfamiliar situations. Had the filmmakers desired, the film could have gone out "to get" the Girl Scouts, to subtly ridicule their activities. Happily, there is no suggestion of this, and *On the Road to Button Bay* is a delight.

Some argue that this low-key type of subject is the only sort suited to direct-cinema techniques. Bluem says, "The very success of Drew's method in *Button Bay* stressed the reason for its failure in almost all the News Documentaries which Drew's unit produced." He feels that in *Button Bay* "the unity of climax and resolution was inherent in the story," and that more controversial subjects do not lend themselves to traditional dramatic forms.[44]

While agreeing that direct cinema is eminently suited to situations with little news value, I believe that the rest of Bluem's structural analysis is pointed 180 degrees in the wrong direction. It is

On the Road to Button Bay

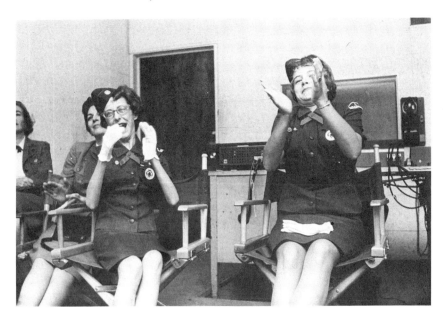

On the Road to Button Bay

the *Button Bay* kind of story where "the unity of climax and resolution" is *least* inherent in the story. A suggestion of the usual
Drew structure comes up often (cutting between the preparations
of each of the girls for the trip, the mini-crisis previously mentioned), but there is too much happening to allow it to take
charge. Because no dramatic course of events overrides lesser
activities, the film is hardly committed to a crisis structure. In
more controversial situations, eventual climax and resolution are
the elements that initially determine what the story will be.

Regarding *The Children Were Watching,* a film that Bluem dis-
likes, he argued in quite contradictory fashion, saying in effect
that crisis and conflict were *too much* in evidence in the real
events. So when Bluem says he likes *Button Bay* for its "inherent" structure, what he is really saying is that drama may be present in more controversial subjects, but it is better left to "human
interest" stories of little public consequence. He skirts the central
issue of the extent to which the crisis structure is suited to *any*
subject, whether large or small, preferring instead this veiled suggestion that matters of public concern are best left to the "creative" documentarians. His discussion of structure is simply ration-
alization to support this narrow view.

By the time of *Button Bay,* the equipment of Drew Associates
was as flexible as it would become. Shooting everywhere and in
synch is now quite normal, but it is easy to forget how much this
adds to a film like *Button Bay.* Being able to record one girl's difficulty in getting up at 5:30 AM for a practice camp-out, to follow
them on a train,[45] and always to catch their mumbled comments
and cute expressions gives the film a personal intimacy sufficient
to sustain what otherwise might have been dull in the extreme.
The relationship of the camera to the people it records will continue to be a matter for consideration, but the fact of the filmmaker's ability (should he choose to exercise it) always to be with
his subject should not be ignored.

On the Road to Button Bay is a good place to point up once
more the difficulty of assigning creative responsibility for a par-

ticular film. Besides Drew's customary credit as Executive Producer, the credits list six filmmakers, two assistants, four editors,
and two assistant editors, making a total of fifteen acknowledged
contributors. To call the film Drew's, Leacock's, or anyone else's
is quite a simplification. (Admittedly, in some cases it is not so
difficult.) When so many people shoot different portions, which
others may edit, the best we can do is pin final responsibility on
Drew, who did run the whole show, and note individual contributions when appropriate.

On the Pole and Eddie

Many writers have assumed that *On the Pole* and *Eddie* are al-
ternate titles for the same film; in fact, they are two different films.
(However, such is not the case with *Mooney vs. Fowle* and *Football,* two names for one film.) *On the Pole,* except for a brief portion, was filmed at the 1960 Indianapolis 500 race. The first half
of *Eddie* is taken from *On the Pole* material, and the second half
was shot in color at the 1961 Indianapolis race. The distinction
is necessary because the second film is not merely a sequel.
Both films are about race car driver Eddie Sachs, but the manner in which the second is shot and edited, and the film's division
into half-and-half coverage of two races, are important distinctions.

   On the Pole begins with some newsreel footage of an Indianapolis race, and we see a car spin out. It is now a year later, the
narrator says, and Eddie Sachs is back to try once more. We
first meet Sachs as he drives a passenger car, telling the camera
about the advantages of the pole position (first row in the race,
on the inside). The early part of the film has several scenes in
which Eddie speaks directly to the camera, explaining different
aspects of the race. There is also a poolside interview with
Eddie's wife about his past accidents (narrator: "Dark memories
that return on a sunny day"), where she tells about the operations
he had after a particularly bad crash: "They even put holes in
his eyelids so eyelashes could grow. I think it's a wonderful

thing." In theory unsympathetic to using interview material, the Drew films used it on occasion but generally (as in this case) only to supply information of a nonfactual nature, not as a substitute for action. Also atypical in the first part is a shot of a newspaper headline, carrying in a glance more about the town's excitement than any scene could show. In big letters the paper reads "Sachs Wins Pole"; below this and smaller: "10,000 Turks Repulsed." Not dwelt upon, it is quite humorous, but fortunately they did not try for laughs like this on other occasions.

As race time nears, action begins to dominate talk. Following a printed title, "4:00 AM—Day of the Race," a fine unnarrated sequence of early preparations is an effective suspense builder. A large number of cars are already on their way to the track. We also see an early mass for the drivers (as with the bullfighters in *Bullfight at Malaga*) and shots of souvenir peddlers and program sellers. Nicely inserted is a quick shot of nurses walking onto the track, the sort of journalistic detail that Drew wisely chooses not to comment upon.

Eddie becomes less concerned about the camera as the race gets closer, but because the audience has already seen his normally assured manner, it realizes his present quiet nervousness. Busy taping his goggles and lost in his own private thoughts, he jumps up late for the "Star-Spangled Banner." As he gets into his car, he silently clasps his hands, closes his eyes, and mutters a prayer. He's in tears, and it is inconceivable that he could be concerned with the presence of the camera at this point.

The footage of the race is hardly more than competent, but a couple of points are worth noting. Near the start of the race, a grandstand collapses. There are only two brief shots of it and the sound of the track announcer calling for a doctor, and then back to the races. In an interview a couple of years later, Leacock said that eight people were killed in that mishap.[46] The incident is all but ignored in the film, a fact worth mentioning in the face of criticism about the Drew films that they always exploit dramatic incidents. Here, it was not part of Eddie's story, and it wound up

a wholly understated moment. Also interesting is the simple difference in filmed life-and-death situations when the audience feels
close to a protagonist. In *X-Pilot* it was hard to care about the
outcome of an equally hazardous task. In *On the Pole,* even if
you don't like Eddie you still care what happens to him. He is not
a neutral personality.

   Eddie has to quit the race because of car trouble. This unpredictable outcome had no bearing on the film's opportunity for
resolution. Like *Primary* and many of the other films, whatever
happened, win or lose, there was still an ending. As the winner
is being cheered, Eddie stands alone on the track. The action at
this point is described by Colin Young as follows: "He becomes
aware of the camera, tries to pretend he has not seen it, but we
become aware of his bluff—we see him putting on an act, we see
him gradually becoming resentful of the camera he had earlier
accepted and welcomed; and because of this we see more
clearly below the surface of a man who lived to win and lost—
precisely because, when Sachs was no longer lost in his own
task, the camera became an intrusive element."[47] This explanation may be overinterpretive, but an important point is made—a
subject can be aware of the camera, and in spite of that (or because of it), we can learn something about him.

   In *On the Pole,* Sachs shows three different levels of camera
awareness. The first is in speaking directly to the camera, as
when he discusses some aspect of the race. Here he tries to put
forward a positive view of himself, though we may still feel differently about him from what he might wish (as we could in the
scenes of the white colonialist in *Kenya, Africa*). The second level
is found in the scenes just before and during the race, where he
is so wrapped up in other things that we truly feel he forgets the
camera. The third level is this last case, when Sachs sees the
camera and pretends he isn't noticing it, but we realize that he
does.

   Young feels that *On the Pole* is the most articulate film that
came from the Drew-Leacock association.[48] I would agree, but

with the provision that *articulate* not be equated with *best. On the Pole* is of particular interest for the reason just cited, the rich interplay of camera-subject relationships. Also, the subject is most suited to the usual structure of the Drew films, something close to a traditional storytelling method. (It is worth noting that, as in *Primary,* the subject was chosen by Drew.)[49] The issue of "finding" or "forcing" a story is an extremely tricky matter, but here the conception was whole, and the structure seems precisely right. *On the Pole* showed conclusively that this kind of recorded reality could be as exciting as any fictional drama. One may well ask if that is the best use of direct cinema; but given that purpose (which most of the Drew films have), *On the Pole* fulfills its dramatic dimension admirably.

With such a smoothly flowing structure, though, there is always a nagging feeling that something is wrong. That a cinema-verite

On the Pole and *Eddie.* Eddie during the race.

On the Pole and *Eddie.* Eddie after the race.

film is dramatically satisfying may be even more reason to suspect it of sacrificing some aspects of truth on the altar of entertainment. Leacock takes issue with the very scene Young likes so
much, saying that it is too easily misinterpreted. He thinks that
"in fact, Eddie was just damn well pleased to be alive."[50] There
may be some room for this interpretation on the basis of the
filmed evidence, but the emphasis on winning throughout the film
naturally leads to the assumption that he is heartbroken by the
loss. *On the Pole* might have left a little wider possibility for less
clichéd interpretations. As it is, the dramatic resolution tends to
limit the ambiguity of the outcome. Eddie fits the role of the tragic
hero too closely.

The rationale behind the "crisis" format includes more than its dramatic efficacy. Justification for this structure (as it is expressed in the narration of some of the films and also by several critics of the films) includes the feeling that a person's true nature comes out in crisis situations. By seeing a man in crisis, the argument goes, we learn things about him that would never be apparent in less hectic situations and that he himself could never express in direct interviews. Consider, for instance, this explanation of the closing moments of On the Pole: "After the race, his thoughts of retiring are gone. He will, of course, try again. Why does he race? He never tells us, but we know, in an intimate and complex way that defies verbalization. We know because we have been close to Eddie Sachs during a crisis in his life."[51] Like the "moment of truth" in bullfighting, the crisis is supposed to be a man's ultimate test.

In On the Pole, this idea holds up. It worked so well, in fact, that it came close to being a formula, with less than satisfactory consequences in situations not so well suited to this structure. Further, we might question the philosophical (or rather, psychological) basis for this approach. Do crises indeed show the "true" nature of man? Can we really assume anything about a person and his motives from how he acts in a crisis?

Summing up on this point, three advantages are generally claimed for the crisis structure:
1. The subject is less aware of the camera during these difficult moments, and hence he acts more naturally.
2. The building up to the crisis, the crisis itself, and its resolution provide an exciting dramatic structure.
3. By seeing the subject put through a test, we learn things about him that we couldn't find out through other means.

On the Pole is the quintessential Drew crisis film, and the one in which these attributes are most apparent. There are Drew films where the subjects seem less aware of the camera (Football), where the structure is more satisfactory and the resolution more complete (Crisis: Behind a Presidential Commitment), and where we learn more about a person in a crisis moment *(Jane)*; but never is there so harmonious a combination of these elements as in *On the Pole.*

On the Pole has a *Primary*-like conclusion, with Eddie and his wife leaving for another race in Milwaukee. The last words of the film are an open invitation to a sequel; Mrs. Sachs tells her husband as they drive away from Indianapolis, "Next year, Eddie." The "next year" Mrs. Sachs spoke of comes in *Eddie,* where condensed *On the Pole* material makes up the first thirty minutes. The narrative bridge between one year and the next is continued: still photos of four drivers who were killed that year, superimposed over a shot of a car crashing. The narration intones their names and tells where they were killed. (The risk of death was not overstated, as Sachs himself was killed in a crash several years later.) Part Two bursts into living color with some rapidly speeded-up shots of the parking lots and grandstands filling up on the day of the race (a gimmick that was used in *Primary,* and which Chris Marker later employed in *Le Joli Mai*). Seeing Eddie in color requires some reorientation. The color gives him more presence in a literal sense—making him seem more in the present—but the color feels overly obtrusive and unnecessary. When we see the releasing of hundreds of balloons as we did in *On the Pole* (a yearly ritual before the start of each race), the difference color makes is too large; it detracts from the narrative. Further, everything in this half (shot at the 1961 race) is outdoors. Apparently, color also kept the camera crew from going inside, an unfortunate restriction since the chance to stay with the subject as much as possible should be more important than the beauty of color.

This half is nearly all of the race, unlike *On the Pole,* which used the race as a climax to a long series of preparations and scenes that let us get to know Eddie. The 1961 race is shot very differently from the preceding year's, which was more conventionally executed. Here, there is a constant intercutting between the race's action and Mrs. Sachs's reaction as she watches from the stands. As Eddie pulls in for a tire change, for instance, cut to Mrs. Sachs yelling for them to hurry up. When there is a car crash, we hear the sound of her screaming before cutting to see her expression. Throughout the race, we see almost as much of her as we do of the race itself.

This kind of editing raises serious questions. It isn't simply that there is crosscutting between two actions, but that we are to believe that the cuts are "honest," that the two actions are wholly simultaneous. There is a great deal of intercutting in the Drew films, as between Kennedy and Humphrey in *Primary,* or the black family and the white segregationists in *The Children Were Watching,* but usually these cuts do not necessarily require our believing that the two events are occurring at the same moment. Here it is essential, for if we do not feel that Mrs. Sachs's scream comes at the exact moment it is put on the sound track (at the time of the car crash), we feel manipulated and cheated. An acceptable device in fiction films, crosscutting is possible in direct cinema employing a narrative structure only if we believe in the simultaneous occurrence of the two events, because drama arises *solely* from that fact.

Leacock and Drew claim absolute synchronization in this case,[52] and there is no reason to doubt them. There is, at least, a specificity to Mrs. Sachs's responses that leads one to believe that the editing has been honest. One must note, though, that the drama in the race depends upon a certain omniscient view; two simultaneous events must be covered in order to appreciate either. This is a fundamentally different approach to the recording of an event (by means of multiple camera crews and later compilation of overlapping material) from the technique of shooting with one camera and trying to contruct a narrative from that. *On the Pole* and *Eddie* (or the two halves of *Eddie*) are good examples of these two prevailing tendencies in storytelling (and editing) techniques. The first tells a more or less continuous story of one

person. The second seeks to provide a fuller view of an event
through cutting between what are, in effect, two stories occurring at once. In each case the event is the same (the running of
a race), but the methods chosen to cover it are different.

Eddie ends with Sachs coming in second, and once again there
are concluding scenes stressing his determination to try again.
This ending is probably the worst of the possible outcomes (in
terms of drama) because it is so close to what happened the year
before. Because of that, the whole second half seems superfluous. So, the weakened dramatic tension and the unreconciled
editing differences between the two halves of the film combine
to make Eddie less satisfactory than On the Pole.

David

David is about an ex-addict living at Synanon House, where
similar individuals voluntarily join together to help each other
stay away from drugs. We are with David for a week (or so the
narration states), waiting to see if the young trumpet player will
be able to stay off heroin. His story gets sidetracked a couple of
times by episodes of two other addicts, both of whom eventually
leave, presumably to return to drugs. This works neatly, suggesting only too obviously the possibilities for David.

There is the inevitable go at a crisis moment. At a time when
the stories of all three addicts are coming to a head, the narrator
says that "emotions are building up to an explosive Synanon
session." The session turns out to be little more than a dull
encounter group situation lasting for at least a fourth of the film.
The experience is less than enlightening and not a satisfactory
resolution to the manufactured crisis. The film ends as it begins,
with shots of David swimming in the sea. This week (says the
narrator) has been a victory for David.

David is redeemed by a tangible degree of concern for its title
subject's fate, a feeling of cameraman's love for his subject.
Where in On the Pole our interest in Eddie as a person is closely
tied to the excitement of the race, in David we care more for the

nature of his struggle than for dramatic titillation. There are a couple of beautiful scenes with David and his wife and child, the tenderest moments in any of the "Living Camera" films. David's music is also skillfully employed, a fittingly melancholic sound that is used for mood in several well-edited sequences that seek to do nothing more than convey the feeling of the place at that time. (However, some find this contrived. Henry Breitrose, for one, objects strenuously: "It is as if the style screams to the audience 'Isn't this poetic and moving!' It may very well have been, but the qualities of poesy and emotion are destroyed by its obviousness.")[53] The moments when plot is not advanced are invariably the most interesting in *David.*

The better qualities of *David* are due to D. A. Pennebaker, and credit is given here only because *David* is indicative of a particular sensibility that is evident elsewhere in Pennebaker's films. In its own way, Pennebaker's work is equally as distinctive as Leacock's, and while his range of interests is more limited, his style is no less identifiable. Louis Marcorelles even goes so far as to say that only Pennebaker, among all those who worked on these films, was able to assert a personal style, and that he accomplished this in *David* and *Jane.*[54] While Pennebaker's accomplishment is not so unique as Marcorelles asserts (because Leacock displays a personal style as well), anyone familiar with his later work would know who is responsible for *David.*

The Hemingway-like ending of *David* brings up a touchy issue, the degree to which a filmmaker should have control over the material he shoots. Marcorelles, in the same article, raves about the final moments: "The last scene attains an extraordinary plastic beauty; it gives us the nostalgia of a more refined classical cinema, of a Frank Borzage enriched by nuances of direct: David's success is in the balance, he goes bathing in the California waves, entering almost timidly into the water. And Pennebaker's camera follows him from a distance, trembling imperceptibly, as if at the mercy of the waves which carry him."[55] Pennebaker, however, dismisses the ending completely, saying

David. David with his family.

David. David in encounter group session.

David

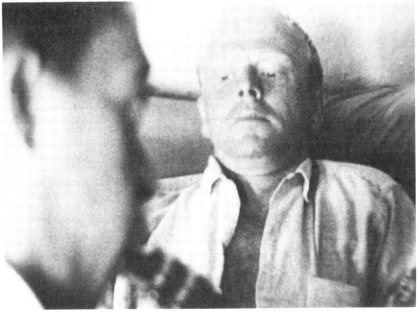

that it was forced on him against his objections. He thinks it falsely suggests that David is better off at the end of the film than he was at the start, which simply wasn't so.[56] Whether or not Pennebaker is correct in his interpretation, this is a good place to assert what should have been assumed from the first: the edited film should not contradict the filmmaker's view of the event. Marcorelles may be right about the beauty of the last scene in *David,* but if the person who shot it doesn't think it's a true representation of the event, then it shouldn't be there. Involved in this case, of course, is the possible conflict between honesty and drama, a matter that goes well beyond the more obvious question of creative freedom.

Petey and Johnny

Petey and Johnny belongs to that category usually labeled "interesting failures." Tackling a particularly difficult subject, a teenage gang in a New York slum area, the film falls victim to the incompatibility of the subject matter with the enforced dramatic form. This is the reverse of a common problem. The subject clearly encompasses a surfeit of gripping incidents. Rather than having to inject interest into seemingly banal material, the problem here was to find a form that could make sense of a mass of footage that lacked the preferred type of crisis situation. Patricia Jaffe, who worked on the editing of the film, confirms what is obvious from the final version:

. . . there were volumes of material with no real core idea. Petey Thomas's daily contact, as a youth worker, with East Harlem gangs was the one thread running through the film. The footage, shot during six months, was diffuse and dealt with diverse individuals. Some of it was concentrated on one of the more prominent gang members, Johnny, an older youth in trouble with the police for illegal possession of weapons. Drew decided that Petey's relationship to Johnny should be the film's central idea, a concept that the material did not support. In an attempt to structure this difficult film, all the exciting moments were pulled from the footage and strung together with a force

that did violence to the final film. Sequences relating to Johnny
were juxtaposed to others dealing with a wide variety of individuals. The sequences themselves were never allowed to play
out but were instead cut to the bone, so that only the "moment"
remained. The film has no air, no connective tissue. . . .[57]

Colin Young puts it more diplomatically when he says "Drew
chose what he considered the best of two betrayals"—that is, he
slicked up the subject for the sake of the audience.[58]

However one puts it, the problem is structural. Ideally, of course,
no "betrayal" should be necessary in editing; a structure should
be possible that is both true to the subject and interesting for an
audience. But between conception and realization a lot of things
can happen, and the dual goal of honesty and interest is not so
easily attained given the many uncertainties of undirected situations. Whether the problem is pinpointed as too much shooting
of peripheral material, fundamental unsuitability of subject matter,
or a clichéd structure, the result is little bits and pieces of fascinating material that even by themselves are finally unsatisfying.
The film tries to cover too much and winds up being about not
enough. Perhaps some small part should have been expanded or
a simpler story line found that would not suggest so many possibilities ultimately thwarted. Trying to tackle challenging material
requires a willingness to break from old methods. As it is, *Petey
and Johnny* looks like the result of substituting unclassifiable
unknowns into a standard formula.

Petey and Johnny is the only Drew film to employ a device common in the work of some other direct-cinema filmmakers (especially William Jersey): narration read by a participant in the film
rather than by an announcer. In this case it was essential, but
it signals a failure by admitting that an insider's view is necessary
to make sense of the story. Given the constant shifting from incident to incident, the audience has to be continually supplied with
a point of view. Petey, the social worker, provides a running commentary throughout the film. To some extent this is a useful approach, but the narration ventures well beyond the expository

to interpret states of mind of the participants and to pass judgment on them. Further, as a dramatic character Petey is a failure.
Paragons of virtue are as unacceptable in direct cinema as in
fiction, and Petey compounds the felony through excessive
moralizing.

 Skillful moments remain. Drew and his people were able to capture some feeling of the street. Sequences of the funeral for a
boy stabbed in a gang fight (reportedly filmed by Leacock),[59] a
street corner singing group, and a pool room scene all have a
power that isn't quite lost in the structural quagmire. However,
a few good moments culled from six months of filming simply
aren't enough. But direct cinema would not be as interesting if
every project yielded predictable results, and *Petey and Johnny*
could not have failed so thoroughly had it not been (because it
was shot in a genuinely unpredictable situation) such a daring
attempt in the first place.

Football

Football (actual title: *Mooney vs. Fowle,* but known under both
names), about a game between two Miami high schools, is primarily the work of James Lipscomb. Although it takes full advantage of the prodigious resources the Drew team had at its disposal (at one point there were eight camera crews in action),[60]
the film avoids the *Petey and Johnny* problem of voluminous
footage chopped to pieces in search of a controlling idea.
Football is successful because its makers understood that freedom in direct cinema does not mean unselective shooting. It is
not just the story of a football game filmed from different points
of view and then edited together.

 In the same way that filmmakers working in fictional genres
like the western or gangster film can respect formula restrictions yet move beyond them, Lipscomb gets around the limitations of the crisis structure. Although the film rushes forward
to a sure resolution (since the game will end), the focus is on
what the people in the film do out of a desire to win. While we

cared (or were supposed to) whether Eddie Sachs would win his race or Scott Crossfield would bring his plane home safely, in *Football,* though it is similarly based on a contest, who wins isn't of crucial importance. This perspective is achieved by deliberate selection. By making the film a story about two teams and their coaches and emphasizing parallels rather than differences between the two, Lipscomb de-emphasizes the final outcome. If, instead of *Mooney vs. Fowle* (the names of the coaches), the film had been *Mooney,* for example, then this would have been *On the Pole* all over again.

A widely held assumption about direct-cinema films is that they are often only as good as their choice of subject. In the present case, Colin Young states the basic argument: *"Football* exploits a situation of straightforward conflict. Given extroverts in front of the camera a skilled crew cannot miss."[61] This is too easy an assumption. On the one hand, the most unlikely subject can become interesting in the proper hands (Leacock's *Happy Mother's Day* comes most quickly to mind). Likewise, potentially exciting material can elude even the most skillful filmmakers. There are no sure-fire subjects, nor is there any telling what might turn out to be of interest. One would not expect a film about a high school football team to present such interesting possibilities, but the unexpected dimensions within routine subject matter are strictly a matter of the filmmaker's sensibility, not of having "extroverts" to film.

In *Primary,* the differences between Humphrey and Kennedy were emphasized by cutting from one to the other while they were engaged in similar activities. From a tense and quiet Kennedy on election night, cut to Humphrey laughing and enjoying a television show. Earlier, from the folksy atmosphere of a Humphrey phone-in TV program, cut to a television set in the middle of a stately, prepared speech by Kennedy. Devices like these support a structure that continually tries to play upon the personality differences of the candidates.

The same method of comparison through editing during

parallel activities is employed in *Football* for precisely the
opposite purpose, to show that the views from both sides are
identical. One well-executed scene shows the setting up of a
camera from a local television station and the beginning of
an interview with one of the coaches. In the middle of the interview, there is a cut to the other coach during *his* interview,
with the camera in the same TV-like stationary position. Besides the similar content of the interview halves, the cut to the
other coach shot from the identical camera position implies
that the same setting-up procedure also took place. Likewise,
a cut from one coach to the other and back during their pre-
game pep talks reveals the essential similarity between the activities of the two men. And like their coaches, the boys on both
teams and the kids in their schools are wholly homogenous.
Sometimes it is even difficult to differentiate the two sides.

These editing choices liberate the film from a preoccupation
with personality quirks and (since the outcome of the game becomes inconsequential when the opponents are interchangeable)
permit content to dominate structure. The emotional intensity
behind each side's desire to win and the pressure on the kids
to perform are illustrated in dozens of ways, from locker room
harangues by the coaches to players' tears. The active nature
of the participants (Young's "extroverts") is the raw material,
but Lipscomb and company knew (or found) what they were
after; the extroverts become indistinguishable in this study of
mass hysteria.

Because life does not always conform to dramatic conventions,
cases do occur when people do things that are "out of character" or that seem unmotivated. One example of this comes during
the closing moments of the game, when the winning coach is
twitching more nervously than his assured victory would suggest
he had to. A fictional writer would have to justify this reaction,
but it is pure gold in direct cinema. The problem is shifted to
establishing the credibility of the event, to showing conclusively

that the twitch (in this case) did indeed come in the closing moments and wasn't simply a shot from earlier in the game cut in at this late moment. In fact, one perceptive writer (who understood the film's parallelism) accused Lipscomb of exactly that device.[62] Establishing the truthfulness of the shot was taken care of in advance by one of direct cinema's surest weapons, the continuous take. As Lipscomb said in a letter replying, in part, to the previously mentioned article, after the close-up of the coach there is an outward zoom as the crowd counts out the last seconds, and the coach is then carried victoriously from the field.[63] While the filmmaker had to notice the tic in order to first zoom in on it, its veracity in terms of when it happened cannot be questioned. It is subjectively selected but no less accurate for that.

Small details are emphasized very effectively in *Football*, because the details (such as the tic) support the more apparent determined frenzy. The scene of a pre-game locker room prayer was easy to get. More interesting is the cheerleader's huddle before the game, as one girl whispers a hastily improvised prayer (". . . Help us win, God, because You know we are the greatest"). It has been reported that the filmmakers didn't even know what the girl was saying until later; someone just held a microphone up, and afterward they found it was a prayer that had been recorded.[64] Such methods are bound to turn up surprises, and they require a structure that can include them without overemphasizing their importance. (*Football* is also the classic example of one level of camera consciousness, often suggested to be the only valid one, of people so wrapped up in their own activities that the effect of the camera's presence is negligible.)

Finally, then, the film's prime attributes boil down to credible content and meaningful structure. *Football* is a social document, a case where journalism and cinema (supposedly the two opposing forces that Drew and Leacock represented) coexist easily.

It is in the company of a select few films that are successful in illuminating the American life-style through direct-cinema techniques. *Football* is firmly rooted in the ordinary, but it manages to maintain a high level of excitement without compromising its material.

Susan Starr

Susan Starr is one of the more predictable Drew-Leacock films. Given the subject, a young girl preparing for the finals of the Dimitri Mitropoulos Piano Competition at Carnegie Hall, there is little that can't be anticipated if one is familiar with a few Drew films. It is not a bad film, just not a very interesting one.

The dramatic structure is taken one step past the conventional to the thoroughly polished. After seeing Susan during her cab ride to the auditorium and at the beginning of her performance, there is a "flashback" to two days earlier, leading back to the point where the filming began and then continuing from there. The film intercuts Susan's preparations with the parallel activities of two of her competitors. (Sensing that it may have been a bit much, the narrator says that we are only seeing three of the four final contestants.) Thus, when Susan is in bed with a sore throat, there is a cut to someone else practicing. This technique, cutting between people preparing for the same event (whose conclusion will provide a sure ending for the film), is scarcely advanced beyond the *Primary* structure. This convention can be excused if it frees the filmmakers to do something else, but *Susan Starr* is consistently unsurprising. Perhaps the structure of the film is at fault, because the most mundane occurrences in films are acceptable provided they are not formula reinforcements of clichés. There are certainly suggestions of interesting possibilities that were not followed through. Susan's pushy parents, who started her practicing when she was very young (one of whom is a frustrated pianist clearly living vicariously through Susan), were worth further investigation. Within the crisis structure, though, they were left only a small place.

The one unexpected occurrence turned out to be Susan's on-camera meeting with a boy (another contestant who was eliminated earlier) whom she was later to marry. This is a happy advantage in direct cinema, to be sure, except that it is exploited to its fullest. In one of the trickier transitions in these films, there is a cut from the announcement of Susan's placing third in the competition (as voiceover on a shot of Susan riding in a train) to the sound of her playing again over a quick montage-like rehash of the scenes in the film where we saw Susan with her eventual husband, leading up to scenes of their marriage. Her loss is inconsequential, it seems, since the competition found her a husband. Since the marriage presumably took place some time later (because we see them meet two days before the event), there is reason to object to its tidy use to wrap things up with a quick, happy ribbon. Although the ending isn't false, since their earlier scenes set it up in terms of motivation, it's a little too cute. Being open to the unforeseen is certainly a part of direct cinema, but when the unexpected occurs, one shouldn't pounce on it like a cat devouring a rodent.

Nehru
Nehru is almost an open admission of failure by the Drew team, a shift from the avowed intention to make a film about the Indian Prime Minister to a self-critique of the problems encountered in following him and the difficulty they had in maintaining the relationship they wished to establish. The result is something of a disaster but one that lays bare important unstated assumptions behind the "Living Camera" philosophy.

The original idea was for Leacock and Gregory Shuker to film Nehru for fifteen days prior to an election, providing the dual opportunity to observe Nehru during a crisis period and get a firsthand look at India as he traveled. The idea is a familiar one for the Drew group. Besides *Primary, Kenya, Africa* tried the same approach. So, from the outset, they expected a familiar kind of conflict. To put it mildly, things didn't happen quite as they had envisioned. Leacock describes the problems: ". . . we had thought that because there was an election coming up there would be some kind of tension . . . but the election of Nehru was such a foregone conclusion that you barely noticed it."[65] Lacking that conflict (no mention is even made of election opponents), another was found in the editing room—between Nehru and the filmmakers.

The film begins with Leacock and Shuker introducing themselves on camera and then explaining what their relationship would be with Nehru and the manner in which they would work. (This was shot afterwards in New York.) Leacock says that the arrangement would be that "He (Nehru), for his part, would ignore our presence," while the filmmakers would promise not to interfere with his activities in any way. Shuker (who was to record sound) tells of the need for getting the microphone in close and demonstrates the method used to obtain synchronized sound, tapping the mike.

And so the action begins. Leacock and Shuker provide the narration. The first scene shows Nehru at some sort of reception. Shuker says: "Nehru greets his guests but ignores our presence. The deal is on." During a meal, Shuker reports what is said, explaining that he couldn't get close enough with his microphone. The scene continues with what almost looks like a parody of the pitfalls of direct cinema: a dog starts barking at Shuker, and conversation at the table stops as the guests watch his loud canine encounter. Normally rejected gaffes like this one are a major component of the film.

One almost envisions editing room conferences about which of several scenes is most embarrassing, thus meriting inclusion in the finished film. At one point, Leacock narrates: "Nehru notices something. Now I pan over to see what it is (the camera pans over to Shuker, then the shot of Shuker is frozen for several seconds). . . . A slip on his part of the bargain," for not ignoring the filmmakers. A scene that rivals the dog-barking scene in terms of self-parody involves a struggle by Leacock and

Shuker to hop on a jeep in the midst of a surging crowd. Leacock manages all right, but Shuker tells of first having to throw the tape recorder on and then getting his hand stuck under a bar on the jeep. Soon after, Leacock shows Shuker covered with flowers that have been tossed in the direction of the Prime Minister.

Things go on like this for most of the film. Shuker taps on the mike, Nehru notices the camera or makes an explicit reference to it, and so on. Then, a final crisis occurs, or is created. Says Leacock in the narration, "We were moved with an overwhelming desire to talk to the man." Shuker continues by saying that to interview Nehru would jeopardize the chance for further filming, but they will take that chance. In a strange way, the relationship of subject to filmmaker is treated as a mystical spell that can be broken with a single word. An interview is set up, one that fully justifies the general reluctance of direct-cinema filmmakers to resort to interviews. The questions are ludicrously uninformed and the answers unrevealing, as in this tepid exchange:
Shuker: How do you feel about the kind of life you have to live?
Nehru: Generally it's a satisfying life.
The film ends with a final reminder of the filmmaking process, Shuker again tapping the mike.

Clearly, some drastic measures were taken in putting the film together. Drew made the decision to edit the film in this manner because, he says, they had "run the risk of starting to tell a story about a person during a period that was not a key or important time in his life," and that it wasn't apparent from the footage that this was indeed such a crucial period for Nehru. He feels that the interaction between the filmmakers and the subject was evident and says, "At some point I crossed the Rubicon and decided that was more relevant and interesting, and a better frame of reference, at least for an American audience, than simply to see what Nehru was doing along with conventional narration."[66] Or, as Leacock briefly sums it up, the form is "a gimmick Drew dreamed up to save a boring film."[67]

There has been a strong divergence of opinion as to the source
of error, whether it was in the choice of subject or the manner
in which it was edited. Jean-Claude Bringuier, a French critic
who has written astutely about American cinema verite, feels that
the fault lies in the incompatibility of filmmaker and subject, that
Nehru lacks the "champion" personality of a John Kennedy or
an Eddie Sachs. Nehru's Indian sensibility, this argument goes,
is not sufficiently akin to the kind of American character that is
on the go all the time and able to tolerate more easily the presence of the camera. The error, then, was in believing that this
method is "absolutely and universally valid."[68] (This view is perhaps supported by Leacock's observation in an interview that
Nehru "was just doing what he usually does day after day." He
excused the film as a result of inexperience, claiming that they
were not yet at a point where they could make films in other than
"high pressure situations.")[69]
  Others saw the fault elsewhere. Colin Young calls the structure
a "hold-over from conservative classical drama" that is totally
unnecessary. His conclusion has far-reaching consequences:
"It ought to be enough to spend fifteen days with Nehru, so long
as the film maker is telling us something we did not know before,
and probably could not know by any other means."[70] This is
perhaps the single most promising sentence in all early cinema-
verite criticism, one of the few statements that encourage cinema-
verite filmmakers to become more adventurous, rather than
suggesting that their work is too "emotional" (as Bluem and
Shayon say) or their goals impossible to achieve.
  It may not be clear that the two points of view represented by
Bringuier and Young here are mutually exclusive. The former
accepts the effectiveness of the Drew films where the subject is
suited to the crisis structure and claims that the successful films
will be those that recognize the limitations in subject possibilities.
In other words, structure dominates subject matter. The latter,
on the other hand, implies that any subject that interests the filmmaker is suitable material, and that direct cinema should reject

traditional theatrical forms and search for new ways to structure the films. In this view, what was wrong with *Nehru* was not the Prime Minister himself (as Bringuier asserts) but the filmmakers' lack of faith in the possible interest of their subject for its own sake, without a story to prop him up.

Each argument makes a valid general point, but neither is entirely applicable to this specific case. The fault, in fact, lies in the filmmaker's interest in Nehru solely as a public figure, a man of action. They want him to conform to their own image of what he should be like. To this extent Bringuier is correct: Nehru is not John Kennedy. But the error lies in their thinking he could be, not in any inherent unsuitability of the subject. Young is partially correct in this instance—it should have been possible to make a film about Nehru. This is not, however, a structural problem. It is a matter of the subject's having sufficient confidence in the filmmakers' acceptance of his normal activities. Leacock and Shuker were not ready to do that; they were expecting action. In a way then, *Nehru* is a very honest film, reflecting the filmmakers' awareness of their inability to win the confidence of the subject. But admitting your mistake is not equivalent to transcending it, and *Nehru* remains an unsatisfactory work, albeit a very curious one.

It should be kept in mind that economics required every film experiment, as all of these are, to look like a success. One does not send a film crew to India to have them come back and abandon the project in the editing stage. Unlike a scripted film, which can be written and then abandoned if it looks unsatisfactory or unrealizable, a direct-cinema film involves far bigger risks. With *Nehru,* Drew Associates gambled and lost. But a failure costs as much money to make as a success and has to fill the same amount of television time.

Jane

Perhaps the most common criticism of direct cinema is that a person constantly subjected to a camera can never truly forget its presence, that he is never "natural." The situation is not quite this simple, for *natural* tends to remain an undefined term. The tension between filmmaker and subject is dependent upon several variables, but of importance here is that whatever the nature of this tension, to a large extent it is visible on the screen. Use of the word *natural* implies an ability to judge off-screen manner, but only the filmmakers have the information necessary to make such a judgment, not critics or viewers. Unless we can see several films about one subject made by different people or possess personal knowledge about the subject, we are in no position to judge naturalness. At best, we are able to judge varying degrees of subject response to the camera, employing no norm other than previous moments in the same film.

A degree of awareness of this problem is already apparent in these films. The very fact of the Drew group's preference for people accustomed to the limelight (politicians, actors, musicians) suggests that they felt this sort of person would be less affected by the presence of a camera than a noncelebrity. (A more obvious consideration in their selection is, of course, audience interest in famous personalities.) These are the people who are "on" all the time, whether playing to one person, a roomful, a large audience, or a camera. And because we see them as public figures, we can be aware of this facet of their personalities, their inclination to perform.

This notion leads to *Jane,* for this film follows the question of acting in front of a direct-cinema camera in a natural direction. The film shows Jane Fonda in rehearsals for a Broadway play, *The Fun Couple,* through its second-night closing. The degree to which Jane is acting is always apparent; in fact, it is a primary interest in the film. Continually present is the obvious contrast between her on-stage acting style and her off-stage manner. We must, then, consider the possibility of an on-camera and off-camera difference—the first comparison invites the second. And as soon as we recognize this, it ceases to be a problem. The role playing and deception become, instead, a key concern. When you know there is distortion in a measurement, you are able to compensate for it. (This is an analogy Leacock also likes to make, no doubt a reflection of his early physics training.) The game of who is aware of what (the viewer aware that the subject is aware of the camera) sounds complicated, but in practice it is readily comprehensible.

We mentioned before Louis Marcorelles' feeling that there is a discernible style in the two Pennebaker films, *David* and *Jane.* While he doesn't go on to explain what he means by this, we are now on the track of it. The two films both push their subjects' defenses to the limit. As can also be seen in *Don't Look Back,* Pennebaker's film on Bob Dylan, he is particularly adept at filming people when they are doing very little, in direct oppositon to the cinema-verite maxim about trying to film people when they are involved in other things so that they will forget the camera. Pennebaker's camera expects its subjects to pretend they are ignoring its presence, for through that pretense we learn something about them.

Jane Fonda was interviewed a year after the film was made, and there is a good indication she came to understand this. In part, this is what she said:

Jane was a nightmare because I was filmed rehearsing and act-ing, and *there were moments when I didn't know when I was acting and when I wasn't.* There was the camera all the time, from start to finish; it was very strange. It was only when I saw the film, a good time after, that I understood what I hadn't real-ized during the experience. The film was truer than the exper-ience itself . . . .My terms with the play were false and ambiguous. Thus on the whole, in a sense, *this film was a false thing about a false thing, and it is that which was true* . . . . I learned many things as an actress from this film. *I saw that the best way to make something happen is to do nothing* (my italics).[71]

This excerpt shows Miss Fonda's keen insight, after the fact, of the revelatory power of Pennebaker's camera, her realization of the possible paradoxes in his way of filming. (There have also been reports that Miss Fonda was greatly upset when she saw the film for the first time.[72] Even if exaggerated, they lead to an interesting speculation on the power of direct cinema. Actresses should be accustomed to seeing themselves on the screen, but, of course, Miss Fonda had never really seen herself in this way.)

The film certainly does catch her during a hectic period. The play itself looks like an obvious disaster from the first moment. The fascination throughout is in the effect that the impending catastrophe is having on the company and in their blind faith that they may somehow have a hit on their hands. Jane is romantically involved with the play's director, and the strain on their relationship brought about by the play's difficulties is convincingly captured. The traveling from city to city for tryouts, the endless rehearsing, the backstage tension before opening night: the theatrical clichés are subverted by the complete mess they are

Jane. Jane Fonda and Director Andreas Voutsinas.

Jane. Jane "alone" in her dressing room.

trying to perfect. Nominally another crisis-oriented structure, *Jane* has a full hour of the same feeling that the last moments of *On the Pole* had, the observation of someone caught with her de-fenses down because she isn't able to maintain publicly her own self-image. The best moments are surely played for the camera: Jane in her dressing room mugging in front of a mirror, Jane and her director in a taxicab (she whispers something to him when she doesn't want the microphone to hear), and an excellent scene of Jane reading the reviews of her performance. Louis Marcorelles raises a question that one hears frequently: Couldn't this be done better in a fiction film? Isn't, in this case, Lumet's *Stage Struck* a more persuasive portrait of a young actress than *Jane?*[73] This is an interesting offshoot of the earlier question of book versus movie concerning *The Making of the President 1960* and *Primary.* On one hand, cinema verite is faulted for not being close enough to written journalism, on the other, for possibly being less effective than drama. Marcorelles is only partially convinced of *Jane's* superiority: "At the level of immediate perception, the physical sensation that something is really happening as it is being filmed, *Jane* holds all the cards."[74] Left unsaid, however, is the implication that beyond the "level of immediate perception," fiction films are superior.

Direct cinema does not seek to displace the fiction film any more than it does written journalism. But if the defenders of the older forms feel threatened, perhaps it is for good cause. A better comparison with *Jane* than *Stage Struck* is the scene in *Citizen Kane* of Susan Alexander Kane reading *her* bad reviews. Welles's scene is a skillfully edited interplay between Susan's yelling and Kane's quiet reactions. Its effectiveness is heightened by lighting and camera position to enforce the relationship between the two people, especially in the last moments when Kane literally overshadows Susan. In *Jane,* the corresponding scene is remarkable in its understated simplicity. Stripped of fictional invention, Jane's thinly masked restraint, her near-tears reading, is even more theatrically powerful. Not scripted or rehearsed, there is no need for the scene to justify itself dramatically, no need for camerawork to emphasize what is already abundantly evident. Superior to fiction film or not, a scene like this at least deserves recognition for its legitimacy.

An annoying little "subplot" is added to *Jane,* and it sticks out obviously and artificially. Near the beginning there is a brief shot of then *New York Herald Tribune* drama critic Walter Kerr, who isn't heard from again until close to the end of the film, just prior to the play's opening. We then follow his journey from the *Tribune* office to the play and then back again. The old technique of parallel editing is then trotted out, and from this point to the scene of Jane reading Kerr's review, the story lurches back and forth between Kerr and Jane (him typing in his office, her par-

tying at Sardi's, etc.). This comes as an unnecessary intrusion
at a time when Jane's story alone has more than enough mo-
mentum of its own. The Kerr material is a hedged bet, reflecting
uncertainty as to whether the rest of the story could stand alone.
Jane, like *On the Pole,* is able to sustain interest without editing
devices to impose conflict.

A scene of Jane alone in her dressing room is quite unlike any
other in the Drew films, very close to a sort of actor's improvisa-
tion in front of the camera. Jane, sitting before a mirror, is not
content to remain still and launches into a series of grimaces,
looks, bits of impersonations, and the like. According to Pennebaker, there was a dispute between him and Drew while editing
this scene as to whether the sound of the camera should be
filtered out as much as possible. Pennebaker felt that the noise
should remain, making it clear that the audience was not seeing
Jane alone in her dressing room, but Jane alone in her dressing
room with a camera observing her.[75] Drew apparently won out,
as the sound of the camera is scarcely heard in this scene.
Pennebaker was right, of course, but his intent still comes
through. No pretense is made of "invisible recording," a notion
brought up more frequently by cinema verite's attackers than
by its practitioners or defenders.

Jane, then, is not typical of the Drew films, for the nature of its
probing stems from a different notion of the possibilities for di
rect cinema. It is the product of a camera style that does not wish
to minimize its presence, instead serving almost as an instigator
of the action. It is safe to assume that such fine distinctions were
lost on the majority of *Jane's* audience, but the difference between, say, *On the Road to Button Bay* and *Jane* is unmistakable
in retrospect. They are characteristic of two wholly separate
approaches to this kind of filming, beginning with different assumptions about their subjects that result in entirely separate
relations between the cameraman and what he is filming. The
former is closer to journalism, a kind of surface reporting that

is often all that is necessary for a very likable, effective film when the subject is cooperative; the latter tracks the elusive, openly questioning both the subject and the recording method.

Direct Cinema and News—A Brief Note
The final two films of the Drew-Leacock association once again relate (as did *Primary* and *The Children Were Watching*) to specific news events. In both cases, however, there was a substantial gap between the occurrence of the event and the television appearance of the film. Although over time this gap has come to seem unimportant in relation to the value of the films as historical records, when they first appeared the films must have had a feeling of stale news. The immediacy of direct cinema, partially akin to television news reporting, is enhanced by the proximity in time between event and film.

In the case of *The Chair,* about the attempt to save Paul Crump from the electric chair, the events took place in July 1962, and the film was not shown on American television until October 1964! Lacking network sponsorship, it was finally aired as the last in the "Living Camera" series. (It had been shown in Europe as early as March 1963, a full year and a half before American screening.) *Crisis: Behind a Presidential Commitment,* concerning a confrontation between George Wallace and the Kennedy administration over desegregation of the University of Alabama, covered events that took place in June 1963. While it was shown on television only four months later, this is still a serious delay when the subject involved is an event that was front-page news at the time.

The potential of direct cinema in relation to newsworthy events (admittedly only a tiny segment of the direct-cinema spectrum) has scarcely been touched. In situations where audiences already are familiar with a good portion of the circumstances (and come to the film with an interest in the subject that doesn't require suspense to be maintained), there could be greater opportunity for this intimate sort of coverage. Of course, even these fledgling attempts were met with an avalanche of criticism (especially *Crisis*), so the possibilities are substantially limited by widespread negative attitudes about the components of this kind of filming. With some widening of the television market in recent years and the possibilities of cable television in the future, perhaps there will be renewed interest in applying these techniques to news events and greater freedom for these experiments to continue.

The Chair
The Chair is a hybrid of the two main tendencies in the Drew films—it falls between the multiple camera coverage approach to an event of short duration and the method of closely following a single person for a long period of time, ultimately capturing particularly intimate moments. It is clear from the final film that an enormous amount of material was shot (reports vary between 60,000 and 70,000 feet of 16-mm film, roughly 30–35 hours when projected, compared to 18,000 feet for *Primary*), for there are a number of extraordinarily personal moments that one would think had to be culled from many hours of filming. The blending of these two approaches might conceivably suggest an ideal synthesis, but, in fact, it shows the incompatibility of mixed viewpoints. The film raised an issue that was to have a good part in what eventually led to the end of the Drew-Leacock association, a fundamental breach between their conceptions of the possibilities for direct cinema.

Once more, the film revolves around a highly tense situation.[76] In this case it is literally a life-and-death matter: Will Paul Crump, a black man sentenced to death nine years previous but now (according to many who know him, including the prison warden) substantially rehabilitated be executed, or will his lawyers be able to have his sentence commuted to life imprisonment? This is surely powerful material, with strong emotional content and opportunity for discussion of basic social issues, all tied together by a certain conclusion (and possibly a very upsetting one). What, then, goes wrong? It is not that what is there is so bad, but that it conforms too well to dramatic expectations. Despite the power of some individual scenes (among the best the Drew group ever shot), the raw material seems seriously diminished.

The story begins five days before the scheduled date of execution, and the principals are introduced quickly. Don Moore, a Chicago lawyer, along with Louis Nizer, brought in from New York to assist, are to prepare a last-ditch effort for a hearing that will decide whether or not to recommend a commutation sentence to the governor. The warden, who, we learn later, will pull the switch if execution is to be carried out (by Crump's request because the warden has become his friend), tests the electric chair. (This is another of the famous tracking shots, down one hall, into an elevator, down another hall, and into the room with the chair.) The prosecuting attorney, his case all prepared, practices his golf swing at a driving range. And, of course, there is Crump himself, visiting with the editor of a novel he has been preparing. (Another good scene: Crump is asked to do some rewriting. The look on his face as he asks, "Do you want me to do that now?" is quite moving.)

Topping even these fine scenes, in the first part of the film is one of Leacock's great pieces of work. It is a very long take in Moore's office. He receives a phone call telling him that the Church will issue a strong statement of support for clemency. It is apparently something Moore has been trying to get for a long time. After hanging up, he begins to cry but then holds back, pauses, puts out a cigarette, and then really cries. The camera moves away, as if in deference to the power of the emotion, and then the shot ends.

A shot like this could only come about in an atmosphere of great trust between filmmakers and subject and as the climax to a long period of shooting. Leacock (with Drew taking sound in this case) seems able to film intimate situations without provoking them, minimizing the importance of the camera's presence in a self-effacing manner that is communicated to an audience through the restrained but purposeful selection of camera movements. It is a style as personal as Pennebaker's but more in keeping with the flow of events. Leacock's skill is evident in the more open actions of his subjects, Pennebaker's, through the tension between camera and subject. (This is a rough generalization rather than a strict differentiation. It is more accurate in characterizing the best moments of each than as a description of their total work.)

On the day of the decision, the suspense is played up for all it's worth. Sample narration: "At the County Jail, Paul Crump waits twenty feet from the chair." The warden conducts practice drills with the chair while waiting for word. There is a shot of the governor reading through some papers, others of Moore waiting in his office. Near the warden's office, cameramen set up for a possible news conference. Moore receives a call that commutation is to be recommended. Elated, he talks about going to the races and sends his secretary to get a racing form. At a press conference, the warden announces that the sentence has been commuted to 199 years. Crump appears before the press: "What have you got to say, Paul?" "I thank God." "A little louder." Over the noise of clicking cameras, someone asks Paul to smile, but he is visibly shaken by the experience and not able to respond to the clamor of the scene. The film ends with shots of Moore at the races and then of Crump being transferred to the prison where he will begin his life sentence.

The Chair certainly has no shortage of effective moments. The initial problem, though, is that it exploits traditional courtroom and death row clichés to the hilt: the young lawyer (Moore) serving for no pay because his cause is just, the star defense attorney, the specter of death, the warden with a job to do. It may well be true that real life is full of high drama, but *The Chair* deals in too many clichés when the film's evidence indicates a tension of an even higher order. An event may be *too* dramatic, as well as not dramatic enough, to adapt to conventional forms.

The Chair. Paul Crump in his cell.

The Chair. Defense attorneys Donald Moore and Louis Nizer confer during clemency hearing.

The Chair. Lawyer Moore during famous "crying" scene (photographed by Leacock).

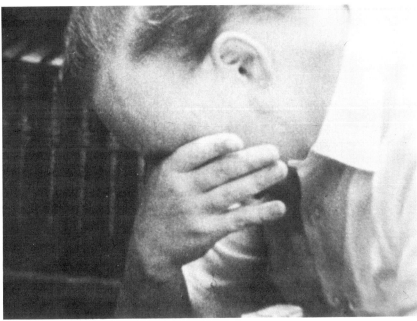

There have been several explanations posited as to what goes wrong, each close to the heart of the problem. Louis Marcorelles speaks of the shift in interest from Crump to Moore (partly necessitated by the shooting conditions), resulting in the sacrifice of "simpler human truths" for suspense-through-editing.[77] It would be more correct to say that given the shift from Crump to Moore, it was not a sufficiently committed shift. Had it been more completely Moore's story (or Crump's, as Marcorelles would have preferred), simpler human truths might still have been evident. The difficulty arises out of the balancing act between separate stories. In another article, Marcorelles admits that the suspense may be strong and well intentioned, but that nevertheless it is arbitrarily introduced, and it deceivingly toys with a man's life.[78] Robert Vas implies that *The Chair* is either edited too much or not enough, saying that it "is no longer the raw material nor is it the final, shaped product." His next metaphor is crude, but the point is well-taken: "Somewhere between the two extremes of raw material and final product lies the banana-skin on which this technically so progressive way of looking slips artistically."[79]

Godard, in his previously mentioned blast of American cinema verite, is particularly vituperative in his use of a familiar argument: "After having seen *The Chair,* we know less about the electric chair than in a mediocre film starring Susan Hayward that follows melodramatic techniques (referring to Robert Wise's *I Want to Live*)."[80] This is part of the same editing argument, since *The Chair* apes the fictional courtroom and prison stereotypes in a format all too recognizable from film and television dramas. But Godard is wrong, for the problem with *The Chair* is not that we "know less" about the people and institutions here than in comparable fiction films, but that we know them equally poorly. His argument suggests the superiority of fiction films in dealing with social issues, where actually it is the dependence on fictional conventions and imitation of fictional editing techniques that is *The Chair's* crippling error.

One could believe that the suspense orientation and stereotyped characters of *The Chair* are an outcome of the choice of subject and/or the resulting footage. This argument would continue by saying that the editing possibilities were then rather limited, that they were dictated by the material then at their disposal. This is an inviting interpretation, but, in this case at least, it is a false one. We can pinpoint specifically the evidence against this, in support of a stronger feeling that reality was too powerful and presented in a way they were not accustomed to dealing with.

The prime responsibility for *The Chair* belongs to Gregory Shuker, who had the original idea for it and maintained his supervisory role through to the editing. Pennebaker and Shuker (on sound) covered Crump and also Nizer. Leacock and Drew (sound) were on Moore, and together they all covered the parole board hearing.[81] This split meant that neither group knew what the other was getting. Especially in a situation of brief duration (here it was a couple of days), structure must come after the fact. The relationship among the parts, the points of transition among them, the overall thrust of the narrative: these are editing, not shooting, decisions. *The Chair* is not a unique case in this respect. Nearly all the Drew films were shot with at least two camera crews, often many more. What is unique is the incompatibility of the separately shot material and the preference for maintaining independent narratives, and not supplying much of any particular one.

The Chair should have been either the story of one person or else eight hours long. Pennebaker's two good scenes of Crump (with his editor, at the press conference) and Leacock's two with Moore (two phone scenes, one when the Church supports them and the other when commutation is recommended) are highlights for which one craves details. It is unsatisfying for the audience to see displays of emotion without having been sufficiently prepared for them. Juxtaposing such moments (not even considering problems of different shooting styles) means simplification of ideas; one conflict after another is a device of melodrama.

In the midst of this falseness, anything is possible. It comes as no surprise in this context to learn that the great shot following the warden on his inspection of the electric chair was actually done a month later.[82] When direct cinema comes from bits and pieces, this opportunity for deliberate falsity within a supposedly chronological narrative can be an irresistible temptation. And to make matters worse, part of the shot is used a second time. When a structure leaves room for such manipulation, we must categorically reject its use. Without credibility at the base of our response to a cinema-verite film, its prime source of strength is cut off. The unquestioned power of individual scenes in *The Chair* makes the falseness of the overall structure all the more apparent. It's simply too exciting to be true.

  Even more tantalizing are the suggestions that some of the events in the film might not have been as stereotyped as they appeared. Leacock says in an interview: " . . . many things were omitted because they did not fit the conception required of the film: 'Will he or won't he?' Will Paul Crump be saved from execution? For instance, the young lawyer was terribly pissed off when Louis Nizer came in on the case. And said so. 'Who's this s.o.b. coming out from New York?' And he was terribly concerned with the racetrack all the way through it. And sometimes you wondered, 'How the hell is this guy ever going to get out?' He was never going to get the bloody brief written."[83]

  Even allowing for possible exaggerations here (although Pennebaker has also expressed similar feelings), this statement still indicates an inflexibility in the editing that is anathema in direct cinema. Editing can conform to a filmmaker's personal vision, but that vision becomes highly suspect when it coincides so closely with traditional drama. Further, when someone edits material he didn't shoot, the chance for falsity is clearly greater. At this stage, obligation to reality is more than likely to take a back seat to efficacy as entertainment.

  The Chair was the subject of an accusation that has since been leveled many times at cinema-verite work. It is surprising, in fact, that it did not come up earlier and more often. The issue is privacy. A BBC-TV executive in discussing American direct cinema said that *The Chair* "illustrates more clearly than any other film the danger of this kind of filming—that it may degenerate into a sort of voyeurism, a hunt for any situation where people are stripping themselves emotionally."[84] Except in rare cases (so far, at least), this seems like a manufactured problem. Provided that those being filmed give their consent, where is the immorality? The most private moment in *The Chair* is the look on Crump's face while he is being callously treated by reporters at the press conference. It is hardly an incident of voyeurism. The issue of privacy becomes a matter of viewers being sensitive to situations they would prefer not to watch or acknowledge.

Crisis: Behind a Presidential Commitment
For three months in 1963, basic issues of direct cinema were discussed on newspaper editorial pages and elsewhere throughout the country. The brouhaha caused by *Crisis: Behind a Presidential Commitment* is perhaps more interesting historically than aesthetically, but the curious case is worth some examination.

Two weeks before the scheduled court-ordered integration of the University of Alabama, Gregory Shuker visited Attorney General Robert Kennedy and requested permission to film his activities during the anticipated crisis. Following his approval, the cooperation of President Kennedy was secured. Shuker said that Drew Associates had long wanted to do "an inside story" during a national crisis, one involving the President but where national security was not at stake.[85]

A month after filming took place, a story appeared in the *New York Times* which simply reported the facts in the preceding paragraph, related Shuker's description of some incidents in the film (then being edited), and briefly explained their shooting methods. Two days later, the following editorial appeared in the *Times.* Remember that this was written solely on the basis of the newspaper report that a film was shot, not from having seen any of it.

NOT MACY'S WINDOW

It is astounding that a documentary film (for TV use) was allowed to be made last month in the offices of the President and
the Attorney General while they were engaged in actual decision-
making conferences on how to handle Negro registration at the
University of Alabama.

Under the circumstances in which the film was taken, the use
of cameras could only denigrate the office of the President. How
can anyone—even or especially the President—act and talk without some consciousness of the camera and the tape recorder?
The process of decision-making is not the occasion for the creation of an "image." The propagandistic connotations of this
filming are unavoidable.

The "Tour of the White House" with the First Lady was of an
entirely different nature. So are TV interviews with the President
or the Attorney General in their offices. But to eavesdrop on
executive decisions of serious Government matters while they are
in progress is highly inappropriate. The White House isn't Macy's
Window.[86]

As if that weren't enough, the *Times* published a letter a short
time later expressing "deep appreciation" for the editorial and
adding, "It would seem that those really qualified as officeholders
of importance in our national government would, by nature, have
some feeling of humility, and be not without some sense of dignity of public office, particularly as to the dignity of the law."[87]
That was the only letter the paper printed concerning the editorial. Plainly then, a sensitive nerve had been touched.

The news article had quoted ABC as saying it hoped to present
the film soon and that they were trying to obtain a sponsor. Whatever the reason for the delay (whether in completion of editing,
ABC hesitation after the outcry, difficulty in finding a sponsor),
Crisis was not shown until October 21, 1963, almost three
months after the news article appeared. The early furor, as we
shall see after discussing the film itself, had not died down a bit.

Crisis: Behind a Presidential Commitment begins with narration
that says, in part: "You will see a historical document. In conformity with the agreement under which this film was made, the
sound in certain scenes in the President's office has been omitted

to protect the essential right of Presidential privacy during the decision-making process." The narrator then assures the audience that the "essence" of the discussions will be conveyed by narration.

What this meant was that in the two scenes in the film that involve the President, only the first few moments of each included any conversation recorded on the spot. (The longest portion of synch sound involving the President, JFK talking with Ted Sorenson about whether to give a television speech concerning the crisis, lasts about thirty seconds.) The narrated "essence" in each case does not include anything particularly private, leading one to wonder at the reluctance to include actual sound. It might be recalled, though, that in the 1961 *Adventures on the New Frontier,* the same problem existed on a more extensive scale. (We might also note that the earlier Kennedy film produced no reaction whatsoever. Presumably, it takes a crisis to get the newspapers interested.) The fault here might be attributable to hesitation in the midst of controversy or meekness on the part of the film's producers. It is certainly strange that they should want to film a crisis expressly involving the President, but then not record his voice. I have questioned several of the participants in the making of the film regarding this matter, but they either don't see it as a problem, are reluctant to discuss it, or express opinions involving personal blame that could not be substantiated. Suffice it to report that this issue was heatedly discussed during the editing of the film.

The President, then, is a minor character in the drama. Much more prominent is his brother, the Attorney General, and there is no use of "essence" narration where he's concerned. The story unfolds in a traditional Drew manner, here very effectively employed. The first few minutes consist of parallel editing of two similar scenes, Robert Kennedy at his home, then going to his office and considering his strategy, and Governor Wallace engaged in similar pursuits. It would appear, as with *Primary,* that there was an attempt at equal time for the two sides to expose their views. Wallace is not treated as the villain of the piece, and, in fact, he comes across very well. There is an amusing moment with him as he leads a brief tour of his home study. He describes a picture on his wall of a Confederate general whom he quotes to the effect that it is better to die young having lived a life of principle than to have a long life of compromise, after which he adds to the camera crew, "Of course that may not mean much to you fellows." In a meeting with his officials, he explains their strategy and insists that there will not be any violence (a good close-up of his hands, as he hits his palm twice while he says, "Those are my orders. We are going to keep the peace.") Bobby, of course, is no weak personality either. Arriving at his desk, he rolls up his sleeves and gets on the phone to General Abrams, who is in charge of the troops that are ready to assist if necessary. The resoluteness behind the manner of RFK and Wallace is an effective suspense builder: the irresistible force and the immovable object.

The first of the two JFK scenes, as mentioned, shows him discussing whether to give a speech on national television. He sits in his rocking chair, looking quite tired. Related civil rights problems are discussed, but we hear of them only through narration. Also in this "second act" of the film, the two Negro students who will attempt to register talk about what's to occur, and Deputy Attorney General Katzenbach briefs federal marshals. The second JFK scene, a long discussion of alternative strategies for the confrontation, is described almost entirely by "essence" narration. After this, we do not see John Kennedy again, except for his face on a TV screen at the very end.

The film so far has been preparation for the "crisis," the actual confrontation at the university steps between Wallace and Katzenbach. Activities on the day of the crisis comprise most of the film. This section is the finest example to date of the possibilities for compiling a record of an event through later cutting together material shot simultaneously in a number of locations. This method is germane to one of the film's key points, that decisions

Crisis: Behind a Presidential Commitment. Burke Marshall, Robert Kennedy, and John F. Kennedy.

often have to be made that could be better implemented if more complete information about related events and decisions was available quickly. In the edited film we have a fuller knowledge of the event than any single person had at the time. (*The Chair* tried to do this, too, but succumbed to the dangers of simplification because the event was so complicated. In *Crisis,* the shorter and better-defined period of crisis is more manageable.) Occasionally the editing makes this point a little too deliberate (repeated cutting back to RFK during the time of confrontation, as he keeps asking questions over the telephone to someone who is reporting the event to him), but the honesty of the editing appears to be unquestionable. There is also an excellent scene that shows both sides of a phone conversation between Robert Kennedy and Katzenbach, in which Kennedy interrupts their strategy discussion to let his daughter talk to "Nick." (According to Leacock, they didn't even know they had both sides of this conversation until they looked at the footage when the shooting was all over. Leacock had a half hour of Katzenbach's nodding and occasionally replying, without even knowing what Katzenbach was talking about. Happily, it matched up to the Pennebaker-filmed Kennedy half.)[88] This conversation includes the most disarmingly personal evaluation of the film, when Kennedy tells Katzenbach that he "can almost dismiss Wallace as a second-rate figure. He's wasting your time; he's wasting the students' time."

The confrontation itself takes place in two stages. The first is Wallace's refusal to move from the doorway as Katzenbach tells him he is in violation of the law and then repeats this again. Katzenbach backs off; cut to RFK trying to get in touch with him a short while later. He finally contacts him by means of a car telephone, and though Katzenbach tells other cameramen and reporters to get back, we still see and hear him talk to Kennedy on the car phone. The crisis is concluded when Wallace steps aside in the face of National Guard troops. From there, it's a simple journey to the conclusion, as the President goes on TV about the incident, Wallace gives his opinion, and a couple of days later two more blacks enter another Alabama university.

So, as this deliberately detailed summary should make clear, the view of the Kennedys "behind the scenes" is hardly scandalous, and the film includes favorable Wallace material as well. *Crisis* (like *Primary*) puts personality into governmental processes, a worthwhile contribution since it certainly has always been there. We are able to realize that the names in the newspapers are more than just public figures—they are people. It is reassuring to know that alternative courses of implementation are discussed, for government tends to appear so automatic. And even though this is an unusual case, it does show how the Executive Branch can enforce a law. With all of these pluses, and apparently no minuses in terms of content, one might think that the original controversy was allayed when the film was finally shown on television. Surprisingly, the uproar grew even louder.

In New York, because the Drew Associates approach was considered such a departure from accepted practices, educational TV station WNDT (which was not the station *Crisis* was shown on, since it was an ABC special) followed the showing with a discussion titled "Presidency by Crisis." Editors from *Time* and *National Review,* CORE Director James Farmer, and documentary filmmaker Willard Van Dyke gave their views on the film. Farmer considered the whole event staged and said that Wallace was playacting. Opinions ventured by others included the feeling that this technique made actors of everyone, that television filmmakers (unlike print editors) should not be allowed to edit what they shoot, and that the President was responsible for the scheduling of the program, timed to aid his own political purposes. Of the four panelists, only Van Dyke felt it to be a worthwhile project. The others objected to both the techniques and the purposes of the film.[89]

Newspaper editorials were still harsh. One, running under the headline "No Business in Show Business," asked: "Does anyone for a moment suppose that the participants in these events . . . were unaffected by the cameras . . . ? The public . . . will never know to what extent it was all play-acting."[90] The *New York Times* television critic termed the program a "peep show," voiced the same criticisms as the editorial just quoted, and added a host of other negative remarks, including the suggestion that Robert Kennedy's statement to Katzenbach that Wallace could almost be dismissed as a second-rate figure (which is paraphrased here as "that he should be treated as a second-rater," a loose rephrasing with an altered connotation) detracts from the "essential honor" of the Administration's conduct.[91] And to top it all off, the *Times* editorial page reminded everyone of its original opinion expressed at the time of filming and added that its "worst fears were confirmed by the critics." Echoing a common cry once more, the editorial concluded, "It is improper to make a stage-show of the inside processes of government."[92]

It is frightening to imagine what the response would have been if Shuker and the others had executed their original intentions —if an "inside story" had really been made. First, as has been noted, Presidential secrecy prerogatives were not violated in the slightest. Newspaper and magazine accounts of the event included more detailed strategy analyses than *Crisis* even attempted to convey. More obviously, *Crisis* does *not* deal with Presidential decision making (nor, for that matter, with decision making by the Attorney General). The events in the film are related to implementation of decisions *already made,* and that is a crucial distinction. Rather than going "Behind a Presidential Commitment," *Crisis* deals with events *subsequent to* the commitment. The decision to enforce court-ordered integration has been made before the film begins, and Wallace has also previously committed himself to opposing it. There is never any discussion as to whether either side should change its mind, if their course of action is proper, or what political ramifications could result. In *Crisis,* we find how their plans work in practice and do see some flexibility in logistical terms (whether to use marshals or troops, etc.), but in no way is the private discussion of national policy violated.

The main thrust of the argument advanced by critics of *Crisis* in regard to "playacting for the camera" is so remarkably naïve and poorly thought out that we shall examine the question once more. The initial confusion stems from use of the word "acting" or, even worse, "playacting." The suggestion, of course, is that the people being filmed are behaving differently than they would if no cameras were present. But different in what way? Would Robert Kennedy not let his daughter on the phone in the middle of an important conversation? Would he not say that Wallace might be dismissed as a second-rate figure as far as Katzenbach was concerned? Are these activities caused by the camera, and would they not occur in its absence? (This concerns only the part of the argument relating to governmental situations. When the statement is made that "For the Attorney General to tolerate cameras in the privacy of his home during the height of a national crisis borders on the unbelievable,"[93] then the critics are revealing the true extent of their paranoia. To see the Attorney General ever so briefly at a meal with his family is hardly a breach of national security or a severe imposition on Kennedy's personal life. It certainly does not, as is specifically charged in this instance, "impart a feeling of play-acting.")

The acting accusation concerning *Crisis* disintegrates more fully the more closely it is examined. On the one hand, these observers question the credibility of certain scenes, and then, on the other, admit to the truth of some remarks and then say they are improper. What they see and don't believe is acting; what they see and believe is disreputable because it should be private. One cannot have it both ways.

And, as before, if one thinks the camera is affecting the action, why can't that be taken into account in evaluating the actions of the participants? If, as Jack Gould says, "Time after time a viewer could see for himself that participants were conscious of the lens, which automatically raised the question of what was being done solely for the benefit of the cameras,"[94] then why is that not a valid question? This is where Drew does himself a disservice when he says that "In *Crisis* I am quite convinced that the cameras did not, in anything that was seen in the film, influence people's actions."[95] Whether he is correct or not, even where there may have been some influence, it is not necessary to discount the response of the subjects. As has been suggested before, those times when we feel there is certain influence can often be the most revealing moments.

The final point in this regard is one of perspective. *Crisis* attempts to establish the relationship between executives who want their decisions enforced and the people below them who must carry out their directives. It shows the links, in other words, between the generals in Washington and their soldiers in the field. So, a good deal of *Crisis* showed public, rather than private, events. The crisis itself, the confrontation at the university, was a national spectacle already. Drew Associates did not cause it to happen or affect it. Participants in the confrontation were already involved in public manipulation, or there would not have been the publicity-making confrontation in the first place. The cameras, then, were only recording an event in which people were already cognizant of their own image. Although that fact seems patently obvious, none of the film's critics seemed to be aware of it.

After *The Chair* and *Crisis: Behind a Presidential Commitment,* Leacock and Pennebaker left Drew Associates. Time-Life support was terminated following the "Living Camera" series, and by this time substantial differences had developed between Drew and the other two. Before going on to consider other cinema-verite films, we need to evaluate the period of the Drew-Leacock association independently because of the strict aesthetic in the films and the special circumstances that led to their production. It is incorrect to assume that what is characteristic of the Drew films is characteristic of direct cinema. Their consistent but particular attitudes toward suitable subject matter and structure embrace only one possible approach to uncontrolled documentary. But as the basis for a critical model and in their own right, the films produced in this period merit close study.

Direct Cinema and the Crisis Structure

The Drew films are a synthesis of cinema-verite techniques and fictional conceptions of character, action, and structure. This is not just a way of saying that filmed reality is subjected to traditional plot structures. The union is considerably more intense. Essentially, it is a grafting operation performed by maintaining the purity of filming methods and applying them in the service of particular theories of what these films ought to be about and how they should be put together. But this does not provide a sufficient description of the process, as each step is affected by those before and after, and the interplay between fictional notions and real situations exists at each stage.

The Drew films are consistent in structure and subject matter. They represent a personal vision in the same manner that fiction films can express the world view of their directors. We shall not worship on the altar of omniscient objectivity, for direct cinema in its very quest for a closer relationship with the world around us becomes an intensely personal form of communication. It is not the propriety of Drew's assertion of choice that will be considered, but rather the nature of that choice and its limitations.

A phrase that has been in constant use during discussion of the Drew films is *crisis structure.* We have noted many examples of stories whose forward movement was propelled by an anticipated crisis moment. The basic organizing principle behind a Drew film can usually be stated in the form of a success or failure question. Will John Kennedy win the election, or will Hubert Humphrey? Will Eddie Sachs win the race? Will Paul Crump be saved from the electric chair? Will the Kennedys' integration strategy work? This description of plot may sound overly simplified in that the same device can often be applied in explaining the structure of fiction films, plays, and novels, at the expense of ludicrously distorting the complex concerns of the work. (Why did Kane say "rosebud"? Will Hamlet avenge his father's death? Will Ahab find and destroy Moby Dick?) But the point is that this *is* a traditional fictional structure and not an inevitable conclusion of direct-cinema methods and intent. There is no eternal verity in human existence that forces one to structure films in this manner. As in fiction, the Drew films take advantage of devices that provide a skeleton to build upon. Were it otherwise, each film would have a particular and unique form.

Since this chapter emphasizes so strongly the specific choices made in selecting subjects and editing, it is necessary to restate that the crux of the films, the reason they are worthy of serious study in this context, is their strong faithfulness to a key direct-cinema concept, namely, recording real people in undirected situations with live sound. To examine the choice of subjects and the editing methods, and to subject them to at times harsh criticism, is in no way to denigrate the Drew team's prodigious ability to enter a world scarcely accessible to film prior to their work. But because the filming technique itself is so potentially powerful, these related areas require examination.

The Crisis Structure—Its Origins and Justifications

The initial basis for the form of the Drew films actually predates the development of their filming techniques, a fact that is difficult to reconcile with the view that their fictional tendencies were something of a compromised afterthought. For Drew, the films became an extension of his earlier background: "I worked at *Life* for a number of years, practicing a form of photojournalism which required you to be constantly present with your photographic subject *in order to capture the exact place and time when the climax occurs* (my italics). I came to conceive of the idea of a movie journalism done in this way with simultaneous sound."[1] *Key Picture,* the title of his early pilot film for television, suggests the attempt at extending the photo techniques.

This was a natural, and inevitable, idea. The *Life* picture essays tried to tell a continuous story that had a dramatic impact; why not take advantage of film for the same purpose? The concept is mass oriented certainly, designed to package reality in an attractive form. But the best photo-articles were always aware of their limitations. They were the pictorial counterpart of the journalistic human-interest story, though they were often accompanied by lengthy stories.

This same recognition of limitations carried over into the films; from the very beginning there were no illusions as to goals. Those who speak of the drama in the Drew films with an accusatory tone often imply that he wasn't aware of what he was doing. The structure, however else it may be described, was anything but accidental. Given Drew's objective (as expressed in the quote above), one should at least note his consistency in realizing it. We are confronted with a forthright, determined approach, and muddled execution of their basic philosophy is a rare occurrence.

Drew, like the *Life* photo essayists, saw the crisis moment as both the ultimate goal of shooting and the conclusion of the story. This was a pragmatic structure, then, because the sequence of events in the finished film could correspond to the chronology of filming. The filmmaker would be "recreating reality" by acting as a witness and not juggling events out of sequence or deliberately falsifying the record of his experience. And, obviously, this structure can conform to traditional storytelling methods. It is a familiar form that maintains audience interest and responds to deeply felt human needs for story resolution and unity.

The requirement of a crisis moment appears to do no more than specify a period in which to film, providing in return a workable structure. An event is picked up at some arbitrary "in progress" point (narration filling in earlier details if necessary), and from there to the crisis there are seemingly no restrictions. The positive aspects of this framework go beyond structural convenience, for although a story comes about through the crisis structure, the story itself is ostensibly a vehicle for another kind of revelation: "The story for me has to go someplace, something has to happen. At the start, I've got a good idea of the things that can happen, but that's not the determining thing because whatever happens, I'll have a story. What really happens in any of these stories is that something is revealed about the people."[2]

The crisis structure, then, was seen as a way to study people through a method that attempts to subsume both reporting and storytelling. At worst, the story would be a fictional element to support a nonfictional result. At best, the story would be a true representation of an exciting period, a key time in someone's life. A final quote from Drew, in an interview recorded shortly after *Yanki, No!* but well before most of the product of the Drew-Leacock period, sums up the goal of all their work: "What makes us different from other reporting, and from other documentary filmmaking, is that in each of these stories there is a time when a man comes against moments of tension, and pressure, and revelation, and decision. It's these moments that interest us most. Where we differ from TV and press is that we're predicated on being there when things are happening to people that count."[3]

So, the objective inherent in the crisis structure has been extended: get that crisis moment, but only so that we can see how people react in such situations.

The Crisis Moment in Practice
It is fine to say that one should strive to capture crisis moments, but what does this mean in terms of filmmaking? Presumably, one could follow anybody and eventually a crisis situation would develop. There are obvious drawbacks to this procedure, not the least being that it might take years for this to happen. But more interestingly, how could the filmmaker anticipate which events are dramatically relevant as preparation for the crisis? For example, if a love affair turns out to be the drama you are after, would you have known to film the earlier stages of the relationship? Short of filming a subject's every waking moment for months on end, such a loose method might not even result in a dramatically interesting film. Clearly, this method is too diffuse and haphazard when one wants to build around a crisis moment.

What happens, then, is quite logical. Situations are selected where a crisis is inevitable, even if the precise outcome cannot be foreseen. As Drew said, "Whatever happens, I'll have a story." In other words, "crisis moments" could more practically be referred to as "different possible outcomes in a situation certain to be resolved." One has only to recall the Drew film that most clearly failed to meet this requirement. In *Nehru,* there was no inevitable crisis. A true crisis situation could conceivably have developed but did not, and so the filmmakers manufactured one—the interview with Nehru himself. Beyond the question of control, this was an unsatisfactory solution because it was transparent and hence dramatically unsatisfying. For a Drew film, an imposed crisis moment is disastrous.

The Drew films are even more specific in situation than a general crisis orientation might indicate. They belong primarily to one category of inevitable crisis events: *the contest.* A bullfight, a primary election, an auto race, a musical competition: these are all contests. Several of the other subjects, a Broadway opening, a jet plane test, initial enforcement of a law, come very close to contest situations as well. These are all events where a person tries to win a set objective, so the result is decisive in one way or another (win or lose) and always certain to occur.

Contests are crises from start to finish. There is no problem of waiting for a crisis moment to occur; it has already begun. There may be points of greater intensity, but even the slowest moments are still part of a general crisis situation. The end of the contest can be a pronounced crisis moment also, but it may not be the only one nor the most interesting. In *Crisis: Behind a Presidential Commitment* or *The Children Were Watching,* the outcome never seems so important (whether the schools are integrated) as the activities leading up to it. The supposed crisis moment is almost anticlimactic because of the intensity of what precedes it.

This method begs the question of the crisis moment's impact. Even when part of the film covers a period preceding the actual contest *(On the Pole, Football),* there is no difference in intensity. What we have come to, then, from "crisis moment" to "different possible outcomes in a situation certain to be resolved" is now simply "pressure situation." Part of the attractiveness of the crisis moment as originally conceived is the assumption that what comes before is *not* a crisis, that some dramatic change takes place that will enable us to get a fresh look at the people involved. Revelations in crisis combined with opportunities to observe activities at other times can provide a multifaceted view of the subject. When the whole film becomes a crisis moment, however, we lack a point of behavioral comparison in a noncrisis situation, and the conclusion of the film is simply the outcome of structural crisis, and not the anticipated time of character revelation.

On the Road to Button Bay does give a suggestion of noncrisis life, and it is present here because the girls are irrepressibly themselves in any situation. But that film is a special case anyway, one of the few that do not try to generate interest through conflict. But even in *Button Bay* one feels a crisis mentality at work, as a portion of the film covers the problems of one of the girls assuming the responsibility of leadership, culminating in a scene where she cries over her difficulties. Almost always, the Drew films are a series of crisis moments of relative intensity, sufficiently distributed so that one never sees an extended segment without pressure. It is not quite correct, then, to compare the Drew structure to "traditional" or "classical" dramatic form, for despite their shared propensity toward crisis resolutions, the means of development are scarcely similar.

Another way of obtaining a crisis moment is, of course, to cause it yourself. Very much to Drew's credit, he was rarely guilty of direct tampering with events. The distinction between perhaps artificially creating a crisis situation in editing (as in *Nehru*) and physically precipitating one at the time of filming may seem like hairsplitting, but there is an important difference. The latter goes a long way toward destruction of the whole direct-cinema aesthetic; the former is only a means of potentially transforming it. Drew could honestly say, in reference to the dramatic element, that "We don't introduce this element, we discover it."[4] To him, the crisis moment was to be found, so that rather than create an imagined reality, he chose those aspects of reality that interested him. The method is assailable only for its limitations and when the crisis moment isn't honestly "found" (that is, during the filming stage), and not as a direct subversion of truth through deliberate tampering with the subject.

In addition to having great dramatic potential, the pressure situation method is also supposed to be desirable because people will be less aware of the presence of the camera. In the tension of perpetual crisis, the influence of the camera is theoretically considerably less important than whatever else is going on. This is a point well taken, even though it simplifies the problem of camera influence. The curious aspect of this argument is that, in effect, it says by choosing an uncommon situation in which to film, you minimize the chance of uncommon influence. If the sole interest were some sort of unhampered observation, a more likely approach would be to find the situations that in themselves interest you. The argument concerning camera influence in crisis situations is justification after the fact. It appears to say that the camera does not distort the event any more than the situation itself does, that is, that the camera presents the undistorted record of an inherently distorted event.

Another outcome of using the contest is the likelihood that the film will cover events that last no more than a few days. The period before a crisis moment can naturally be expected to be a time of intense activity, and the films often start here. *On the Pole* was shot in four days, the day of the race and the three before it.[5] *Susan Starr* took the same length of time, *The Chair* a day longer, and *Crisis* a bit longer still (according to the narration in each). Interestingly, if there is any quantitative difference in shooting methods among the films, the increase is in the number of crews filming rather than the length of time any one person is covered. In other words, there is a stronger tendency to increase simultaneous coverage over a brief span than there is to follow a single event through a longer period of time. The result: instead of a traditional sort of character development (or even dependence

upon character change for dramatic value), the films take advantage of the opportunity to provide a view of reality not available
to any participant.

In this regard, the contest is well suited to direct-cinema methods.
Films shot over long periods of time that try to tell the continuous
story of a few people without extensive narration are incredibly
difficult. The single event viewed from many perspectives is
much easier to edit; you simply cut from one place to another
at parallel moments. And continuity is also easier in a short period of time, since there is a greater likelihood that events will contain their own logic. For instance, a cut from Paul Crump on death
row to his lawyer in his office is more acceptable when it takes
place shortly before the scheduled execution; we immediately
make the logical connection between the two events (that while
Crump is waiting, his lawyer is trying to save him). Were it months
earlier, however, we would have to be told the reason for going
from one place to another because the pressure of time would
not then provide an "automatic" link.

The brief duration of a contest and its generally self-contained
nature (little traveling around, fewer peripheral activities) has another important advantage over the film covering a longer period.
When shooting lasts many weeks or months, the natural tendency
is to select the best moments, to condense a greater mass of
material. This is not direct cinema's forte, condensation being
more a fictional device. Direct cinema excels in whole chunks
of life, long takes full of many possibilities. A moment, like Paul
Crump's lawyer crying, is nothing without the context of the rest
of the scene. Events of shorter overall duration are more likely
to allow space for these fuller scenes to play themselves out.

One has only to look at the cases when shooting lasted a long
time to understand the difference. In *Petey and Johnny* (shot over
a six-month period) the resulting material had a formlessness
not conducive to a crisis structure, and more events occurred
than could be effectively handled within the time period of a one-

hour film. The result was doubly unsatisfactory—the episodes were chopped up, and a form was imposed to build to a crisis. The story could be told, and the different episodes joined together, only by a great deal of narration.

Theoretically at least, the short filming period should serve cinema verite by also tending to prevent the filmmaker from growing attached to his subject in such a way that his conception of the material becomes unduly biased. Unlike Flaherty's interpretation of nonpreconception, which came to mean finding the story in the course of shooting even if it meant starting all over once you hit on the essential elements, the direct-cinema approach is closer to the actual meaning of the term. These film crews were practically thrown into unfamiliar situations, with little planning or preparation. The spontaneity of this approach should have served to make each assignment result in an entirely different kind of film, but the similarities of subjects and situations in the Drew films tended to lessen this possibility. The Drew filmmakers carried preconceptions from film to film.

There is yet another reason for short time periods in a crisis structure—longer ones provide no added information, while they decrease the sense of drama. In *The Chair*, for instance, there would have been no reason to begin the film at an earlier point. The drama was in the proximity to the final moment of decision and, in fact, one might wish for still more information as to what occurred during that brief period. *Eddie*, compared to the earlier *On the Pole*, demonstrates the same point. Repeating the race a second time accomplished no more than repetition of action without added character revelation or increased dramatic excitement. While a structure of repetition can be a means to break out of a linear narrative (as in the Maysles' films), repetition for its own sake is purposeless and ineffective.

The contest situations also led to another device that made editing much simpler. The films could be the stories of several people who were rarely, if ever, seen together. *Primary, Football, Susan*

Starr, Crisis, and others all show this trait. Again, it was a useful way to get around the difficult single person continuity problems. (Reportedly, it was Leacock who first recognized the practical advantage of this method.)[6] Like the simultaneous-moment cutting mentioned earlier, when a part of one person's story was missing, not interesting, poorly shot or recorded, then one simply cut to the other story. Transitions were easy; they were frequently performed on parallel actions. From Kennedy making a speech, the cut is to Humphrey doing the same thing. From Susan Starr practicing the piano, cut to one of her opponents engaged in similar activity. The first story can then be picked up at a later point. (Parallel editing, of course, has been a common cinematic device since D.W. Griffith.) Two stories are advanced that would be much more difficult to develop independently.

A curious result of this intercutting technique is that it is not as forceful a device as one would expect. It would seem to be the perfect way to emphasize conflict, to contrast personalities. In *Primary* and some other cases it occasionally does just that. But more often, it seems, the cutting points up similarities. When a cut is made on the basis of action (from one person doing something to another engaged in a related pursuit), the activity tends to dominate personality differences. Thus, in *Crisis,* when a sequence goes back and forth between Robert Kennedy and George Wallace, it does not emphasize differences between their personalities (or politics) so much as it suggests that they both do a lot of the same things. It is almost a neutral cutting device, good or bad depending upon the affinities of the material on each side of the cut and the sense of editing intention behind them. For instance, in *Jane,* the intercutting between Jane Fonda and Walter Kerr after the play doesn't work because the Kerr segments begin so late in the film that they weaken the story tension already established. There are many cases of the same thing in *Petey and Johnny,* people popping in and out more or less arbitrarily. But when there is already an established connection between the intercut sequences and there is no doubt that these are actually simultaneous events, then the device can be tremendously effective. The cut from one locker room pep talk to the other in *Football,* the RFK–Katzenbach phone conversation in *Crisis,* and precious few others are all we have to begin to get an idea of the power of this technique. Many times, this kind of cutting is simply a bland editing device. For real effectiveness, both elements have to be present: clear connection and certainty of simultaneity.

The main problem with intercutting stories, then, is that it can convey the opposite of what the filmmaker intends. The cutting appears to set up oppositions, to exploit conflict for dramatic purposes. But when the images belie the attempt, when the conflict seems far less rigid than the ordering of the images would have you believe, the images themselves become suspect. This same idea can be expressed several ways, by emphasizing different steps in the process, but these different explanations are all ways of saying the same thing, that the overall structure can imply a view of events at odds with individual segments.

In criticism of the films, this idea has often been expressed by saying that the editing looks "forced." Patricia Jaffe reflects this feeling in her observation that "many of the Drew films were flawed by pushing the material into a mold where none existed"; she considers this characteristic a "result of Drew's inclination and experience," his push to keep the audience at a constantly high level of excitement.[7] What she is saying is that the editing wishes to tell a story not present in the material itself. Her conclusion (very close to that of Breitrose and others) is that the best Drew films are those where the conflict and resolution are already present, as in the self-contained situations of *On the Pole* and *Football.* In other words, given an editing method that seeks to establish crisis, the best films are those where the crisis is already present. This, of course, borders on tautology and doesn't really tell us much about the films.

Louis Marcorelles, with his customary perspicacity, is quite aware of the editing problem in the Drew films; he says that, for him, "the failure of most of these passionate attempts comes from the absence of controlling unity in the editing."[8] He explains the problem as a clash among the styles of the individual filmmakers that manifests itself when their separate parts are combined into one film. Except in regard to *The Chair,* though, it is difficult to support this argument. What he really wants to say, I think, is that he wishes Leacock and Pennebaker had a larger role in editing, feeling they are less crisis oriented than Drew. He does not, then, come to terms with the crisis structure and its editing problems but only suggests that the films would have been better if they were not what they indeed are—films about crises. So, though he senses that something is wrong, he does not provide a satisfactory description of what it is.

What the editing discussions all lead to, in the final analysis, is this: the simple recognition that editing can be as much a form of "fictionalization" as scripting or acting. It is often harder to spot, possibly insidious, and sometimes scarcely credible. Because the integrity of the filming situation is respected (in that no one is directed, no scenes are prepared), the opportunity to play down this aspect, to suggest by implication that the film must still be showing "what happened" no matter how it has been edited, is tempting. Opening narration in the films often plays up the shooting technique, emphasizing that it is a "true story" (said at the start of *On the Pole*), that it "actually happened" *(David),* that "it wasn't planned, it's for real" *(Petey and Johnny),* and that it was made without "any acting" *(Button Bay).* It is, in fact, the sanctimonious repetition of the claim to undiluted reality that wears thinnest in the narration and comes closest to undermining the whole approach. Constantly exploiting the filming method by directly paying homage to it, the narration seeks to legitimize the editing process as an invisible joining together of truths.

To Drew's credit, he doesn't hide the role of editing. In fact, he recognizes its key formative role in the films. The phrase he uses,

however, is not *editing* but *cutting on picture logic.* This is no
euphemistic cover-up but an honest expression of how Drew
sees his role: "I'm interested in one approach only, and that is to
convey the excitement and drama and feeling of real life as it happens through films."[9] The idea behind picture logic, basically, is
that if a documentary can be understood by hearing it alone without seeing the pictures, then it is a conventional film cut on "word
logic." But, on the other hand, if (as Drew once put it) one "turns
off the sound and can follow the logic—*even the drama*—of the
show in what evolves visually, then we are confronted, perhaps,
with a reality that is captured as it happened (my italics)."[10] Drew's
perhaps is a fortunate though hesitant addition, for it recognizes
that picture logic may mean other things.

   Picture logic is an attempt to equate visual storytelling with truth.
The degree to which a story can be followed visually, however,
is by no means a measure of its veracity. In fact, the ease of a
visually flowing story might actually indicate that the rough edges
of reality have been smoothed for the sake of drama. The very
smoothness in the tight suspense of *The Chair* is exactly its fault.
Reality does not always coincide with drama, and when it does
we had better look twice.

   The picture logic idea also ignores the deep, basic difference
between narration and live, synchronized sound. As much as we
can despise excessive narration (an easy target), to ignore the
spoken word is to overlook perhaps the single most crucial difference between direct cinema and other forms of filmmaking:
that we are able to hear people saying things that no one has
told them to say. There is nothing at all wrong in the "logic" of a
film evolving (which must mean the way it is edited) through what
the people in it say; no betrayal of the direct-cinema ideal is involved. In fact, it is just as incorrect to assert the supremacy of
the visual over the aural as vice versa. Separating the two aspects,
thinking in mutually exclusive terms of picture logic and word
logic, are only two ways of justifying artificial structures.

   When credibility is questioned as a result of editing, the house of cards is ready to topple. When uncontrolled events are fashioned to meet fictional conceptions, then the shooting process itself is equally open to question. One simply no longer knows where falsity begins, once it is clear that it has affected the ends. Andrew Sarris describes a showing of *Jane* and *The Chair* in Montreal where National Film Board people were skeptical about some of the crudities of the films, and he attributes these (presumably occasional sound difficulties or wandering zoom shots) to "an attempt to con an audience into thinking that something is more real when it is awkward, or rather that awkwardness is truth."[11] While cinema verite is always open to this kind of accusation (in fact, Sarris marshals it in an attack on *Don't Look Back,* a Pennebaker film not from this period), the only atmosphere in which it may have some validity is where other sorts of obvious trickery are present, as in the possibly false conflicts created by intercutting stories.

The Drew Hero

Drew's feeling that the structure of these films was simply a method of ensuring a complete story, that their real purpose was to assist in studying people, has already been noted. If that were true, it might then be possible to excuse certain limitations and rigidity of structure in exchange for substantial variation in the personalities involved and extensive insight into their nature. But, like the situations, the people involved vary only within a certain range. This is no accident. Character and structure are closely bound. We have observed several cases where observation of people may have been distorted by dramatic expectations of what they should be like (especially in *On the Pole* and *The Chair*). Exactly which came first (the subject-types or the structure) is difficult to determine, but their symbiotic relationship is clear.

   The ideal Drew subject is an active, positive hero, for this is the person who will act assertively in a crisis situation. In such moments, the precise action is not so important as the need for there

to be *some kind* of action. An indifferent hero would be unthinkable in a Drew film. Of course, the hero concept is a fictional one,
easily supported by the dramatic expectations of the crisis structure. In *On the Pole,* for example, the camera *had* to stay with
Eddie long enough for him to resent its presence, so we could
then feel his reaction in a crisis moment. Without that moment,
On the Pole lacks resolution. One does not show the events leading up to a crisis without having a character who will follow through
in some way.

Several of the Drew films show their heroes in weak moments
(an exhausted Kennedy, the crying lawyer, Eddie after the race)
but only to reinforce their final resilience in the crisis moment.
That final upbeat is more than a bit clichéd and not always convincing, too much a "pick yourself up, dust yourself off" type of
philosophizing that ties things up rather neatly.

As Jean-Claude Bringuier points out in a fine article about the
Drew films, whatever the outcome of the ordeal in any one of
these films, it is positive. If Kennedy lost the primary election, he
would say what Humphrey does, and what Eddie Sachs does,
that he will start all over again. Bringuier goes on to note how,
in effect, these heroes are perpetuations of American myths.
"America exists in *Only Angels Have Wings* as well as in Leacock's films, and it is the same America."[12]

His reference to a Hawks film is particularly astute, for the image
of the hero in a good number of the Drew films is indeed quite
Hawksian. A male professionalism often dominates: pilots and
race car drivers risking death (both have been subjects for Hawks
films), Robert Kennedy and his deputy Katzenbach out to subdue
George Wallace, fighting lawyers working hard to save their client
against great odds. Success in a Drew film (as in a Hawks film)
is measured by the way you handle yourself in a tough situation,
how well you do your job when the chips are down. And if you
don't quite make it, like Eddie Sachs, well then, next time you'll
just have to do that much better.

As in Hawks films, while the popular images may contain some insight into the American character, the mythical aspects can limit the possibilities for reality. The insights may be less myth than simply reinforcements of American clichés. Even the more exposed moments can add to the deception, for which of the Drew heroes is exposed in an unexpected manner? Their personalities are molded by their professions, but the professions enforce stereotypes that the films exploit. We come to a film about a race car driver with the expectation that his one goal is to win. When we see him lose, we can only read his reaction as disappointment. In a story about a lawyer working to save a condemned man we assume nothing less than all-out dedication to the job. But what happens, in the first case, if Eddie Sachs is really just glad to get out of the race alive, if he wasn't concerned simply about winning? And what happens if the lawyer is more interested in making a name for himself than winning his case, and if he isn't as prepared as he should be to go to court? This is not to say that these are truer interpretations of the events in *On the Pole* and *The Chair,* but it is a serious deficiency of the films that they do not allow room for any interpretations beyond the ones enforced by the hero image. The crisis moment is falsified when the hero is untarnished no matter what happens.

This is where the two films in which Pennebaker asserts his camera style, *David* and *Jane,* are more interesting as human documents than many of the other Drew films. The best Drew films were shot during highly charged situations involving many people (a football game, an integration crisis), at times when personality seemed less important than the drama of the moment. Kennedy may fit the hero image, but the real interest in *Crisis* is the excitement of participating in the event, which is bigger than the personalities involved. In *Football,* the incredible intensity of feeling is expressed by everyone, not just the two coaches. *David* and *Jane,* in contrast, leave their characters vulnerable to the extent that even if David stays away from drugs or Jane's play had been a success, we have still observed them at a time when they were at the edge of control. Though the presence of the camera is more clearly a factor in these two films than in the contest films, the complexities of the characters are more fully brought out simply by the less active nature of the situations.

The tendencies toward stereotypes are not deliberate misrepresentations. Drew, like Hawks, is personally sympathetic to the hero conception, and its presence in the films is more a function of the extent to which he asserted his personal predilections than a measure of preconceived falsity. However, there is no reason to assume that Drew was bound to come any closer to "truth" than Hawks solely on the basis of the shooting techniques. We can wish that Drew had sensed the potential for direct cinema to surpass fictional techniques, but that he did not desire to do so in no way minimizes his actual accomplishments. The same mentality that would ask Drew to be different from what he is would have to ask why no Hollywood director in the thirties used sound as Welles did in *Citizen Kane,* or why no one before Griffith made a film comparable to *Birth of a Nation.* Once potentials have begun to be realized (and in direct cinema this has scarcely started), it becomes quite easy to fault the pioneers for not going further than they did.

For Drew, the use of heroes was a reflection of his personal interests. He hoped to pull television documentary out of the doldrums through drama, and the need for personable subjects to serve this goal is clear. Drew freely admits he had certain "peculiarities and prejudices" in regard to the kinds of people suitable for these films, and he goes on to say, "I hate to see films about people who are mentally ill or are being detained in prisons: *people who aren't free, people who aren't on their own* (my italics). . . . I avoid assignments like that like the plague."[13] That is certainly a point to notice in his films: the people involved submit willingly to the pressure situations. They aspire to heroic stature, if they do not always attain it.

Crisis and Character

The Drew hero and the crisis structure reinforce each other. In fact, they are almost two ways to discuss the same idea. Recall what Drew said: "In each of the stories there is a time when a man comes against moments of tension, and pressure, and revelation, and decision. It's these moments that interest us most." Expressed in this manner, the two ideas are one; each defines the other. The crisis moment is the time when a person responds to this kind of situation, and the type of confrontation is archetypically heroic. The next question, though, is whether the crisis structure requires this kind of main personality.

The answer to the question in its broadest sense is *no,* since there are certainly dramas that are wholly dependent upon a crisis-like structure but that have scarcely sympathetic, much less heroic, main characters. But if the goal of the crisis moment is to evoke audience interest, then the kind of person it best portrays is obvious. (Again, this is not a defense of the crisis moment but rather an explanation of the consequences once such a structure is assumed to be necessary.) In several of the early Drew films, *Bullfight at Malaga* and *X-Pilot,* for example, the supposed crisis moments were rather boring because close identification with the participants was not possible. Certainly bullfighters and jet pilots are potential heroes, but these particular characters come across as too distant, too cold. The difference, the "warmth," found in the later films results from their taking advantage of the intimate possibilities of direct-cinema techniques. We can care about heroes when they have recognizable human quirks, like Eddie Sachs's little prayer before his race or Bobby Kennedy's allowing his daughter to run through his office. The luxury of intimacy (including the moments of supposed weakness mentioned earlier) is the basis for our interest in the outcomes of the crises.

For Drew, this identification has always been necessary and, for that matter, still is. In a conversation with me that took place while he was editing a feature-length film about gliders, he was particularly insistent upon the need for the audience to see events in the film through their effect upon a person they can connect to. His phrase for footage where this identification is absent is *unattached seeing,* material that, however spectacular, lacks a human connection: "When that airplane flies into a storm, I have to know that the central character is in the plane, that he's looking through the canopy, that he's making decisions. *Unattached seeing* is a term that for me reflects a psychological fact, which is that a physical film is boring, while a psychological film isn't."[14] The crisis moment alone is not, in fact, a crisis moment at all without the audience's understanding of its effect upon a particular person and its feeling that that person is reacting in some way to it.

Crisis and Truth

The primary justification for the crisis structure is that it provides a vehicle to discover a kind of truth about people. By observing people in pressure situations, Drew means to put them to the test. There is an intense, unspoken faith in the revelation of character under stress. But is the crisis situation literally the "moment of truth"? Using the films as evidence, what do we learn about people in crisis?

The "truths," it turns out, are often empty or misleading. The basic error stems from the unfounded assumption that external appearances and actions are sufficient to reveal inward thoughts. The connection is tenuous at best and often wholly nonexistent. Motivation is still a matter of complete speculation. We never know why people do what we see them doing, and we have nowhere to turn for motivation but to conventional dramatic formulas.

A key test is the scene in *The Chair* when lawyer Don Moore cries. It is the most dramatic moment in all the Drew-Leacock films and, hence, should be even more revealing than other less intense crisis moments. But what good, after all, is Moore to Crump unless he *acts?* We simply assume that Moore cries out of unselfish devotion to his cause, since we have come to that view of defense lawyers from fictional sources and from a simple human desire that this be his primary motivation. Without more information (perhaps of the sort Leacock says was cut out), we have nothing to go by.

A similar moment is the coach's tic in the closing moments of the game in *Football*. Yes, he's still tense even though his team has just about won, but what are we to make of it? It didn't have to happen, but it is hardly an action of any depth, as exciting as it may be to see it captured on film. It could never have been acted so convincingly, but that could prove only that it takes real people to perform truly superficial displays of emotion.

The strongest case for a crisis moment that does reveal character is the scene with John Kennedy on election night in *Primary*. The reason it is effective points up failures in the crisis situations of many of the films. Most important, there is a contrast between the Kennedy we see through most of *Primary* and the one in this scene. He is without the flashy smile, looks considerably more fatigued, speaks more openly, and appears quite different from the familiar public Kennedy we were used to from earlier views in the film. There isn't a single other case of that kind of character change in the rest of the films (except briefly, near the start of *On the Pole*), and crisis situations should be nothing else if not times of considerable flux.

Just what kind of truth the Drew people hoped to discover through the crisis situations remains unclear. Dramatic excitement appears to have been higher on the list of priorities; Drew must have felt there would be no mass audience interest in less intense situations, and truth would take care of itself because of the shooting methods. Their best films are those that do not aspire to any character depth (ignoring the camera influence situations), like *Crisis* and *Football,* and excel instead on a sort of superjournalistic level where milieu, a good deal of exciting activity, and possible sociological implications are uppermost. But since most of the films are definitely personality oriented, this leaves us many cases of lots of footage about people we never come to know. Ultimately, crisis moments are probably much more deceptive situations if knowing people is a fundamental goal. The truths are too simple, too easily obtained, often highly suspect, and too consistently misleading.

One possible advantage of the crisis moment moves away from character revelation into ideas. Heated situations may encourage people to speak their minds more freely and display feelings that may be less apparent in calmer times. The white segregationists in *The Children Were Watching* are so angered by the attempt to integrate their schools that they are less reluctant to reveal themselves than they might be in a noncrisis atmosphere. While these situations can make fine films, they operate on a different level. The situations bring out buried feelings, but they do not have any depth. If we seek insight into people, they don't satisfy us. People matter in these films *(The Children Were Watching, Kenya, Africa, Yanki, No!)* only as representatives of ideas and rarely in their own right.

Crisis moments are most revealing in situations that one might think would be less than ideal—cases where the camera is clearly influencing the subject. At best, all we can know of a subject's "psychology" in these films is the degree to which he is aware of the camera. The whole operation is based upon one key condition, that the subject is trying to maintain appearances, attempting to project his own conception of his personal character.

The Drew films' claim to character insight is implicitly twofold: the crisis moments themselves are more revealing (because they put people to a test) and people in crisis situations are less subject to camera influence, which makes the filmmaking process even more direct. In regard to the second premise, minimal camera influence in crisis situations is no guarantee of character honesty. But limiting the definition of the crisis moment can place the relation between camera and character during these times on more solid conceptual ground.

To reach that limited definition, we must make a distinction between what the crisis moment is generally thought to be and those.

less frequent moments of genuine personal crisis. Given the condition of conscious acting for the camera by the subject, the
crisis moment is that time when the subject is stripped of his defenses as a result of failing in some way. Consequently, this moment would come after the supposed crisis had run its course,
after an outcome had been decided.

A moment surely falling in this category (insight into character
through camera influence after usual crisis) comes immediately
after Eddie Sachs's race in *On the Pole.* First, the condition of
previous conscious acting is here: Eddie has been boosting an
image of himself throughout the film. But only when the race is
ended and we see Eddie annoyed by the intrusion of the camera
in his defeat do we really begin to learn something about him.
Theoretically, this should be the time of least revelation, since the
crisis that takes up most of the film (whether he will win the race)
has subsided. In fact, that crisis has only served the cause by
sufficiently weakening Eddie's defenses for the final "kill." After
the race, the complex interplay between the relentlessly following
camera and the off-guard subject is truly a fulfilling moment worth
the hour's preparation. Eddie shows himself afraid to express
disappointment, trying to act "natural," but not being sure what
"natural" means in terms of the image he wants to present of
himself.

Another scene like this occurs in *Jane* when Miss Fonda reads
the reviews after the opening of her show. Her situation is very
much like Eddie's—already defeated, not knowing quite how to
act, and wanting still to maintain an edge of control over the camera. Though this is a moment of crisis, it is not correct to say that
the camera's presence is less important. In fact, we would want
Jane to feel the camera's presence, to be forced finally (though
not directly by any instruction from the filmmaker) to allow pen-
etration of the ritualized defenses she has so carefully maintained
in other parts of the film.

The setting up of defenses is a necessary condition, for if the subject refuses to place barriers between himself and the camera, trying to reveal character is then like pushing into a pillow, it just gives way and moves somewhere else. Someone like Susan Starr is not an appropriate subject for a crisis situation, since she too easily accepts the camera. Likewise, we would never expect Nehru to reveal himself in crisis because he refuses to become involved in the deception of presenting a special image to the camera. Only subjects offering some resistance have the kind of depth that can be rewardingly plumbed within a crisis structure. The revealing moments through camera influence are a reflection of the subject's failure to meet heroic specifications. A more compassionate regard for these people, and a closer relationship with them, would have been a more natural way to observe them. But by choosing to follow them in crisis, the filmmakers judge them according to their level of achievement, a complicity with the very forces that expose these people to failure.

This kind of character revelation demands failure. If Eddie had won the race, the film would have been a trifle. Imagining a scene of Jane Fonda reading a favorable review the morning after a hit play suggests the shortcomings in successful crisis resolution. The tragic dimension, the fall from excessive pride, is nonexistent if victory is the outcome. Thus, this kind of film, while immensely revealing, is only a chance occurrence. It is character revelation through the luck of witnessing failure, an ironic twist in films that generally idolize heroic accomplishment.

The difference between crises of camera influence and the kind Drew prefers is a distinction between psychological and physical crisis. Paradoxically, considering Drew's stated preference for subjects that are "free," this particular form of camera insight comes in moments of greatest restriction. Drew's crises are physical (success struggles, situations of visible pressure); and the moment of truth is considered to be that moment when the subject shows himself bearing the burden of conflict. The other cases of crisis (like those of Eddie Sachs and Jane) are post-struggle situations that revolve around something beyond winning and losing. It is a matter of external versus internal crisis.

Summary

From this analysis of the crisis structure, three conclusions emerge:

1. Crisis moments seek to bring out special kinds of behavior that, through contrast with other moments, will tell us something about the subject. Generally, however, they do not tell us anything that adds to our insight into the person or that is sufficient evidence in itself to broaden our understanding of the character.

2. People in crisis situations may demonstrate contrasting behavior (Moore's crying in *The Chair*) that still might not help us understand the person. That an activity occurs in crisis is not a guarantee that it is inherently revealing of the subject's true personality. Often, because of our own unavoidable dramatic expectations, these actions can be quite misleading.

3. When people attempting to shape their image before the camera are brought through a crisis that does not leave them triumphant, their struggle to maintain a semblance of dignity (involving a duplicity towards the camera) can be informative on a psychological level.

These conclusions are not too encouraging and become even less so when we note that crisis situations are not prerequisite to understanding through camera influence (thus taking the edge off the third point). In *Jane,* for example, the scene of her alone in the dressing room is as revealing as the review scene for essentially the same reason, that we are keenly aware that she is putting on an act for the camera. Observing a person in defeat after crisis is surely only one way to use the camera as a probe. Actually, scenes wholly without dramatic weight (like the dressing room scene) can be even more revealing, since the subject is freer of immediate preoccupations and better able to concentrate on the subtleties of image projection.

But more crucially, we must question seriously the complete efficacy of the crisis structure as a means to learn about people,

because even given that structure, the most revealing (and/or interesting) moments have little or no correlation with the intensity of the crisis. In other words, we manage to learn about people *despite* the crisis situations, even within that rigid structure. Consider a few examples from the Drew "crisis" films themselves of relatively crisis-free moments:
1. Hubert Humphrey talking and sleeping in the car in *Primary*
2. David (in film of that title) with his family
3. Nehru greeting government officials
4. A street corner singing group in *Petey and Johnny*
5. George Wallace in *Crisis* describing objects in his office.
All these situations are revealing for no other reason than that we learn something, however small, about a person that interested the filmmakers and interests us. Freed of the crisis requirement, the moments stand on their own, unbound by the strictures of plot advancement. This is rather a backhanded compliment to the crisis structure, however, to say that it makes less pressured moments that slip through seem more honest.

The related ideas of editing and character conception discussed in earlier parts of this chapter (parallel editing for conflict, the Drew heroes) are so closely tied together that the elimination of either one would undermine the necessity of the other. Less emphasis upon crisis would minimize a hero mentality and would not require the suspense of edited contrasts. Likewise, nonheroic subjects will not fall into crisis situations, and hence different structures will result. When Drew says they "discover" the dramatic element, that discovery means that they locate the conditions (crisis situation, active subject) that they know will result in a certain kind of film. That's an awful lot of baggage to carry around, and it results in a damaging kind of uniformity.

It might be thought that the crisis moment structure is only a vehicle, simply a technique that can be kept constantly fresh through applying it in an everchanging succession of situations. Would that this were so! The Drew films excel in constant reexamination of a particularly limited area of investigation, the lust for achievement that seems so typically American; but we must recognize that it is not the all-purpose form for a great many subjects. It suited Drew's interests, and some fine films have come about through its use, but, to repeat, it is only one possibility for cinema verite. Structure is the greatest variable in this kind of filming, and Drew's is but one kind.

There's still a whole world unreachable by the crisis structure. Drew found certain elements of American life that were easily adaptable to a structure that had its roots outside cinema, in theater and photojournalism. Some day, I hope, the crisis structure will be looked upon as a transitional phase comparable to the early days of the fiction film, when traditional theatrical conceptions had not yet been discarded. Reality is powerful stuff, and Drew and his people got their hooks into only one segment of it. But even the suggestion of future potential would be unimaginable without the necessary groundwork provided by these films. Their importance as a crucial stage in the development of a whole new kind of cinema can only increase, and there will always be a great deal to learn from these seminal efforts.

The Maysles Brothers

The early films of the Maysles Brothers, Albert and David, were the first clear attempt to employ cinema verite (although they prefer the term *direct cinema*) in nondramatic fashion. Unlike the Drew films, the Maysles' work lacks clear dramatic resolution or character revelation through win-or-lose climaxes. Still, their films reflect the influence of the Drew approach and are much closer to his work than to, say, Frederick Wiseman's. Like the Drew films, the Maysles films consistently maintain a personality-oriented structure, and while not dependent upon the same sort of crisis conditions, they do have a sense of people trying to prove themselves (or, at least, to survive) in pressure situations. In Maysles films, however, the pressure never lets up. The contest never ends.

Albert Maysles, like Leacock, showed an interest in an incipient cinema-verite aesthetic before there was any name for it. In 1955, with a background in psychology and almost no knowledge of film, he talked CBS into backing his plan to shoot footage of mental hospitals in the Soviet Union. The resulting short film (about ten minutes in length), *Psychiatry in Russia,* is of little more than historical interest, a brief, diary-like record of his three-month trip. Maysles provides his own narration, in the absence of live synch sound, and all the shots appear to have been taken with a hand-held camera. It is a competent account, but the visuals are generally uninteresting, and the limitations of nonsynch shooting are again evident (as in Leacock's early work). The following year he shot a film about Polish youth with his brother David (who had previously worked as assistant to the producer on a couple of feature films). In 1959, Al Maysles met Richard Leacock and D. A. Pennebaker in Moscow, where they were shooting a film on a Bernstein concert. This association led to his work on *Primary, Yanki, No!,* and *Kenya, Africa,* and David as well worked briefly for Drew Associates. In 1962, breaking from Drew, they formed their own company. For all their films, Al has been cameraman, with David taking sound and supervising editing.

Showman

Showman is a landmark film, the first American cinema-verite work entirely free from the constraints of crisis situations and plot progression to a clear resolution. The Maysles' first film, it is literally a slice of life, a record of some time spent following Joe Levine, a film entrepreneur then rising to the top on the financial strength of his *Hercules.* While there are threads of narrative continuity, there is no real story or dramatic character change. Levine is no different at the end of the film than at the beginning, and he has not passed through a particularly climactic period. The film has the engaging quality of looking caught on the run, with events happening too quickly to be molded into a tightly ordered struc-ture. *Showman* is an almost pure form of revelation through situation; each scene looks as though it was selected for nothing more than insight into the film's main character.

The film is not completely structureless, however. Its prime uni-fying force is the simple convention of chronological continuity,

Showman. Joseph Levine.

Showman. Deal-making.

Showman. Joseph Levine during Boston homecoming.

Showman. Levine presenting Oscar to Sophia Loren for *Two Women.*

with arbitrary starting and ending points. It is matched only by Leacock's later *A Stravinsky Portrait* in placing complete faith in the typicality, the everyday activity of a time period seemingly chosen at random in one person's life. Both films even have a way of making the possibly spectacular into the acceptably routine. Levine's trip to Rome to present Sophia Loren her Oscar for *Two Women* (a Levine-produced film) is given no greater emphasis than his breakfast conversation with his cook: it is just another entry in the filmed "diary." A pattern of life develops, a repetition of response, which argues that we have seen sufficient material to get an idea of what Levine is like.

  Beyond the structure of limited noncrisis chronology, there are some simple continuity threads, though there are just as many potential "little stories" that might develop out of single episodes but never do. Levine's promotion of *Two Women* and his dealings with Miss Loren connect several scenes, and his reunion with childhood cohorts at a Boston dinner has some follow-up. But a supposed meeting with Kim Novak never takes place, and there are a good number of episodes unconnected with any others. (Most memorable is a radio station "debate" between Levine and David Susskind over questions of audience tastes and film art.)

Freed from plot advancement, the film is full of spontaneous moments unmatched in fiction films. The introduction given Levine at the Boston dinner, like the mayor's speech in Leacock's *Happy Mother's Day,* is the kind of florid banality that rings true in a way that a fictionalized incident could never get away with. ("The man with a golden touch has a heart of gold, too.") Cinema verite can make cliché fresh: the ethic of noninterference means that everyday speech and typical relationships are again within the province of film. Levine's "yes men" are a fictional cliché, but their very presence in the film argues for a certain unmanipulated form of observation. ("You were down to earth, Joe." "You should write a book, Joe.") These kinds of clichés are also acceptable in this film because Levine himself provides a running commentary on many incidents (but within the film's action itself, rather than as voiceover), as when he quickly dissociates himself from the aura of nostalgia surrounding the Boston reunion.

Levine's complexity in *Showman* develops from the contradictions of his personality, which are expressed, not through a balance of scenes showing him in a "good" or a "bad" light (the typical "objectivity" of many television documentaries) but directly and discretely in each moment we observe him in action. If one were to take sides, one could conclude that Levine is either a monster destroying public taste or just a very ambitious guy who has won out over other ambitious guys, but whatever one's opinion of Levine, it could be supported by the entire film and not just by selected scenes. No one episode is advanced as being "more" revealing of Levine, in marked contrast to the emphasis placed on the crisis moment in Drew films.

What's Happening! The Beatles in the U.S.A.

What's Happening! The Beatles in the U.S.A. is again an "on the run" film. The Maysles were offered the opportunity to film The

Beatles' first trip to America only two hours before their plane arrived (the first scene in the film).[1] Shot over a five-day period, the film has even less plot continuity than *Showman*. The Beatles are followed through press encounters, hotel rooms, night clubs, and performances, with the skeletal structure of beginning at the group's New York arrival and ending with their return to London. The first full-length synch-sound cinema-verite film completely free of narration (no small accomplishment), *What's Happening* gives the impression of having been almost accidentally recorded, when in fact its structure and thematic concerns are surprisingly consistent.

The film seems so entirely objective, so free of external comment, that some accused it of being little more than a glorified newsreel. The view of Antony Jay, then Head of Features for BBC-TV, is typical of this attitude: " . . . as most documentary film-makers understand the term, it was hardly a film at all. . . . I think it will be hard for anyone who comes fresh to this film in ten years' time to believe that anything so unutterably tedious was ever transmitted: its viewability depended entirely on a nearly obsessive interest in everything to do with the Beatles. . . . Unless there is no difference at all between the documentary producer and the newsreel cameraman, it had almost no relevance to the development of documentaries. . . . It is not about art, it is about keyholes."[2] Jay's ten years have not quite passed, but his anger at the seeming formlessness of the film should be kept in mind during the ensuing discussion, as the impression might otherwise be transmitted that *What's Happening* is *overly* structured. Despite appearances, the film offers a good deal more than private views of famous people. Jay's remarks, however, merit a reply.

A. William Bluem has argued that cinema verite "can nullify an essentially intellectual message—or impede, in annoying fashion, our appreciation and understanding of it" and also that it "can interfere with rationality (it is *designed* to do so)."[3] While Jay would certainly deny that *What's Happening* even has an intellectual message, the two views overlap in an implicit belief in the necessity for overt statement of purpose in documentary. The tone of such prescriptive directives, like many of the films made in accordance with these beliefs, is rather dogmatic. The Maysles in *What's Happening,* and in their work generally, are as concerned about message as Jay and Bluem. Maysles films do not attempt to "hide" a message in a surface of uninterpreted observation; they simply refuse to spoon-feed interpretation when the material itself is open to consideration from a number of points of view. This approach, rather than interfering with rationality, openly encourages it, since none of the thinking is done for you in the form of narration or an easily followed plot. While my view of the film is, of course, personal, one can only hope that the internal consistencies in a film, leading to conclusions in regard to theme, argue effectively against accusations like those just cited.

The idea of The Beatles as a commodity, a marketable product, is certainly clear in the film, but even more apparent is the atmosphere of excessive commercialism that makes it impossible for them to function in any other way. Some critics have claimed that the film fails to differentiate among the four members of the group,[4] but this is not so much a shortcoming of the film as an observation of how people in the film treat The Beatles. To say that the film could express distinct personal characteristics of each of the four would mean that the situations where they were observed would allow for such differentiation. As the Maysles did not plan any of the events they filmed, if The Beatles all come out looking alike, we must analyze the processes that led to this merging of personalities rather than criticize the film for recording this phenomenon. The view of the four Beatles as interchangeable components of a marketable commodity, of individual characteristics sacrificed to commercial group cohesion, is the kind of insight that a preconceived approach to the subject could very possibly have obscured. (One such approach might, for instance, have independent sections about each of the four, thus deliberately stressing their differences.)

The emphasis upon The Beatles as a product is reinforced through

the appearance of numerous commercials and frequent discussions (even some parodies) of advertisements. To give a few examples:
1. As they are driven from the airport, they hear one of their songs on the radio, followed directly by a cigarette ad.
2. In their hotel room, they hear a wine commercial (again directly after one of their songs) and then joke about it.
3. George is interviewed on the phone by a radio disc jockey who has to interrupt to do an ad.
4. Paul objects to the use of ads in news broadcasts and shows for children.
5. John and George perform a mock cigarette commercial.
6. Another radio disc jockey asks each of them to yell the station's call letters and number into the phone.
Whether these scenes were selected from a great variety of material or whether they are an inevitable result of following The Beatles for five days is a moot point. In either case, the thematic pattern persists.

The strongest argument for intentional thematic statement is the inclusion of The Beatles' return to London Airport. They are met by a mob of fans identical to the crowd that greeted their arrival in New York. One would have expected the film to end with their New York departure, as the film is ostensibly a report on their American visit, so the brief London footage comes as something of a surprise. The one shot makes the film circular in structure and reminds us that Beatlemania is not an exclusively American phenomenon. The group is a worldwide commodity.

Theme is nonassertive in *What's Happening* for two reasons: the film lacks specific crisis situations to point up the tensions at work, and it refuses to press for a certain point of view through camera style (or narration). Al Maysles' camera simply follows action, rarely moving in on small details or gestures. Maysles' camera in the early films seems most at ease in scenes of chaotic movement, as in the shot in *Primary* following Kennedy through the crowd or the Peppermint Lounge sequence in this film, when

in one long take we are brought completely into the frenetic atmosphere, made to feel like participants. Louis Marcorelles called
this latter shot "the most revealing moment of the Maysles technique. . . . We are *in,* intensely taken into an action and the emotion
it engenders. For the first time, we catch a glimpse of a camera
depicting *really* physical actions."5 If there has been a progression in the Maysles style, though, it has been away from this kind
of first-person "atmosphere" shooting into what we might call a
more psychologically oriented filming approach, a way of shooting that is concerned with the relationships among a small number of people and with the role of the camera itself.

Some suggestions of this progression are apparent in these first
films. In *What's Happening,* The Beatles, for the most part, refuse
to pretend that the camera is invisible, accepting it as just another
natural element of intrusion. They often perform directly to the
camera, or at least mug occasionally in its direction. Sometimes,
however, the probe goes on a little too long for their liking, as in
a shot of Paul, when he fools around awhile for the camera but
then gets bored, so he sits waiting for the camera to move away.
It doesn't, and the two are locked in a momentary struggle, as
Paul stares directly into the camera, challenging it to move elsewhere. (There is an almost identical shot of Rolling Stones drum-
mer Charlie Watts in *Gimme Shelter.*) There are few such moments, but this element of open confrontation (as we have noted
with Pennebaker) is a far different approach from the concept
of the camera as an invisible (or at least unobtrusive) recorder,
as is the case in *Showman.*

Another departure from impersonal observation is the occasional
tendency to select reactions rather than follow actions. In a revealing scene in *What's Happening,* a manic disc jockey named
Murray the K does a report to his listeners via telephone from The
Beatles' hotel room. At one point he says, "They've got ice in their
pockets. They're real cool!" The camera is on John, staring in-
credulously at the man's performance and way of expressing
himself. There is a somewhat similar camera choice in *Showman,*

when Levine is talking with a group of his subordinates, in which the camera stays on Levine regardless of who is speaking, as if in judgment of the relative importance of the others' comments. These are selections made in the camera, rather than through editing; in the *What's Happening* shot the emphasis upon John is asserted through framing and angle rather than through a cut to him. In scenes filmed with one camera, depictions of nonverbal attitudes to some ongoing event (usually called "reaction shots") must be incorporated·within one shot, as this one is, since a cut will invalidate the credibility of the shot by suggesting an immediate response when a viewer might wonder how much time has in fact elapsed between the two setups. An example of this problem occurs in *Showman,* when Levine looks out a window of his Cannes hotel room, and there is a cut to a girl on the beach, and

What's Happening! The Beatles in the U.S.A. Paul McCartney listens to radio plug for The Beatles.

What's Happening! The Beatles in the U.S.A. George Harrison, Ringo Starr, and John Lennon.

then a shot of Levine still looking out the window. Quite obviously, the footage of the girl was shot some other time, and actually we have no idea at all what Levine was looking at or for how long. Because a scene in a cinema-verite film carries with it its own internal evidence as to whether only one camera is present, be it size of the room itself or lack of continuity between shots within the scene, the traditional suspension of disbelief in regard to cutting in fiction films (that is, the acceptance that the individual shots are, indeed, continuous in time within a scene, though weeks might have separated their actual filming) cannot apply. For this reason, credible selection comes through changes of emphasis within a shot; the cameraman becomes his own editor.

He becomes his own editor, that is, if he wishes to. Generally, as in this film, the cameraman follows action—if someone talks, we see him, and if another person replies, the camera pans over to him. It is when the cameraman decides that the listener may be more important to watch than the speaker, that is, when he refuses to follow action, that selection is taking place. Occasional shots in *Showman* and *What's Happening,* like the examples already given, are the first indications of the potential complexity of this seemingly straightforward shooting style and of the need for new criteria to evaluate these films. A smooth cut to indicate a reaction, an element to be valued perhaps in a fiction film, can be highly undesirable in a cinema-verite work.

Since *What's Happening* doesn't have much of a story (even in comparison to other cinema verite, like the Drew-Leacock films), one might wonder just what function physical editing (as opposed to editing while shooting) does have. Since the primary objective of the film might be termed simply "interesting observation," rather than story advancement, the editing process is not dependent upon a view of progressive development of character in the fictional sense. Ideally, a film like this would consist of *all* technically competent material that was shot, but that specific scenes have been selected to the exclusion of others does not make the film any less "truthful." Since there is little contextual meaning in the film, in the sense that no particular meaning results from the ordering of scenes (as in films with a narrative), editing selections do not alter the meaning of independent scenes. More scenes would just supply more evidence, which would make for a more valid portrait, in the same way that a larger sample would give a statistical survey greater validity.

In crisis-oriented films (or, more generally, films with plot resolution), if a happy scene, for instance, follows a scene of crucial defeat, a point has been made through editing (or in our trust that editing is being faithful to actual chronology). In a film like *What's Happening,* where such dramatic reversals do not take place, the order of scenes is not nearly so important, which is a way of saying that editing ceases to be as powerful a formative device. Each sequence stands on its own, and its relationship to other sequences is cumulative rather than dependent upon direct transitional (or chronological) links from one to another. Several

scenes more or less would not alter the film, whereas such altera-
tions in a *Primary* or an *On the Pole* could result in very different
conclusions about characters, in view of the pivotal position structure holds in those films.

   This may leave such films open to the kind of criticism noted by
Colin Young in the case of *Showman,* from people who say "they
learn no more when it is over than after ten minutes—that it stays
on the surface."[6] This view, in its way, is a compliment to the
Maysles approach, in that "staying on the surface" suggests that
the filmmakers have been sensitive to the fragile chemistry of
camera-subject interaction and have chosen not to upset the
delicate balance implied in such a relationship. An unexamined
concept in the quoted position is just what "the surface" is, and
what kind of insights we can expect from these films. This is a
broad question, but in relation to the Maysles films, there is a faith
in the complexity of personalities that argues that the accumulation of observation (the filming) is an information-gathering process rather than a search for logical structure. In these films the
Maysles are not after "the truth" about Joe Levine or The Beatles;
they are not defining their significance for us. In this sense, the
films are not informational in intent; hence, the accusations that
as the films progress we don't "know more." The Maysles' role
is closer to that of an intermediary between their subject and us.
This does not, certainly, imply an impersonal recording process,
but at least they don't function as creators of fictional structures
in order to reduce experience to recognizable patterns.

   A Hard Day's Night, The Beatles' first dramatic film, was clearly
influenced by *What's Happening.* Semidocumentary in intent, the
Richard Lester film does not use The Beatles as characters, except perhaps to conform to their own popular images. Many
scenes in the film appear to be directly inspired by *What's Happening,* especially those that focus on questions from reporters
and the scene where George goes to an ad agency, only to be
confronted by a guy whose *gear* and *fab* argot is reminiscent of
Murray the K's carrying-on. The fictional film tries to capture the

same sense of claustrophobia, and its use of shots of fans to convey the mystic power of Beatlemania is similar to the Maysles, if a good deal more overstated. Interestingly, in view of the previously mentioned criticism of *What's Happening* for failure to differentiate among the four, *A Hard Day's Night* does isolate each for certain segments of the film, a liberty the Maysles were not free to take. These segments of the Lester film, though, are the most obviously fictionalized and seem rather flat in comparison to the scenes of rehearsal and performance. The film ends with a postconcert escape by helicopter, but unlike the New York departure in *What's Happening,* which only leads to identical chaos in London, the Lester film opts for the rosier view of genuine release, as the helicopter takes off and the film ends.

What's Happening is also the prototypical performer portrait, bearing close resemblances to Pennebaker's film on Bob Dylan, *Don't Look Back.* Both films deal with a performer's tour of a foreign country and are structured on that basis. The newness of the performer to the country he's visiting leads to many press interviews, a way of getting verbal response without the filmmakers' taking a direct hand. In both, the idea of performer as commodity is important, and consequently there are quite similar scenes of their managers negotiating deals (similar, too, to telephone deals in *Showman*). Both films invite interpretation of their subjects as social and cultural phenomena, exploring the milieu they travel through and the responses people make to them. Because these films take performers out of their usual environment, they can be viewed in several ways—as personality studies and as explorations of the stars as products of society.

Meet Marlon Brando
If Antony Jay and others felt that *What's Happening* was hardly even a film, one wonders what they would think about *Meet Marlon Brando,* which challenges even more radically conventional notions of documentary structure. Unfortunately, the film has had

only the most limited distribution, reportedly because of Brando's refusal to permit its release,[7] so the issues the film raises have not been the subject of much critical discussion.

Meet Marlon Brando didn't even start out to be a film at all. The Maysles were assigned to film a battery of press interviews that Brando was giving in New York to local television reporters from various cities across the country to plug his film *Morituri.* As the shooting progressed, the Maysles felt there was an interest in the material of a sort no one had anticipated, and they shot more than their assignment had called for, financing the extra shooting personally.[8]

The half-hour film consists entirely of a succession of these interviews. There is scarcely any direct information conveyed, as Brando is continually evasive in the face of a stream of rather ridiculous questions. Nor is there any discussion of the film supposedly being promoted, beyond Brando's challenging an interviewer who says "It's a great picture" as to whether she's actually seen it, only to get a sheepish negative reply. Typical of his responses to questions about the film are these two exchanges:

Interviewer: Do tell us about your movie.
Brando: Why?
Interviewer: We'll all be watching for Marlon.
Brando: Don't watch too close.

Occasionally he tries to shift the discussion to serious topics like education, problems of the American Indian, or man's essentially violent nature (quoting Dr. Louis Leakey), only to be brought back to more mundane topics by TV hosts who could care less about these subjects. Increasingly exasperated, Brando ends his final interview with this highly sarcastic comment: "For God's sake, go see it. You won't know how to proceed in life if you don't go see *Morituri.*"

The camera style is totally unemphatic, almost invariably a stationary two-shot of Brando and his interviewer. There is never any visual emphasis supplied by pans or zooms (except in one inter-

view done in Central Park) and hardly any cutting within interviews. The deliberately flat visual style, along with the minimal
structure, makes *Meet Marlon Brando* one of the "purest" examples of American cinema verite so far realized.

  On first seeing the film, there's a certain astonishment, after one
or two of the interviews, in realizing that the whole film is going
to consist of nothing but these interviews. This structural audacity,
though, appears less radical when defined and placed within the
context of the Maysles' work to this point. The film can be viewed
as a sort of controlled experiment where external variables are
kept at a minimum. In each segment, Brando is put through the
same process of having to "sell" a film he's not interested in to a
person he doesn't like. Again, one could argue that we don't
"know" any more about Brando at the end of the film than after
the first interview, but in terms of the film's credibility (or, rather,
Brando's), it is the very repetition, the lack of "new" information,
that gives the film meaning. The absence of plot in the Maysles
films discussed so far would be the first indication that the structure of the Brando film, while surprising at first, is only an extension of tendencies previously expressed.

  The repetition of incidents in *Meet Marlon Brando* is a result of
the tendency in Maysles films to separate personality from plot.
To understand this, let us compare the Maysles films to the Drew
films. In Maysles films (with the possible exception of *Gimme
Shelter*), one always has the feeling that people are more important than events, whereas in the Drew films, because of the relative weight given to the situation in which the individual is placed,
personality is defined by action to a much greater extent. This is
not a negative criticism of the Drew films but an observation in
keeping with Drew's stated preference for people who *do* things.[9]
When we think of Eddie Sachs, we think of him as a man who
races cars; he lacks an identity apart from his profession. People
in Drew films are unhappy only when they fail, not because they
are dissatisfied with what they must do.

In the Maysles films, a tension usually exists between a person's "nature" and what he does to make money. (This is most true for Brando, Paul Brennan in *Salesman,* and The Beatles; least for Levine.) Because of this tension, we get a stronger sense than in the Drew films of people whose identities can be discussed apart from their professional activities. We do not necessarily think of Brando in the film as an actor but as a man who is also an actor. (Robert Steele, quite properly, can talk about how Brando "substituted his real personality for his persona.")[10] This distinction is more important than it may seem, for it is the discrepancy between Brando's view of himself and the way others see him that most clearly defines the nature of his situation, and this discrepancy is developed and impressed on the observer by repetition. Brando, unlike Eddie Sachs, cannot "win." There is nothing he can "do," given the situation, to triumph, because the situation itself is so compromised.

Meet Marlon Brando

Meet Marlon Brando

Meet Marlon Brando

In relation to structure, then, because Brando (as well as other Maysles subjects) is not defined by action, it is entirely illogical to say that "nothing" happens for thirty minutes except a repetition of identical situations. In fact, it is the structure itself that makes his predicament clear, in other words, that reveals his personality. One of the interviews alone, perhaps as a single episode in a *Showman*-type film of many different Brando activities, could only express these feelings in skeletal form. If we interpret "knowledge" in this film (using the word in answer to those who would say you don't "know" more about Brando by the end) as a better understanding of Brando's contradictory position, the depth of his compromise, then the form and length of the film are quite important.

The film can also be taken as an ironic comment on the interview process itself. American cinema-verite filmmakers have almost completely avoided the use of interviews, and this film is a useful index of the Maysles' probable feeling in this regard. By running so many short interviews in sequence, they demonstrate the equal inability of all to draw Brando out on matters he would like to discuss. (The interview scenes in Pennebaker's *Don't Look Back* function similarly.) The film is a series of badly directed Brando performances, each interviewer trying to make the actor play his game.

Meet Marlon Brando is further revealing in regard to the actual promotion routine—the curious form of torture that a movie star has to go through. Like *Showman* and *What's Happening* (and perhaps *Gimme Shelter*), the film is also about the merchandising of art or at least its business aspect. In all cases there is a feeling that the people in question have made compromises by giving in so readily to the lust for money. Brando's series of inane interviews, like The Beatles tour, is a crazy idea to begin with, endured only for personal commercial benefit.

Brando, like the others, is aware of his huckster role and of his function as a commodity. He tells one interviewer: "I'm like the hula hoop. It comes along and everybody buys it, and after awhile, nobody buys it any more." Like other Maysles personalities, it is Brando's degree of self-realization which makes him sympathetic. Maysles heroes, when we're not laughing at the absurdity of their situation (and *Meet Marlon Brando is* a hilarious film), achieve an almost tragic stature.

Salesman

Salesman is the Maysles' most ambitious work to date and in many ways the most important product of American cinema verite. (It should be noted that the credits read "A Film by The Maysles Brothers and Charlotte Zwerin." Miss Zwerin played a major role in editing.)[11] It is a vexing, problematic film, however. On the one hand, *Salesman* is startlingly pure, a rigorous attempt to capture aspects of American experience scarcely explored in early films of this kind, refusing to deal with a famous personality or an event of marked significance. On the other, *Salesman* is as neatly constructed as if it were largely prescribed, full of devices heretofore more the province of fiction film. Its ultimate signifi-cance may lie more in the direction it signals and the questions it raises than in its intrinsic merits, but it is certainly a film of crucial importance.

The film depicts the activities of four Bible salesmen. It begins in Boston but takes place primarily during a selling trip in Florida. All four men are shown in independent sales attempts (they go to the homes of people who have stated their interest in the prod-uct by filling out a card at their church), and the great majority of scenes are these one-to-one encounters. At an early point, though, the film begins to focus on one of them, Paul, the least successful of the group. As the film develops, Paul's lack of prog-ress is played off against the relative success of the others, and he appears to become increasingly disillusioned about his work. In the last scene, he stands in a doorway, near tears, in seem-ing awareness of the depressing nature of his situation.

Like many of the Drew films, *Salesman* relies frequently on cutting among the activities of several people, in this case the four
salesmen. Al Maysles has remarked, though without noting the
similarity in approach to many of the Drew films, "We had a ter-
rific advantage in filming four people rather than one, because we
could break away from one person and give him a rest and pick
up with another one."[12] The film begins, for instance, with one
sales transaction of each, all four scenes ending with a name
and nickname ("The Badger," "The Gipper," etc.) superimposed
as titles over a shot of the salesman we have just seen in action.

Paul's emergence as the central dramatic focus is achieved
through a combination of structural choices and events in the
film. One way this is developed is through scenes of him talking
while driving alone (with the unseen filmmakers, of course). He
discusses the other three in turn, and as he does so, each is "illustrated" with another selling scene (Paul, in effect, functioning
here as narrator, in a film otherwise devoid of narration). Clearly,
this is an arbitrary choice, as any of the four might have assumed
this role. From this perspective, the other three begin to look
more similar; they are the ones getting sales while Paul flounders.

An even more important structural choice involving Paul as central character is the manner in which footage of a Chicago sales
meeting is introduced. A scene of all four salesmen together ends
with a line (which looks dubbed in for transitional purposes, as
we don't see the speaker) referring to the upcoming meeting.
The next shot shows Paul on the train to Chicago, and a voiceover begins from the meeting before cutting to the matching visual. A man rises and tells of his optimism for the coming year.
Cut back to Paul on the train, then back to the meeting for a similar speech. So, the first speeches at the meeting are presented
as flash-forwards, presumably as reflections of Paul's fears of not
selling. This construction is a dramatic device, in that the meeting
is used to interpret Paul's probable thoughts prior to his arrival,
an interpretation developed entirely through editing.

This emphasis upon Paul supports the film's central conflict—his frustration at not selling while the others are. As the film continues, there are fewer sequences constructed of successive scenes with each of the four. Instead, Paul is more directly played off against the others. While the film lacks a climax, the last scene is the most expressive of his mounting frustration. Through the structure of contrast, we are made to feel that Paul is at the end of his rope.

Quite frequently in interviews, the Maysles have argued that their films should be judged by the same criteria one applies to fiction films, referring to their work as a cinematic equivalent to the "nonfiction novel" like Truman Capote's *In Cold Blood.*[13] We are certainly under no obligation to judge a film according to the makers' view of how it should be considered, but the suggestion deserves consideration. The statement carries with it a couple of major implications: first, that no special attention be given to the circumstances that produced the film (including the knowledge that these men are really Bible salesmen, that they were not told what to do, that nothing was restaged) and that the question of manipulation in editing is irrelevant. One should, according to this view, consider nothing beyond what is on the screen and evaluate the film evidence accordingly.

Attempting to follow this dictum, the film is wholly discussable in terms of the view of American life it portrays, the metaphoric possibilities in the situation, the contradictions between religion and hawking Bibles, the pervading sense of *angst,* etc. This kind of explication, while certainly fruitful, sidesteps major questions. The crux of this argument seems to be that a cinema-verite approach can lead to superior fiction, when the real question should be why we need fiction at all. To say that the film should be judged like any other means that the approach is important because it gives the filmmaker "better" material than he perhaps could have invented, but that the same necessity for working within a narrative applies.

Salesman. Paul Brennan makes one of his few sales.

Salesman. The "star" is introduced.

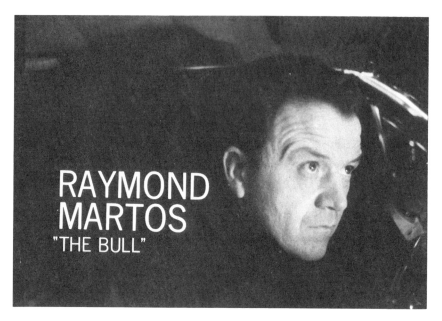

Salesman. One of the other salesmen.

Because of the cinema-verite ground rules, even the basic requirement of not restaging events, the method itself must influence the form of the film. Therefore, to ignore the method in evaluating the film seems a forced approach. If we did employ standard criteria, we might judge the intercutting between episodes of the four salesmen to be a contrived means of comparison. We could wonder why the film jumps around so much when Paul seems to be the dramatic focus. More seriously, if only the usual criteria apply, the many scenes of selling are surely inordinately repetitious. Rather than argue against these hypothetical faults, that is, try to justify the fictional "look" of the film, let's simply evaluate what is, indeed, of interest and importance, and see how these elements are not generally a part of fiction films; this approach will provide the most conclusive evidence against the idea of identical criteria in fiction and cinema-verite films.

Joseph Gelmis relates a very useful quote from David Maysles: "The most exciting thing in life is to watch the meeting of two strangers, to see how they communicate."[14] We have talked already about repetition in *Meet Marlon Brando* and the use of identical situations to explore personality apart from plot development. The selling encounters in *Salesman* function similarly. The patterns developing from repetition in the dozen or so sales pitches, and not the larger narrative in which these encounters occur, are the source of greatest insight. It is the cumulative effect of these scenes and the wealth of detail within each that make *Salesman* such a revelation. These individual encounters, these spontaneous, unrehearsed meetings between strangers, are the major substance of the film.

If anything, the "story" of Paul's disenchantment with his job could be viewed as a gimmick, a perhaps artificial thread to tie the selling scenes together. The need for plot development makes the ordering of scenes suspect, and we can legitimately wonder whether the order is actually nonchronological, structured to suggest Paul's growing ineffectiveness, when in fact the events themselves might not have contained so neat a progression. For all we know, the scenes could have been filmed in nearly reverse sequence from how they are presented, or in dozens of other permutations. The structure itself may be only a framework, but as in the Drew films, it still appears to restrict unnecessarily the complexity of material strong enough to stand unaided by such fictional supports. Where *Salesman* could have been truly radical, but still a natural outgrowth of the Maysles' earlier work, it edges back into the kind of manipulation that American cinema verite was originally reacting against.

The flashforward scenes of the Chicago sales meeting provide a useful point to examine the limitations of fictionalization. As mentioned, the sequence is constructed to suggest that the meeting reflects Paul's fears about failure. We see the scene "through his eyes," clarifying the competitive pressures he feels. The inclusion of the sales meeting footage is, in this way, justified by making it important to the central character. The visual evidence, however, makes clear that the material requires no such justification. Like the police convention in Leacock's *Chiefs,* the sales convention presents a microcosmic portrait of widely shared American values and goals. The salesmen's self-assured promises of great achievement and the extraordinary speech by the Bible's designer make this material strong enough to stand completely on its own. The dramatic framework, the structural insistence on evaluating the event as it affects Paul, forces a more limited view. If we wish to see greater significance in the scene, we must do so in spite of the way it is presented.

The structure is unnecessary because the conflicts are present within the selling scenes themselves, even without the superstructure of motel scenes of Paul discussing his increasing frustration. Again, we don't "know" more from all the scenes of salesmanship than from any one, but as in earlier films, the similar encounters are rich both in variation and in defining overall patterns. The salesmen's forced jocularity, their wheedling for a sale, the petty lies, the playing upon religious values, the accepted clichés — this picture of a way of making a living has no equivalent whatsoever in American filmmaking, documentary or otherwise. As in *Meet Marlon Brando,* no dramatic framework is necessary to support the interest inherent in such material. To develop a structure to support these scenes implies a lack of confidence in their own power to sustain an audience's attention, and I would like to hope these fears were unfounded. If these meetings between strangers are "the most exciting thing in life," one would think they could stand alone.

Because the salesmen are so concerned with success, they appear to be relatively unconcerned with the presence of the camera. The scenes of the salesmen when they are not selling, when they are together at day's end or during meals, find them behaving differently. The camera keeps them moving and talking; although they do not play to the camera as overtly as The Beatles did, they are at least aware they are being filmed. This is not to argue that they respond uncharacteristically, but distinguishing levels of camera awareness is important to evaluating their actions. The last shot of Paul, in fact, is quite like the corresponding moments in *Jane.* The presence of the camera appears to make Paul even more acutely aware of his failure, threatening to expose feelings he might prefer to keep hidden. Still, the scenes where he fails to make sales and where this frustration comes out directly within the context of events seem to be sufficient for recognition of the nature of his predicament.

Salesman, then, carries the Maysles approach several steps forward and perhaps a step back. It is a further exploration of the themes of materialism, success, and commercialism present in the earlier films, developed at feature length without the need for big names or major events. It is easy to agree with David Maysles' evaluation: "The great achievement in *Salesman,* something we were trying to prove to everybody, was that you could take someone from everyday life and make a film about him."[15] Nevertheless, perhaps the major innovative element in earlier Maysles films, the disregard for conventional dramatic development, is at least partially compromised. To achieve one kind of purity, they may have lost sight of another.

Gimme Shelter

Gimme Shelter, like *What's Happening! The Beatles in the U.S.A.,* and *Meet Marlon Brando,* began as a routine commercial assignment. The Maysles were hired to shoot some footage of The Rolling Stones' performance at Madison Square Garden. As with the Brando film, they felt an interest in the material sufficient to film further at their own expense. They stayed on for the remainder of the Stones' American tour, which ended with a large free concert at Altamont (near San Francisco) where a man near the stage was stabbed to death.[16]

The film, like Leacock's and Shuker's *Nehru,* introduces the filmmakers as characters in the film. At the start, we see David Mays-

.

les in front of a Steenbeck editing machine with some members of the group, as David explains the rudiments of their filming approach, just as Leacock did at the start of the Nehru film. *Gimme Shelter* is constructed in a kind of flashback fashion, cutting between the main narrative of the tour and the events leading to Altamont, with the added dimension of filming the participants viewing themselves some time later (as in Rouch's and Morin's *Chronique d'un Eté*). The structure is even more complex than simply moving between these two levels, as parts of planning conferences for Altamont taking place in lawyer Melvin Belli's office are also intercut throughout the film. The highly intricate structure is surprising in view of the Maysles' past work. *Gimme Shelter* seems more closely related to the Drew-Leacock films than to their own.

The structure is reminiscent of *The Chair* or *Crisis: Behind a Presidential Commitment,* films of multiple coverage attempting to present a more complete view of a complex event than was available to any individual participant. Like the Drew films, *Gimme Shelter* is certainly crisis oriented, climaxing with the Altamont stabbing, which is repeated in slow motion (David Maysles operating the Steenbeck for Mick Jagger, the group's lead singer, and the audience). In contrast to the Drew films, though, is the accidental, found nature of the crisis, since the stabbing, of course, was not anticipated.

The Belli telephone scenes, as he makes calls to arrange for the concert, also have a familiar look. Like the phone deals in *Showman,* they also recall the Kennedy-Katzenbach conversations in *Crisis* and the attorney's pleading by phone in *The Chair.* Even Pennebaker's *Don't Look Back* has an extended scene of bargaining by phone. The fascination with behind-the-scenes planning has long been a staple of these films. In *Gimme Shelter,* their inclusion suggests an almost formulaic approach to coverage of an event, although it's a formula first displayed in the Maysles' own Joe Levine film.

Gimme Shelter. David Maysles, Albert Maysles, and Mick Jagger during shooting in London.

More positively perhaps, *Gimme Shelter* shares with *What's Happening* a strong interest in media projections of pop images. Where the Maysles could pan in *What's Happening* from The Beatles themselves to their watching their own arrival (an event we had seen previously) on a Walter Cronkite news show, in *Gimme Shelter* we see Jagger and other members of the group watching themselves on editing screens. Completely open about the manipulative possibilities in editing, since the film shows events being pieced together on a Steenbeck from film and radio tapes, *Gimme Shelter* functions as a critique of its own methods. For-tunately, the people in front of the editing machines make no ver-bal judgments about the events they view, and a wide range of interpretations is possible.

Nevertheless, *Gimme Shelter* is not as interesting, nor as complex, as the earlier Maysles films. A large part of the film is simply records of performances, and the crisis structure, though not planned, imposes its characteristic limitations on the film. It is sadly ironic that this is by far the most widely seen and discussed Maysles film, for it offers only slight indications of the range of their concerns and the rewards of their filming approach. Still, in reporting events of a controversial nature, no conclusions are pressed, no excuses offered. A cinema-verite ethic comes through in this respect.

D. A. Pennebaker

D. A. Pennebaker's films since his period with Drew Associates, especially *Don't Look Back* and *Monterey Pop,* have made him probably the best known of American cinema-verite filmmakers. While he and Leacock formed their own company together in 1963 after leaving Drew Associates, their work since then has been largely individual. Leacock has done some shooting for Pennebaker's films, and the two worked with Jean-Luc Godard on a film that Godard never completed that was to be called *One A.M.,* but their films since they both left Drew have not been collaborative works.[1] Pennebaker has also been cameraman for Norman Mailer on his three films, *Wild 90, Beyond the Law,* and *Maidstone,* and has made several other films that, though not as

D. A. Pennebaker

well known as the first two mentioned above, are of great interest, both in themselves and for the issues they raise.

Elizabeth and Mary

Elizabeth and Mary was originally made for purposes of medical study only. Above its scientific application, it is a deeply moving work. The film is an account of "a day in the life" of ten-year-old twin sisters, one of whom is blind and mentally retarded. There are only two lines of narration in the entire film, identifying each of the sisters. The structure is quite simple: chronological, with crosscutting during the period when the sisters go to their respective schools (Elizabeth to a special school for the blind, Mary to a neighborhood parochial school). The film begins with their getting up in the morning, follows them through this seemingly typical day (no special crises or unusual occurrences), and ends with their going to sleep.

Elizabeth and Mary is one of the finest examples of a cinema-verite aesthetic in action. The goal of the film appears to be no more than to explore how this child lives (the emphasis is upon Elizabeth, the blind twin), how she interacts with her family, and how she acts in school. There is no attempt at generalization, arguing in any way that she is a typical case; nor is there any special pleading in her behalf, singling her out as a "problem child" that society must learn to deal with. The camera just watches, scarcely commenting upon what it sees.

The crosscutting from one to the other while the twins are at their schools does allow for some comparison through editing, an imposed, interpretive device. This is a limited application of the same approach used extensively in many of the Drew-Leacock films: alternating between two continuous chronologies for transition purposes. We see religious instruction at one school, then at the other; a noisy scene at Elizabeth's school contrasts with the rigid order at Mary's. The differences are so obvious, though, that no strong point is made this way. Instead, it seems

a minimal structural device for a part of the film, crosscutting
being a natural way to maintain chronology while showing the
two independent activities (preferable to separate complete sections on each). This isn't even a problem for long, as most of the
film deals with their time in and around the house, with no cutting
back and forth between separate locations.

Again, individual scenes are often quite long; this seems to be
characteristic of all good cinema verite. The film looks almost
unedited, and there is surely no form of "plot" progression or
character development. Less customary, perhaps, is the extreme
mobility of the camera, which goes from room to room without
a cut. There are many scenes of completely routine activity and
even some of inactivity (especially a lengthy shot of Elizabeth

Elizabeth and Mary. The sisters.

Elizabeth and Mary

sitting in a rocking chair, rocking back and forth, issuing random comments). One really feels as if he has moved in with the family, primarily through the closely following camera and the film's respect for real time. While the twins' one day is shown in a hour, the film is remarkably unhurried. (The original version was reportedly eight hours long; Pennebaker calls it "a truly pure film, but unwatchable,"[2] a point I wish I had the opportunity to argue.) By showing an admittedly limited number of events, but allowing the chosen ones to run to some length, the film conveys a sense of actual experience that would not have been possible had more events, but of shorter duration, been included.

The absence of control does not lead to a feeling of detachment or impersonal recording. *Elizabeth and Mary* is moving primarily because traditional film barriers are broken, and we are brought right into the subject's private world. There's an extraordinary shot following Elizabeth down a long school hall, where again (as with Kennedy in *Primary*) it is almost as if *we* are her, so well communicated is the difficulty such a simple trip contains for the child. The film is shot very close, and while it may be harsh to point out that Elizabeth's lack of sight leaves her less influenced than most people by the camera's presence (although this isn't necessarily true), one feels like an invisible participant in a world otherwise impenetrable. By not preaching about her problems and in no way trying to convince us of the significance of her condition, Pennebaker tells us all we need to know.

The lack of direct comment is exemplary. It is easy to imagine the same situation covered by a filmmaker who would be inclined to interview Elizabeth's parents and teacher, her sister, and perhaps even the girl herself. Instead, Pennebaker shows the family at dinner, and the combination of careful attention and deliberate equality accorded her during the meal says more than the family probably could have even articulated. Through other scenes, the love between the two sisters becomes apparent, along with the possible burden this love places on the normal child, as when she tries to play with her friends but still watch out for her sister. In the film's last scene, Mary is doing her homework quietly on her bed while beside her Elizabeth goes to sleep. At first it is curious that Elizabeth can sleep while Mary works in full light, but then, of course, we realize why she can do so. Throughout the film, relationships become clear through our seeing them operate, not through our being told how things are. It is impossible to imagine this film undertaken through any means other than a cinema-verite approach. Its very reason for being derives from a desire for observation without intrusion, and the film is unthinkable as either a prescribed, planned, or otherwise directly controlled work.

One of the surprising things about *Elizabeth and Mary* is its atypicality in relation to Pennebaker's other films. It is fair to say that cinema-verite filmmakers have tended, in each case, toward certain areas of concern, similarities in structure, and even recognizable camera styles. From viewing *Primary* and *The Children Were Watching,* we would know that *Crisis* came from the same filmmakers, just as from *David* and *Jane* we can discern similarities with Pennebaker's later work. But *Elizabeth and Mary* is a stunning surprise, a wholly fresh experience. From this we could conclude that cinema-verite filmmakers *ought* to venture more frequently into new areas of concern, but it would be overly prescriptive to press this point. Nevertheless, *Elizabeth and Mary* is its own justification, a film that could only have come about through an intense concern for people, an unwillingness to tamper with situations the filmmaker enters, and a healthy unconcern for drama or the kind of information supplying usually associated with the documentary form.

Don't Look Back

Pennebaker's feature length film about Bob Dylan, *Don't Look Back,* is a record of his 1965 British concert tour. It is a work much more in the mainstream of American cinema verite than might at first be evident, and it also has clear connections to Pennebaker's earlier films. Once more, the need to consider a film such as this within these broader contexts should become evident, for *Don't Look Back* (despite appearances) is not simply a report of a concert tour or an informal personality portrait.

   The film appears to adhere rigorously to the irrelevant, refusing to treat Dylan as a "documentary subject," someone whose past must be explained, whose present motivations must be explored, and whose significance must be established. Pennebaker's attitude toward direct information is evident in the scene that shows the beginning of a radio interview for the African service of the BBC. Preliminary conversation is seen, but as soon as the interviewer asks his first question ("How did it all begin for you, Bob? What actually started you off?"), there is a cut to very old footage of Dylan playing to a group of blacks and civil rights workers in

Mississippi, not so much to answer the question as to negate the sense behind asking it. Pennebaker is not going to "tell" anything about Dylan, at least not through traditional means.

Don't Look Back owes a great deal to the Drew-Leacock films (besides his own *David* and *Jane*), as well as to earlier Maysles Brothers films. To a surprising degree, *Don't Look Back* looks like a remake of *Primary*. Both films take place in the backs of cars, in hotel rooms, and in public auditoriums. There are the rounds of interviews, the entourage of managers and public relations people selling their "performers," and the same feeling of exuberant ever-presentness in camera style. The famous shot in *Primary* following Kennedy into an auditorium is inversely echoed in *Don't Look Back* after the final concert, when Dylan is followed down a stairway, through a hall, out a door, and into a waiting car—all in a single shot. American cinema verite often glories in the camera's ability to catch action on the run and in the most difficult of shooting conditions, not just to revel in technique, but as a means of expressing a life-style through a camera style.

The influence of the Maysles' *What's Happening! The Beatles in the U.S.A.* is obvious, in terms of both structure and subject matter, but similarities to their *Meet Marlon Brando* are more interesting, as *Don't Look Back* is full of "unproductive" interviews. Even more openly than Brando, Dylan refuses to respond to the interview format. He frequently reverses interviews, throwing questions back at the reporters and ultimately questioning their whole approach to life, as in devastating encounters with a science student and a *Time* reporter. In all the interviews, there is scarcely a single question that elicits any factual information in response. Instead, it is his deliberate evasiveness and disdain for the interview method that cumulatively evokes a portrait of Dylan.

An important question in regard to *Don't Look Back* relates once more to the matter of camera influence. As with *David* and most particularly *Jane,* there is little effort on Pennebaker's part to shoot unobtrusively. Even more than in the earlier films, it would be very hard to argue that Dylan isn't "acting" for the camera. Of course, in the eyes of many, this alone would invalidate the film as a "true" portrait. But again, this view makes certain assumptions about possible (or necessary) functions of cinema verite that have to be examined in greater detail.

Don't Look Back is actually one of the easier cases to consider in this regard. We begin by noting the frequency of situations where Dylan is shown doing nothing. Typical is a scene very like one in *Jane,* with Dylan in his dressing room before the final concert, nervously pacing around the room and worrying about the condition of his harmonica. Were Pennebaker consciously concerned with avoiding situations of certain camera influence, he would surely take refuge in the safer situations where the subject is actively involved in some specific activity. Choosing to film at times when his subject is confined and unable to ignore the camera, Pennebaker not only reduces the relationship to a one-to-one, subject-filmmaker confrontation but does so specifically to make his *audience* more aware of the pretenses involved. That is, a filmmaker may sense that his subject is "acting" for the camera (on the basis of observing him constantly for a period of time), but in those cases the forces at work might not be clear to an audience. In these elemental confrontations—a man in a room with a camera on him—there can be little doubt the subject is reacting to being filmed.

The question then becomes: What good are such scenes, if the presence of the camera is clearly a factor? On the surface, this kind of shooting would appear to be antithetical to a cinema-verite approach. We have noted with approbation many cases where the filmmaker has functioned unobtrusively, as a minimal influence in delicate situations (such as Leacock's filming of Kennedy and Humphrey in certain scenes of *Primary*). One might argue that when people are clearly influenced by the camera, their "performances" are nearly equivalent to those of actors in a fiction film, that to see people "playing" themselves

Don't Look Back. Bob Dylan.

is scarcely different from seeing people play other people. A disturbed reality, to follow this line, is not a reality at all.

Such an approach takes an overly simplistic view of the questions involved, even though when presented in the abstract the argument is appealing. Before we deal with this argument directly, however, there is a counterargument to be refuted, one that comes up in regard to other films as well. A typical filmmaker's response to this question is that, yes, the camera was an influence in a particular instance, but it only served to encourage a "true" (or an even *more* true) representation of the subject's personality. As Pennebaker tells Alan Rosenthal about the people in this film: "They were enacting roles—Dylan as well as anybody else—but they were enacting them very accurately."[3] The idea of heightened responses, the suggestion that the camera can *bring out* latent or incipient emotions, has been frequently pressed into service by filmmakers in answer to this charge.

This is a dangerous tack, however, in that it implies that the filmmaker is capable of judging which incidents of heightened response are characteristic and which are not. It is one thing to judge that the subject is reacting to the camera's presence, quite another to make a decision in regard to the quality of the response. To say that a given situation affected by the camera is still representative of the subject (or, perhaps, even more so) assumes that the nature of a "true" response can be independently defined. In other words, if Dylan responds in anger to the presence of the camera, then Dylan is an "angry person" whose repressed hostilities have been brought into the open. The shortcomings in such logic should be clear. If typical responses can only be brought out through provocation, then in what way are they typical?

A more fruitful approach is to refuse judgment on the typicality of these moments of camera influence but to insist upon clear filmmaker intent in regard to such situations. In this way, the viewer is free to evaluate the evidence on his own. It is here that *Don't Look Back* and other Pennebaker films are exemplary; there is little question that the camera is functioning as a deliberate influence, that the subject is aware of it. *Don't Look Back*, through the very nature of the subject-camera confrontations, is a film *about* this interplay. Although we don't necessarily need verbal support from the filmmaker as to his intent, it is interesting that Pennebaker himself has said that the film is about "a guy acting out his life."[4] And most crucially: "I assume everyone looking at it can instantly tell as well as I can that it's an act."[5] Dylan, like Jane Fonda, is a performer, and the film itself is a performance in the sense that it is clear that Dylan is establishing a persona, reacting to the insistent camera in deliberate ways.

How, then, does *Don't Look Back* relate to aspects of cinema verite discussed so far, rather than being a perversion of them? While the camera is surely an influence, the performance, so to speak, is not determined by the filmmaker. Again, there is the refusal to direct people, to suggest in any way that one action is more desirable than another. The subject remains free to that considerable extent—he's not told what to do or how to respond. If there is pretense in this subject-filmmaker relationship, a game being played, it is pretense chosen by the subject and not upset by the filmmaker. In that sense, the filmmaker functions as in any cinema-verite film, detached through an unwillingness to express any kinds of preferences to the people being filmed. As Pennebaker has said, "I don't feel that because I'm there with a camera I have any special privileges, and I don't feel I should exert any."[6] Despite questions of camera influence, this attitude is clear in the film and remains a primary characteristic of a cinema-verite approach.

These camera-influenced situations are also consistent with a cinema-verite approach because they still allow the viewer the freedom to interpret and evaluate the events himself. Dylan is not "explained" to us; no conclusions about him are expressed. In other words, the film shares the quality of uninterpreted data we have noted previously. Pennebaker again speaks well to this point: "I'm in no better position to judge Dylan than anybody else. I'm not a psychologist or anything. I don't have any particular qualifications for making any judgments of any interest, of any value."[7] The film supports this stated approach, as does the wide variety of responses it evokes.[8] Although camera presence is a factor, the open admission of influence (through the kinds of situations filmed and the manner of shooting) simply makes this another aspect to be considered.

The "problem" of camera influence is eased considerably if our approach allows for the recognition that to some degree the presence of the camera is *always* a factor in cinema-verite films. To say that *Don't Look Back* is not a "true portrait" because of

Pennebaker's aggressive camera is to make the unsupportable assumption that this kind of filming can *ever* be free of such influence. If we say in regard to other films that the camera was not obtrusive, this means that other factors were present to minimize its influence. That is, except in cases of hidden cameras (which all cinema-verite filmmakers reject), there is a continuum, rather than a polarity, between relatively influence-free shooting and cases where the camera's presence is a significant factor. In all cases, then, a triadic relationship exists among filmmaker, subject, and the subject's involvement in other activities, each one of the three affecting the others. Pennebaker's filming in many scenes of *Don't Look Back* is "purer" than many examples of more unobtrusive shooting, in that the camera-subject relationship is more directly open to the audience.

A further necessary distinction has to be made in regard to the relationship between camera-influenced shooting and dramatic structure. We have previously noted the tendency in the Drew-Leacock films to focus on camera influence in immediately post-crisis situations, especially in *On the Pole* and *Jane.* (The last scene in the Maysles' *Salesman* is yet another case.) Employed in this fashion, camera-influenced shooting is difficult to evaluate in that dramatic exigencies collide with character revelation. Because Eddie Sachs has just lost the race, is his reaction to the camera a result of his loss or simply the first moment he is observed outside a crisis structure? Too many possible motives are present to determine the nature of his response.

In *Don't Look Back* and in the dressing room scene in *Jane,* while the subject is under considerable pressure, the lack of immediate win-lose alternatives is itself a form of purity in shooting approach, another means to minimize factors outside the subject-filmmaker relationship. Dylan is freer to concentrate on his projected persona than is Eddie Sachs. Also, *Don't Look Back* is unique in being an extended exploration (in a number of scenes) of this relationship, unlike the relatively isolated moments in *On the Pole, Jane,* and *Salesman.* Through a consistent use of camera-influenced situations, especially without a win-lose structure, the nature of the camera-subject interaction becomes considerably clearer.

Original Cast Album: Company!
Original Cast Album: Company! is an expertly executed work, a natural product of previous Pennebaker concerns and American cinema-verite tradition. The situation the film covers, an all-night recording session to produce the album for a Broadway show, "structures itself" in a fashion close to the Drew films. The whole album must be recorded in this one evening, so the time unity provides a set framework. As the evening wears on, a bit of dramatic tension develops. When the lateness of the hour begins to grate against the quality of the performances, we are back for a time in the recognizable world of success-or-failure, wondering whether the session can be completed satisfactorily. The brief crisis period, however, is only a small part of the entire process, and *Company* is primarily a process-oriented work.

In sharp contrast to nearly all the films discussed so far, *Company* does not focus on particular individuals. Instead, Pennebaker chooses to emphasize the complex coordination of contributions necessary to produce the album. Point of view shifts repeatedly, stopping briefly with the record producer, the writer, the orchestra, the show's producer, and various combinations of performers. *Company* is an educational film as much as a musical entertainment film, so intent is it upon detailing the range of functions involved in the creation of this single record.

Of importance in this approach is the nature of the decisions involved. *Company* might easily have centered on a single individual (there are a number of strong personalities to choose from), thus becoming something like *Jane* or *Susan Starr.* A by-product of audience interest in a main character is a shift away from concern for the process itself. In *Jane,* as we have noted previously, the cut-away after the opening performance to follow Walter Kerr as he goes off to write his review is a maddening diversion once we have been oriented to care solely for Jane's outcome. We find this circumstance repeatedly in the Drew films. *On the Pole* is only tangentially about race car drivers; the emphasis upon an individual's personal struggle makes the precise nature of his endeavor immaterial. It is of only oblique importance that Eddie Sachs is a race car driver. What matters most is that he is involved in a contest and he risks his life. The process itself, of car racing, is not of great concern. Those Drew films that give the most information about processes, for instance, *Primary* and *Football,* do so in each case through minimizing individuality by way of noting parallel activities of its two main personalities. To the extent that processes are emphasized, be they the working of a primary election, a football game, or the rehearsal of a play, the apparent intention of personality orientation loses some degree of force, although this rarely happens in the Drew films.

So strong is the precedence of emphasis upon the individual that an unassuming, straightforward film like *Company* may look more innovative than it actually is. The "natural" way to cover a recording session would seem to be to detail all aspects of it, but *natural,* like *real,* is a relative term. The preference for personality studies in cinema verite, even in films not operating under standard dramatic forms (like the Maysles'), constitutes a strong tradition. And while no approach is more "truthful" than any other, differences have to be recognized.

Due to the essentially repetitive nature of the recording session, the preparation and performance of a dozen or so songs, Pennebaker varies his means of covering each. *Company* is a valuable work for comparing a variety of possible shooting and editing methods in a series of identical situations. Sometimes, a song is shown in a single long take on the performers. In other cases, the camera treats a song as an event as complex as the integration crisis in *Crisis: Behind a Presidential Commitment,* with coverage of many individuals throughout the studio. For several of the songs, the preparation period is covered in detail; occasionally, rehearsals and more than one take of the same song are included in order to give a fuller sense of the developmental process. Where *Lambert and Co.,* an earlier Pennebaker film about a recording session, would randomly intercut background action into the studio performances, *Company* is methodical in its purposeful integration of complementary functions. Further, its range of filming methods to cover individual songs is itself a creative process, a study of the options available even in a situation so limited in time and location.

Monterey Pop and *Keep on Rockin'*

Pennebaker's two films of rock music festivals, *Monterey Pop* and *Keep on Rockin',*[9] are entertainment films which at first seem to relate only peripherally to cinema-verite questions. Given the staged nature of the events (even though they are not set up or controlled by the filmmaker) and the overriding intention of presenting effective performances, the two films might be thought of as little more than newsreel-like records of the shows for the benefit of larger audiences. While the films do have rather specific intentions, a comparison of the two brings out familiar questions. Filmmaker decisions about the nature of the subject matter, the manner of "fidelity" to the event, and the role of editing continue to be pertinent.

Monterey Pop is built up from many short segments; no group does more than a few songs. The approach is impressionistic, a broad collage of performers and onlookers who together express a certain hip California life-style. Seen today, only a few years after it was made, the film already looks charmingly dated. Along with the music, there are a few attempts at filling in local color. Pennebaker includes several sequences of postcard-like shooting, providing a general impression of the people in attendance, and also a couple of brief interviews. It's all pleasant to watch but, in terms of cinema verite, rather trivial. Pennebaker feels free to use music as "mood" over nonsynch material, and the overall random structure of performances (cut together primarily out of consideration for musical pacing) contains neither a relation to real time nor any organic development of its own.

Because of the similar nature of the material, the two films provide a classic framework in which to consider once again the role of editing. The standard defense of *Monterey Pop*'s fragmented presentation would be to argue that the high degree of selectivity regarding individual performances reflects the event more accurately than a less rigorously structured work could have done. In other words, given the varied nature of the whole event, the preferred method for expressing that variety would be to show bits and pieces of as many facets as possible. This is quite a plausible argument, but one that runs counter to several key cinema-verite concepts.

The respect for the long take and the attempt to keep cutting at a minimum in most cinema-verite films stem from combined desires to approximate the feeling of being an actual witness to the event and not to force a specific interpretation through editing upon the filmed material. Taken back a step, the films on a theoretical level share a faith in the complexity of actual experience, which the filmmakers attempt to carry over into their finished work. Stated simply, this can be expressed as a desire to "interfere" as little as possible in editing as well as in shooting.

Monterey Pop contrasts sharply with *Keep On Rockin'* in regard to editing. The second film is a very able critique of the first. *Keep On Rockin'* is a clear application of well-defined cinema-verite principles, and the best way to understand the shortcomings of the earlier film is to study this one. Instead of creating a mosaic structure, Pennebaker here limits himself to only four performers, each seen at some length. The independent sequences have a development that only real-time, relatively uninterrupted shooting seems able to provide, and consequently the whole film has a completeness that is inevitably missing from *Monterey Pop*, with its highly selective editing approach.

A sense of duration, of lived experience, has always been a crucial aspect of American cinema verite. Whether it is the slow back-
and-forth of windshield wipers on Hubert Humphrey's car as he
drives between campaign stops in *Primary* or the repetition of
sales pitches in the Maysles' *Salesman,* cinema verite has attempted to go beyond the reporting of facts and telling of stories to
do nothing less than re-create personal experience. This aim is
generally intuitive, but the desire to eliminate barriers between
subject and audience leads to the camera's acting as a human
observer would, making viewing selections on the spot and not
at some later point. The long take or long episode is a reflection
of the personalized camera.

 Keep On Rockin' does give one a sense of actually being present at the event. This sounds like either a trivial accomplishment

Keep On Rockin'. Pennebaker filming Bo Diddley.

or a critical commonplace, but the film's immediacy is a direct reflection of Pennebaker's re-evaluated approach to structure (since *Monterey Pop*). A trust in nonselection within perform-ances yields a film rich in the kind of spontaneous observation characteristic of good cinema verite. *Keep on Rockin',* while loose in structure, is less random than *Monterey Pop.* The full-ness of real-time development serves up a continuing succession of internally related events, which is more satisfying both cine-matically and musically than a collage of fragments.

An example of the advantages in this approach occurs during the Chuck Berry segment. At the start of his set he does a song called "Johnny B. Goode," and the performance is quite clumsy. Playing with a group put together especially for the festival, he is clearly ill at ease. As they continue, there is a gradual coales-cing of talent, and at the end of the segment, they again play the same song. This time the result is definitely more satisfactory. However, we can only tell the difference by having been witness to the progression that led up to it. Traditional editing practices would surely have cut out the first performance of the song as mere inferior duplication, and any selection of "best" songs from the forty-five-minute performance would give no idea of the subtle "drama" inherent in the entire presentation.

The surface similarity of the performers (all are male rock stars associated with the fifties) and their equal periods of screen time suggest the same structure of repetition noted in the Maysles' films. The film builds through comparison the contrasts beneath the identical situations of a "meeting" between musician and audience. We can compare the nature of each meeting by ob-serving how each singer establishes rapport, following the de-velopment of each full performance, and noting the audience response each elicits. *Keep on Rockin'* is four musical portraits rather than the series of sketches that make up *Monterey Pop.*

While *Keep On Rockin'* appears less personal than other Penne-baker films because of the minimal editing, its driving force is the same preoccupation found in many Pennebaker films—the nature of the creative process and the personality of the artist. *David, Jane, Don't Look Back, Lambert and Co., Company,* and *Keep On Rockin'* all share this interest. While the artist, especially the musician, has been Pennebaker's primary concern, he has explored this area in diverse ways. Some of the films emphasize the creative process itself, be it a play or a musical performance, not dealing closely with particular personalities. Others, especially *Jane* and *Don't Look Back,* subordinate the creative product to a probe of fragile, defensive artists—the films of deliberate camera influence. *Keep On Rockin',* while a special film because of its strict concert format, does evidence concern for both the mystique of the artist and the intricacies of public performance.

The Children's Theater of John Donahue

The Children's Theater of John Donahue is a work in progress at the time of this writing, but in a preliminary version it is characteristically Pennebaker and should be included in the previous list of films about the creative process. The film deals with the preparation for a production by the Minneapolis Children's Theater Company. It is a "remake" of *Jane* but without excessive concern for either the win-lose aspects of putting on a play or the problems of one star. Instead, the emphasis is on the nuts-and-bolts hard work behind a theatrical production, broadened somewhat to include material about the city's response to this experimental theater project. Of great interest are the frequent long scenes, sometimes out of all proportion to dramatic or plot necessities. One of the best scenes in the film is a lengthy reading from the play to be performed, where one feels Donahue's (director of the company) enthusiasm being communicated to the kids. The segment lasts at least ten minutes, propelled by nothing beyond an individual's excitement in creativity. More than ten years after *David* and *Jane,* Pennebaker's commitment to cinema verite remains intact.

Richard Leacock

Richard Leacock

Happy Mother's Day

Happy Mother's Day (originally called *Quint City, U.S.A.*) was
Richard Leacock's first film after his separation from Drew
Associates in 1963. Leacock was hired by the *Saturday Evening
Post* to make a film about the Fisher quintuplets, then two weeks
old. Along with Joyce Chopra to take sound, he went to Aberdeen, South Dakota, and shot the film in three weeks. When he
showed the completed film to his sponsors, they did not approve
of it. After various legal hassles (primarily because of a contract
with Drew that Leacock was not to do any network filming for a
year), ABC acquired rights to all the footage he shot and made
their own film from the same material that Leacock edited into
Happy Mother's Day. These unfortunate difficulties do allow us

a unique opportunity to contrast Leacock's approach with a network documentary department's handling of the same footage. This is an ancillary concern, however, as Leacock's film is important regardless of the ABC film.

Happy Mother's Day begins with a brief sequence of TV news footage taken on the day the quintuplets were born. (Leacock was not yet on the scene.) After some aerial shots of the town (the wryly extraneous narrator: "Aberdeen, South Dakota, is a prairie town, and the land is flat"), we are told it is now two weeks later, and Mrs. Fisher is seen watching a parade in celebration of "Gypsy Day." Back at the Fisher home, Mr. Fisher tends his cows (no longer needed, because of a local dairy's gift of a year's milk supply), and the Fisher children play with their cat. In a charming scene shot in a dark barn and in full synch sound, Mrs. Fisher and her children examine five (!) kittens that have just been born. The film to this point has the appearance of being a nice "folksy" portrait of the Fisher family.

The near-idyllic tone is short-lived. First a reporter from *Ladies Home Journal* arrives, then a *Saturday Evening Post* photographer. A bevy of cameras around his neck, the *Post* man photographs the family driving around in a Model T Ford. Mrs. Fisher is taken to buy some clothes by the wife of the local Chamber of Commerce head, and she very briefly and uncomfortably tries on a mink coat. Back to the house, there is a close-up of the photographer giving directions from the top of a ladder; cut to a full shot showing that he is taking pictures of all the gifts the Fishers have received. ("Do you want another row of milk, or is that enough?") The narrator raises the question of invasion of privacy, and apparently in answer to an interview question (not shown), Mrs. Fisher says that her children "will never be on display."

The film to this point has been directly concerned with the Fishers; they are in every scene (except the gift pictures, taken in front of their house). In the remainder of the film, roughly half of its thirty-minute length, the Fishers become peripheral figures.

The rather droll (but slightly annoying) narration of the first part is dropped, most scenes now running with no commentary at all. Concern shifts to the impact of the births upon the town and the town's attitudes toward the Fishers. A group of businessmen talk among themselves about the potential influx of tourists, the adjustments the Fishers will "have to" make, and the commercial benefits the town can expect. Next, a woman's club member talks to Mrs. Fisher about what she will wear to their luncheon in her honor. Commercial questions are even more overt in the next scene, a Chamber of Commerce meeting. They discuss the sales of Quint souvenir items and whether newspaper ads to push them would be "too commercial." One man says that if they run an ad, it should indicate that the proceeds will go to the Fisher Foundation, only to be informed by another fellow that there is no "Foundation"!

Narration then tersely announces: "Morning of the parade honoring the one-month birthday of the Fisher quintuplets." A staged preview of the parade is held for the benefit of newsmen and photographers. Fisher family members pose with a congressman and then an Indian. At the luncheon in their honor, the mayor gets up and delivers an extraordinarily inflated speech, shown entirely in one take, beginning "Never in the history of the United States has a city official had such a great responsibility as I do today." A woman then sings a horrible song, and it's time for the parade. The Fishers ride to their place on the reviewing stand, the American Legion band and a few floats go by, while a man hawks Quint City hats for fifty cents. Rain begins, abruptly ending the parade, and the Fishers and everyone else run for cover. Over shots of the event breaking up, narration ironically informs us, "It was a typical day of celebration in Aberdeen, South Dakota, Quint City, U.S.A."

So, there is a clear shift in the film from being about the Fisher family to a concern for the impact of the births upon the town. That the film could have continued as a personal portrait had Leacock chosen to do so is clear from the ABC film. When

Happy Mother's Day. Rain starts as Fisher family watches parade honoring birth of their quintuplets.

broadcast, the ABC film was sponsored by Beech-Nut, and the movie looks like a half-hour baby food commercial. There is a good deal more footage of the babies themselves, generally just shots of them in their incubators while voiceover interviews with their doctor and nurses are heard. When Quint souvenirs are shown, the guy selling them is interviewed and says, "I don't want to make a killing; I just want to help the children." All references to commercialism are followed by similar disclaimers of that motivation from the people involved. The last part of the film appears to have been shot after Leacock's departure, as there is a scene in the hospital when the babies are eight weeks old, with quite a bit of further discussion about their condition.

The most interesting thing about the ABC film in comparison

with *Happy Mother's Day* is that whenever identical footage is used, it is always greatly cut down. There are no scenes in the ABC film that are also in Leacock's that run longer. The mayor's speech, for instance, which Leacock shows in its entirety, is just a brief snippet on the ABC film and leaves one with an entirely different impression, of its being simply a routine introduction. The parade that ends *Happy Mother's Day* is no more than a few shots in the ABC film. In the latter film, emphasis is altered not solely by throwing in some more footage of the babies and taking out some Leacock material on possible exploitation of the quin-tuplets but also by extracting particular, singular meanings from brief excerpts of Leacock's longer scenes.

   This difference is crucial. Leacock, certainly selective (shooting ratio for the film was 25 to 1),[1] still presents scenes of some length. In so doing, he allows the contradictions in the events to come through, especially the possible conflict between the town's genuine concern for the Fishers and the commercial potential involved. As Pat Jaffe puts it: "The footage is allowed to take its head."[2] Louis Marcorelles surely overstates the case by saying, in regard to this film, "At such a point, cinema has disap-peared,"[3] but there is a faith in letting scenes run that is entirely absent from the ABC film. This is not to argue that the Leacock film is more "truthful," but that its selectivity is of an entirely dif-ferent order. The ABC film, despite the subject, looks didactic; every shot, every interview, has one point to press. *Happy Mother's Day* seems to say: "This is what it felt like to be there and what seemed important from everything that we witnessed." As Leacock says, one aim of his approach is to reveal "things that are different from what is expected,"[4] whereas the ABC version seeks to confirm what you probably would have antici-pated anyway.

   This leads back to the question of nonpreconception and the filmmaker's relationship to the people and events he witnesses and what processes of selection are involved in films of this kind.

Happy Mother's Day is a useful case in which to consider these questions once again, for their importance in cinema verite can not be overemphasized.

The following statements by Leacock deal with one question — the attitude of the cinema-verite filmmaker toward what he is filming.

The two of us, in three weeks, shot the entire film, and we never asked anybody to do anything; we were simply observers.[5]

(In regard to an incident during filming when Mr. Fisher asked Leacock whether he wanted a particular action and Leacock refused to tell him what to do) You see, once he does *that,* he will do something else that pleases me. I'm not interested in his pleasing me. I don't care how unhappy I am, *I don't want him to please me.* And once I start asking him to do things, I'm dead.[6]

One of the things that distorts things the most is that people usually are basically trying to please us. So they tend to do what they think you want them to do, which is why you have to do a great deal of not filming, because you have to wait until they get that out of their systems. And if you don't film and don't film and don't film, then they finally say, "Oh, screw this idiot. He doesn't know what he wants anyway." And they go back to doing what they have to do.[7]

As the last two quotes suggest, being "simply observers" is not simple at all. Leacock's shooting, here and elsewhere, is not "intimate" in the same sense that material shot by Al Maysles or D. A. Pennebaker often is. It is not a matter of waiting for people to drop their defenses (as sometimes happens with the other two filmmakers), but one of not permitting the physical presence of the filmmaker to be a tool in observation. Leacock's work is a cinema of self-effacement, of waiting for situations where his presence is not a significant factor. (Only Leacock, of all the filmmakers in this book, could say, "I find filming rather embarrassing at times.")[8] One feels from many scenes he has shot that a great deal of patience must have been required, that he had to stand around a long time before he felt that what he was shoot-

ing was not affected by his own participation. This observation
sounds banal, but there are many moments one could cite—
Kennedy on election night in *Primary*, the lawyer breaking
down in *The Chair*, the Venezuelan family in *Yanki, No!*, the birth
of the kittens in this film. This is another point where cinema
verite avoids being an impersonal recording process. Few filmmakers are capable of maintaining relationships with their subjects that would enable them to film such material; and there are
few who could recognize the advantages of being "simply observers."

Shooting obviously involves selection, but in Leacock's films the
decisions are made in the camera. Sequences are not shot with
an idea of how they can be put together in an editing room; his
shooting, very frequently long takes, seems almost choreo-
graphed. Pat Jaffe, herself an editor, puts it well: "When you have
marvelous shooting (like Leacock's in this film), you can edit the
film almost as it comes out of the camera. When the cameraman
is really operating smoothly and moving from one image to another with ease, the footage has the quality and rhythm of a
ballet, and whole sequences may be left intact."[9] It is this approach that leads to a feeling like Marcorelles' that "cinema
has disappeared," and in a sense it has, if one's conception of
cinema embraces a notion of directorial control, of planned shots
and prearranged effects. "You can't have a director with this
kind of film. You even have to edit your film as the event is actually happening. You have to decide it's this and this and this I
want to look at; and not this and this and this. . . . You have to
make the decisions yourself, you can't alter anything afterwards;
nothing can be reshot."[10]

What is the function, then, of the actual editing process? In
Leacock's case, it is minimal. Leacock's description of this step
supports Jaffe's view quoted in the preceding paragraph: "I start
at the beginning and I go all the way through it, making almost
no judgments, simply making work everything I can make work.
It's fairly simple actually. You look at the first cut, and that's

very close to the finished film."[11] *Happy Mother's Day* supports
this description. The film looks untampered with; whatever selections have been made are part of the way things are shot, not
how they are put together.

  Again we ought to note the importance of having editing done
by the same people who made the first series of selections, that
is, those who shot the footage. The shift in *Happy Mother's Day*
from family portrait to town portrait is very probably a reflection
of Leacock's own shifting interest as an actual observer, the film
itself thus recreating his own experience. The ABC film looks
like what you'd expect to see about the birth of quintuplets, as
if editing were performed to make the material conform to audience notions of such an event. In this case, there's no need for
cameramen to be editors, since fidelity to their own experience is
not a criterion. Leacock's film is concerned with human qualities
expressed in individual moments, small spontaneous "surprises,"
such things as Mrs. Fisher's reactions to trying on a mink coat
and the mayor's attitude as he delivers his speech. The ABC
film seeks to cover a significant event in a "serious" fashion
(meaning conformity with a standard network documentary approach) that precludes Leacock's level of close, uninterpreted
observation.

  Sometimes, though, Leacock's ironic sense of humor may get
the better of him. This is a delicate issue, but there are times in
the film when one can possibly believe that people are being
laughed at, being made objects of derision.[12] The woman who
sings the horrible song at the luncheon borders on the absurd,
and the mayor's well-meaning but pompous speech leaves him
looking bad. But in selecting such things, is Leacock making
jokes at their expense and at the expense of presenting material
still left open for viewer evaluation? There are several responses
to this question. The least satisfactory, I think, is that the people
themselves don't find their activities funny, that they would not feel
they have been unfairly treated. This view implies a certain snob-
bishness then, of superiority to the subject. (We know it's funny,

but they're too dumb to realize it.) A more useful response might be that, yes, they're ridiculous, but it is the uniqueness of the situation (the birth of the quints) that brings out these qualities, and their very absurdity is more a comment on the crazy nature of what's happening than a judgment of their personal qualities. I don't think the comic elements in such moments are intended to be cruel, but they are admittedly a troublesome aspect of selective filming. This kind of suggestion of smug superiority comes up too frequently to ignore it (not just with Leacock, but also with the Maysles Brothers and Frederick Wiseman), and there's no easy answer for it. When the detachment of a cinema-verite approach is translated by a viewer as implying a superiority, especially in cases where people look ridiculous, it is difficult to justify. Still, as in all cases where "bias" in cinema verite is charged, the implied assumption that these films do not reflect the values and attitudes of the filmmaker is not a well-considered position. At best, we can say that Leacock sees these activities as ridiculous (just for having selected them), and the manner of presentation does not prevent us from disagreeing.

While *Happy Mother's Day* seems personal, the material is not judged in any kind of restrictive fashion. The camera is just *there,* and no forced or limiting structure is imposed afterward. Leacock finds a form growing out of the events themselves, and there is drama in *Happy Mother's Day* of a kind we're not used to. In part, this comes about through Leacock's willingness to go anywhere, however apparently trivial. Few filmmakers in this situation would even care about filming the birth of the kittens, and fewer still would save it from the cutting-room floor. The film tantalizes, makes you wonder from sequence to sequence what will happen next, but does not encourage you to *expect* any kind of dramatic resolution. There's perhaps little we can extract from this in terms of general principles, but that in itself may be the point. Leacock's films, even more than Flaherty's, suggest the real meaning of nonpreconception. *Happy Mother's Day,* so innocent and engaging, is an advance in cinema verite and in cinema.

A Stravinsky Portrait

A Stravinsky Portrait is a model application of a cinema-verite approach to a personality study; while it is entirely free of dramatic structure, it is not random filming. As in *Happy Mother's Day,* Leacock gives the impression of having absorbed himself in his subject completely, but without making his own presence a factor to be reckoned with. There is an unusual acceptance of the camera in situations where one might expect, because few people are present and the only activity is conversation, that it would have been a more disturbing influence.

Again, the relationship between filmmaker and subject is important. Leacock clearly was not a disruptive element, and in talking about the shooting period he articulates what one feels from watching the film:

> We (Leacock and Sarah Hudson, who took sound) became members of the household. We spent a lot of time going swimming and listening to music, eating together and enjoying each other, and to heck with cameras. We became an accepted part, an enjoyed part, of the scene we were invading. We were not people who were aggressively trying to get something out of him. Filming, in a sense, almost became secondary, which resulted in a very different level of intimacy than you normally get. Often this tends to sound arrogant, but it's terribly important and seldom understood. If you come barging into a room, I don't care what's going on, and you behave like technicians, a lot of people retreat. These technicians like to be festooned with braces and supports and look like sort of a zombie. They really do. A lot of people hide behind this. And I'd rather not have a camera at all. Just be there.[13]

A Stravinsky Portrait is more than just glimpses into Stravinsky's private life. In fact, it is not what one would call a private view of him at all. It is a film about Stravinsky the artist, a study of his relation to his work. There are no shots of Stravinsky puttering around his garden, taking a swim, or engaging in any activities not relevant to his creative life. For this reason, perhaps, it is even more intimate than more cliché "private" moments would have been.

Much of the film takes place in Stravinsky's Beverly Hills home, where he is seen in conversation with a good many people, including Robert Craft, Pierre Boulez, and Rolf Liebermann (a musician as well as producer of this film). A typical scene, and the sort of thing one can imagine only Leacock including, is a long discussion between Stravinsky and Boulez (a conductor noted for his interpretations of Stravinsky) about a possible error in the printed score of *Les Noces.* The entire conversation is in French, and the primary quality the episode communicates is their intense concentration on this matter. Such a moment is hardly a crisis situation or even an event of any great significance. It is simply a fascinating, highly revealing glimpse of Stravinsky.

While some of the sequences are brief, fully a quarter of the hour-

A Stravinsky Portrait

A Stravinsky Portrait

long film is devoted to an absolutely extraordinary rehearsal session in Hamburg prior to a taping of Stravinsky's conducting his
own *Variations Dedicated to the Memory of Aldous Huxley.* The
scene at first seems only incidentally about Stravinsky. We see a
kind of mini-film about the rehearsal process—Stravinsky going
over a difficult passage with a violinist, then another part with two
cellists, and eventually the complete work with the whole orchestra. All conversation is in German, and no narration is added,
nor is any necessary. The process eloquently speaks for itself.
Stravinsky is so determined, so joyous when conducting, that
further comment would be extraneous. Brief shots of him alone
conducting without the full context of the rehearsal (as a more
traditional TV documentary might present) could not communi-

cate the full meaning of these activities. Leacock, bold enough to let such a lengthy scene run its course, allows us to share in Stravinsky's creative joy.

The narration in the film, spoken by Leacock himself, is a model of conciseness. He restricts himself to simple designations of place, identification of people, and a few very brief translations of foreign language conversations. We are never given any information about Stravinsky through narration, just enough background to follow what's going on in a particular scene. While this seems hardly a revolutionary approach, one is hard-pressed to think of another instance where narration is so sparsely and properly applied.

The camera movement and cutting in the film are as rigorously minimal as the narration. Every movement carries with it its own motivation; we feel as if the camera's eye moves in the same way ours would if we were present. Many times a shot is quite steady, with Leacock possibly moving in on Stravinsky almost imperceptibly (for instance, when he pours over the *Les Noces* score). This kind of camera work is difficult to describe when done properly; it is only in cases of irrelevant panning, excess zooming, and unnecessary cutting that the difficulty of capturing unobtrusive but interesting footage becomes apparent. The sureness of style in *A Stravinsky Portrait* is further demonstration of Leacock's faith in his subject, a faith that the finished film (and the subject himself) fully justifies.

Campaign Manager

In discussing *Primary,* we noted Leacock's feeling that the film did not achieve what it set out to accomplish: to show the inner workings of a political campaign. *Campaign Manager* (also called *Republicans: The New Breed*) tries to explore that very territory. Instead of focusing upon a candidate, the film moves to the edge of the spotlight, dealing with Barry Goldwater's campaign manager during the 1964 presidential election, John Grenier, the Executive Director of the Republican National Committee. The film consists mostly of Grenier on the telephone and in meetings with his associates, trying to organize Goldwater's activities. It is a low-key presentation, without ambitions as an exposé of smoke-filled rooms or a heroic portrait of men under pressure.

Where *Primary* explored the campaign process through a struggle between contenders in one specific contest, *Campaign Manager* is practically a structureless film. Grenier is followed for a brief period of time, well before the election, and we see nothing of the Democratic opposition. Goldwater himself is hardly seen, just in brief shots at a couple of rallies. Even without a crisis structure, the film lacks any moments of great pressure or drama. Grenier is not an intense personality, and the film is really nothing but an account of some aspects of behind-the-scenes operations in a political campaign. The conversations are routine and rarely

Campaign Manager. John Grenier, campaign manager for Barry Goldwater during the 1964 presidential campaign.

deal with political topics. Grenier's time, according to the film, is mostly taken up with arranging schedules for greatest effectiveness without overtaxing the candidate and trying to raise money to support the campaign. It's not quite the complete "inside" story Leacock wanted (on the basis of his comments about *Primary*), but what is there is quite interesting.

Audience identification with the main character and interest through dramatic structure are rigorously suppressed. The film's value is in taking us someplace we couldn't go ourselves, giving us a glimpse into an activity we've never seen before. The film makes no judgments about the process it observes and presses no arguments about its importance. Leacock has likened the cinema-verite approach to the deliberate restrictions of the sonnet form,[14] and *Campaign Manager* plays it strictly by the rules, almost reveling in its unvarying succession of similar activities and absence of crisis moments. There's scarcely even a question of camera influence in the scenes we're shown (although the camera is never privy to any discussions of a particularly private nature), given the depiction of deliberately routine tasks.

While *Campaign Manager* is pure in these respects, its dependence on certain cinema-verite conventions is clear. In conception, the idea of exploring behind-the-scenes politics through sticking with one person is still a notion derived from the Drew films, a personality-orientation not found, say, in *Happy Mother's Day* or in Leacock's later *Chiefs*. In other words, a social question is explored through following one person. This choice does have some influence on the film, as in the scene where Grenier talks to someone about how he got into politics, a discussion telling us more about the man than the political process (although, admittedly, something of both). The film is never entirely sure whether it is a portrait of a politician or an exploration of a political process; this sort of problem seems endemic to this "representative individual" approach.

Campaign Manager is one of a good number of American cinema-verite films where telephone scenes appear. This seemingly trivial connection is far from coincidental. Telephone conversations also occur in the Drew-Leacock films *The Chair* and *Crisis: Behind a Presidential Commitment* (figuring prominently in each, with Leacock filming in both cases); the Maysles' *Showman, Salesman,* and *Gimme Shelter;* Pennebaker's *Don't Look Back;* and Wiseman's *Hospital.* The most obvious reason for their frequency is simply as a result of the importance phones have in daily life, particularly in politics. In this film and in *Crisis,* telephone scenes could not have been avoided. More broadly, though, such situations are a way of getting around interviewing or narration, as they often bring out verbal information without the filmmaker's having to intervene directly. They also reoccur because of the simplicity of the situation. The cameraman has no decisions to make (as he would were the other person present); these scenes are usually straight-on close-ups. The shots of Robert Kennedy in *Crisis,* the two doctors in *Hospital,* and Grenier here, are unexplainably strong images—we somehow feel closer to the subject, more involved in these scenes.

If there is any typical Leacock scene in the film, it is surely one where a strategy session breaks down when room service arrives and there's confusion about whose lunch is whose, where issues once again are submerged by human idiosyncrasies. It is a lesser version of the *Crisis* moment where Robert Kennedy's daughter comes running in on a previously serious discussion. The scene runs on, as Grenier and his associates deliberate at some length who ordered their meat cooked medium and who medium-rare, and Leacock includes the whole thing. The scene is funny in a droll, Leacockian way, but it's an acceptable humor in an otherwise serious context because it is so obviously unrelated to anything else in the film. There is no wider principle to be formulated from this, but the oblique mark of filmmaker personality in so unobtrusively detached a film is worth noting (along with Leacock's willingness to forgo ostensible concern in favor of an activity that interests him).

Campaign Manager is not a highly significant work, but in its insistence upon a modest goal, it achieves no small measure of success. Leacock avoids a number of possible pitfalls the subject matter easily invites (opportunity for high drama, dependence upon famous names, taking an exposé approach), quite content to observe an interesting process. Cinema verite need not attempt to deal with grand subjects and major events, and *Campaign Manager* is a good example of the potential benefits of limited aspirations.

Ku Klux Klan—The Invisible Empire
In 1966 Leacock shot a good deal of *Ku Klux Klan—The Invisible Empire,* shown on "CBS Reports." The film was edited and supervised by CBS News in a traditional television documentary fashion, heavily narrated and full of interviews. Still, there is some characteristic Leacock footage of Klan activities, especially of a fascinating, bizarre initiation ceremony. Leacock is again able to film highly controversial subject matter in a way that does not appear to impose his own opinions upon the material. His feeling about this kind of filming is revealing:

Film can really be a sort of research data. This leads to interesting problems, like how do I spend eight weeks with the leadership of the Ku Klux Klan, where obviously I don't agree with them. But I find them very interesting, and this gave us a sufficient ground in common so that they tolerated me and I tolerated them. Now some people think that this is sort of immoral. You have to have some basis of respect for each other, and with me, I think, it's just that these are fellow human beings. I may disagree with them tremendously, but still I find them extremely interesting. I want to know why they do the things they do. I want to know what they're like.[15]

The argument about possible immorality through taking a detached approach and therefore refusing to comment upon the people being filmed is again one-half of a squeeze that some cinema-verite criticism imposes. This view says that if cinema verite *does not* express a point of view, it should. An interesting aspect of this argument is its ready admission that unbiased filmmaking is possible (though, by this view, undesirable). The other side is more common, saying that cinema verite *should not* express a point of view but inevitably does. The answer to the former objection is in asking how point of view should be expressed, whether, in this case, clear hostility to the Klan would have produced the "research data" necessary to evaluate their activities. The fact that the filmmaker remains detached does not mean an audience will follow suit. In regard to the latter argument, that cinema verite inevitably expresses point of view, one must ask for clear criteria as to how this comes about. If cinema verite is always so loaded with inevitable interpretation, why is there frequently such widespread disagreement in regard to the filmmaker's point of view in a particular film? Judgments on the people and events themselves in these films are too often translated into judgments about the filmmakers. Given the uncontrolled nature of situations in these films, at least some distinction between content and style ought to be possible.

Chiefs

Chiefs is a twenty-minute film of a police chiefs' convention in Honolulu. On the surface, it is practically a straight report of the convention. Activities shown include speeches, informal conversations, and numerous demonstrations of special police equipment. The film seems very typically Leacock in several ways. Like the white colonialist in *Kenya, Africa,* the KKK members, and some of the Aberdeen townspeople in *Happy Mother's Day,* the people in *Chiefs* express opinions that Leacock very possibly doesn't agree with, yet they are given an opportunity to voice their opinions without interference. In one conversation, between Police Chief Tom Reddin of Los Angeles and Chief Charles Gain of Oakland, the two speak at some length about the menace of college radicals, the bad influence of professors, and the attachments of these groups to Communist beliefs. In a relatively lengthy speech to the convention, Reddin speaks of "the increasing tendency toward permissiveness toward those who would change society through revolution rather than through evolution," adding, "We draw the line where the question of freedom arises, and we draw it where anarchy takes place." Leacock does not take speech excerpts out of context nor ridicule any statements of political philosophy. The filming approach does not in any way seek to condemn the subjects' spoken ideas; they are simply allowed to present their views.

There are other moments in the film, equally as typical of Leacock, which have just enough ironic edge to make point of view clear. A police choir sings "Battle Hymn of the Republic," and Leacock's camera lingers awhile on the face of a completely bald, rather ridiculous-looking choir member. A police drill team performs in close-order drill, and the camera zooms in on the tight-lipped, overly pompous expressions of two marchers facing each other as their pinwheel pattern revolves. Over the opening shot of a policeman on the Capitol steps, a couple of lines from Gilbert and Sullivan's "A Policeman's Lot Is Not a Happy One" are heard. During a minister's speech about the 1968 Chicago Convention riots ("There were terrible provocations"), there is a cut to a long shot from the back of the room to show the meager size of the audience. None of these moments are what one would call detached, and whether they are more than just small bits of humor in an essentially serious film is surely relevant to a consideration of filmmaker point of view.

The riot control equipment demonstrations are particularly troublesome in this regard. The factual information — the nature of the weapons, their specific potentials for killing and wounding, the range of available equipment — is hardly a laughing matter. Yet, there are humorous moments in these scenes, like a plastic handcuff demonstration where they can't find the release device, or a fellow trying on a bullet-proof vest of the wrong size. The tension between the horrific possibilities in this equipment and the breezy way it is discussed and demonstrated surely seems a quality Leacock sought to capture. He prefers this more palatable presentation of a rather grim subject, which may itself be a reaction to more traditional approaches. One can easily imagine a humorless

Chiefs. Weapon demonstration.

depiction of the same demonstrations, and whether the scenes would then be more or less credible is open to question. My feeling is that Leacock's approach in no way damages the serious side of these events, but the main point here is that the personal nature of his approach is not covert but clear from the very first shot of the film.

There is a distinctively Leacock moment during one of these demonstrations that allows for a useful comparison with the earlier Drew films. While a man is trying on some special body armor, there is a shot of a young child watching him. The shot is brief and not repeated. This understated point is in marked contrast to the Drew-Leacock *The Children Were Watching,* where this same visual connection was repeatedly made and, in fact, became an organizing principle of the film. In the later Leacock films (those discussed in this chapter), the camera very rarely makes points through specific visual emphasis. Nevertheless, the greater sense of detachment, the refusal to permit personal interpretation to obtrude visually, does not mean the film lacks a point of view. But we must redefine what "point of view" means in regard to cinema verite and consider whether we would ask for completely dispassionate filmic responses (assuming these were possible) to an event such as this one.

Like *Happy Mother's Day,* the wry sense of humor spread through *Chiefs* and the absence of narration leave the viewer a bit uncertain what to make of the film. Is Leacock being patronizing to his subject and inviting the same attitude from viewers? Is he out for laughs at the expense of stimulating interest in the important questions the film raises? I think not, but the issue must be examined, as it is a natural criticism. We can first consider Leacock's rather persuasive response to this question:

We were not being ludicrous. We picked very consciously and carefully the most serious policemen in America, and those are the cream of the crop. We could have just put all our emphasis on the sort of old-fashioned, beer gut, tough cop. We had hilariously funny material on some of them, but it wasn't interesting. Tom Reddin was Chief of Los Angeles and Charles Gain from Oakland—these were the cream of the crop. These were the leading, modern-type chiefs of police in America. The film really is a warning: "If you're going to go fight the cops, know what you're up against and what they're after you for." I know people tend to laugh at it, but if it's a sugar-coated pill, it's still a pill. What they say in there is what they mean and it has a very direct police chiefs' message: "Our goal is to find the revolutionaries and destroy them." It's deadly serious, in this sense. There's really very little emphasis on the ludicrous aspects. We could have done miles and miles of them doing those hula dances; there were lots of goofy things going on there. We didn't show them drinking; that goes on at any convention. I like drinking, too. I'm not going to put them down for that. Because just making asses of people is too easy. And Tom Reddin is no ass. He's a very serious guy.[16]

One of the main arguments in this statement is especially interesting, since it is a quite common reply to charges of this sort. To paraphrase, Leacock is saying "If you think the film ridicules its subject, you should see some of the footage we didn't use." (The Maysles Brothers and Frederick Wiseman have responded similarly in particular cases to this charge.) What's interesting in this is Leacock's open recognition of his powers to manipulate the material if he so chooses, his awareness of developing an argument in the film. In other words, less important chiefs could not be taken as seriously, a preponderance of unflattering shots would have strained credibility, and so on. Leacock is fully aware (as surely an audience is, as well) that this is not simply a report on a convention (just as *Happy Mother's Day* is not a report on the birth of quintuplets) but a deliberate means to deal with important social issues in somewhat indirect fashion.

At this point, because of certain common factors in approach, we might compare *Chiefs* with Frederick Wiseman's *Law and Order.* Both films are about the police, and although neither comment directly on issues raised in their films, overall attitudes of the respective filmmakers seem pretty clear. Leacock warns about the police chief's position in regard to dissent and the technological sophistication of their weapons for response to it. Wiseman does not deal with overt political questions, instead concentrating on the day-to-day activities of the average cop. Leacock explores the ideas of the top police in America in a special situation. Wiseman works with more typical police pursuits and few direct statements of police philosophy.

Neither film attempts to be "objective," in the sense of presenting "balanced" arguments on two sides of an issue. Both films are personal in a number of ways. First, their structure clearly derives from methods employed previously, that is, we can identify similarities between each film and other films by their respective filmmakers. The selections made in regard to subject matter used to explore the common social question (the role of police), as they affect the nature of the issues raised, are surely personal—

Leacock's, a film of conversations and somewhat humorous situations, Wiseman's dealing with street activities in a generally
grim fashion. Still, both Leacock and Wiseman respect the nature
of their films as evidence. We can disagree with what the chiefs
say in Leacock's film, but we cannot, I think, argue that their views
are unfairly represented. We can disagree with the way police
function in *Law and Order,* but we cannot say that police do not
perform the activities Wiseman includes. Because of the refusal
in both cases to intervene directly in the activities being filmed,
both films function as a source of information entirely apart from
questions of bias. They raise issues and perhaps lean toward certain opinions in regard to those issues, but neither film reaches
conclusions. For this reason, the films cannot be said to contradict each other. The issues involved are certainly of sufficient
complexity to allow for these investigations of different aspects
of the same question. Despite the very different appearance of
the two films, their common commitment to an uncontrolled approach leaves them entirely open for debate and differences of
interpretation. Point of view expressed through editing selection
and possibly camera style in regard to events the filmmaker does
not control still allows the events themselves, the subject matter
of the film, to maintain an independent existence. In controlled
films, direct manipulation generally precludes such possibilities.
Because the police convention was not created to be filmed, our
position as viewer of this account of that event, however wryly
it is presented, still leaves us free to talk about the *police chiefs'*
ideas, rather than just wrangling over Leacock's view of them.

   The importance of the filmmaker's lack of direct control is crucial. Although *Chiefs* is not *the* truth on the role of the police, the
simple presence of Leacock's irony and humor does not invalidate this approach. What must be guarded against is an attitude
that would suggest that because the filmmaker has been selective,
these choices in subject matter and in editing are equivalent to
manipulation at the source, whether through scripting or using

actors. As Leacock's films demonstrate, there are possibilities in cinema verite that have only begun to be explored, and large, gray areas of critical questions for which we have no final answers do exist. Leacock is surely on the frontier of what is still a new kind of film, operating under its own set of rules.

Frederick Wiseman

Frederick Wiseman is not a direct product of the artistic cross-breeding that connects all the filmmakers discussed so far. His films do not share the strong personality orientation that characterizes even the Maysles films, our previous paradigm of a purified cinema verite. Wiseman's films are free of both extended concern for specific individuals and dependence upon familiar dramatic forms. (This is not to argue that Wiseman's films are a higher level of cinema verite, a term he rejects, but that his films are a departure from structural approaches previously considered.) Wiseman has specific intentions in his films, and his work is so surely of one piece, full of interconnections to a strong degree, that we shall have to examine the possible conflict between the continued commitment to open, spontaneous shooting and purposeful point-making within a tightly controlled structure.

Wiseman's background before he began making his own films was primarily in law but also included some film experience. He produced *The Cool World* from Warren Miller's novel about Harlem, directed by Shirley Clarke. While teaching law at Boston College, he used to take his students to Bridgewater State Hospital for the Criminally Insane, where he was eventually to make his first film, *Titicut Follies*. His reason for the visits was that he knew many of his students would become judges and district attorneys, and he "wanted them to see the inside of the kind of institution they might someday be committing someone to."[1]

This sense of purpose is typical in Wiseman's film work. Except for his most recent, all of Wiseman's films have dealt with public, tax-supported institutions: a mental hospital, an urban police department, a high school, a metropolitan hospital, and an Army training camp. In all cases, Wiseman explores the institution through a unique mosaic structure. Each film is a series of unnarrated independent sequences, separate events tied together by their common locale and whatever thematic connections we choose to infer. If a person appears in more than one sequence, it happens usually by accident rather than by dramatic necessity.

His films are structured through overall patterns, repetitions of certain kinds of incidents, and a concern for exploring the relationship between the institution and the people it serves. Beyond that, as Wiseman puts it, "I'm trying to see if you can pick up reflections of the larger issues of society in the institutions."[2] A by-product of this search for larger issues is a cumulative sense of the common qualities shared by the institutions in terms of both problems and methods of responding to them. As a result, the institutions, and therefore the films, are closely related. To discuss Wiseman is to talk about six variations on the same theme — the quality of American life as it is expressed by its institutions.

Titicut Follies

Wiseman's first film (codirected by John Marshall), *Titicut Follies,* deals with the most sensational material (in a journalistic sense) of any of his films. Like all of Wiseman's films, its basic structural unit is an encounter between an institution employee and a person he must serve. Patterns of bureaucratic insensitivity established in *Titicut* continue throughout Wiseman's work, and it is the first where the point comes through that the problems are too large, sensitive, and complex to be handled by an institutional bureaucracy, that the institution itself is a friction point. A doctor's attitude to a patient, a guard's response to an inmate, the kinds of supposed insanity, embrace a range of personal, institutional, and social questions. Despite the undoubtedly ghastly nature of the subject matter, *Titicut* does more than encourage revulsion for Bridgewater.

The film's first apparent quality is its refusal to deal in stereotypes. On the basis of prior cinematic experience, one surely expects to see guards as sadists and inmates as victims (or else some other black-and-white definition of roles), but one has to feel an ambivalence in *Titicut* toward people on both sides. They are caught in an institutional trap. While a hospital for the criminally insane is surely necessary (as are the institutions in most

Wiseman films), it is a place where pressing problems receive less than satisfactory treatment, due to the complexity of the problems the institution is expected to treat and the lack of public knowledge or concern about its workings.

A scene in *Titicut* suggests the need for complex response to seemingly direct material. A man committed for engaging in sexual activities with children, including his daughter, is questioned by a psychiatrist. The man's story clearly indicates that he has serious emotional problems that require medical treatment, but implicit in the doctor's questions is a certain lewd suggestiveness beyond a strictly professional interest. In the middle of the scene, Wiseman cuts to a room where inmates are directed to strip and are then searched. Back to the doctor and patient, where stripping and searching take place on a mental level as the prying investigation delves into the subjects of masturbation, the man's relations with his wife, and his homosexual activities. The scene ends with the man saying, "I know I need help but I don't know where I can get it." The doctor's reply: "You get it here, I guess." It is the first of many instances in Wiseman's films when one knows that the buck has been passed as far as it will go. The problem gets dealt with here or it doesn't get dealt with at all.

A scene like this allows the viewer freedom for a number of simultaneous responses. The doctor must ask questions, but he seems to do it with a brutish insensitivity and an undeniable relish for detail. The patient, toward whom we'd like to feel sympathetic, becomes difficult to relate to as he details his clearly serious and socially dangerous sexual problems. There are no "answers" in such an encounter, and Wiseman does not attempt to supply any. *Titicut Follies* is neither muckraking nor propagandistic in ultimate effect, because the solutions, or even whether any are possible, are by no means apparent.

The doctor-sex molester scene also indicates a structural difficulty Wiseman had yet to resolve, an interesting problem from a cinema-verite point of view because its solution has led him toward a more complete refusal to judge his material, which, in turn, has resulted in structures allowing more openness to audience interpretation. When he cuts from the interview to other inmates being searched and then back again, he implies a comparison which forces a singular response. Strictly through editing, we are made to consider each scene in terms of the other, that is, to note the doctor's verbal stripping of his patient. This runs counter to the cinema-verite notion of attempting not to reduce the complexity of filmed events, instead trusting the power of the material to be its own statement (and perhaps not the same statement for each viewer).

This problem is again apparent in a scene of an inmate being force-fed through a long rubber tube inserted into his nose, as a doctor's cigarette ash haphazardly dangles over the opening. Into this scene, Wiseman intercuts several flashforwards of the same man being prepared for burial. While this manipulation may serve to keep our attention on a grisly spectacle we might otherwise avoid and also makes a quite valid point—that more attention was paid to the man dead than alive—this is editorial editing of a crude sort. Wiseman's refusal to work in this vein in subsequent films places him more squarely within a cinema-verite tradition, for he has since replaced such contrived juxtaposition with far from obvious connections between scenes, giving his later work a quality much more of information gathering than point proving.

Titicut Follies takes its name from a variety show performed by the inmates and guards. Wiseman uses acts from the Follies as opening and closing sequences, also cutting back to it at other times during the film. The unnatural theatricality of the scenes permeates the rest of the film. Again, this is a tendency that Wiseman keeps under control in his later films, although he still leans toward "summing up" shots, which bring together certain themes of the film. *Titicut Follies,* then, is well on the way toward a structure able to deal with the complexity of institutional relationships but still exhibiting tendencies of over-control, which Wiseman later reduced considerably.

Law and Order

Wiseman's first film was about an institution few people knew; his second, *Law and Order,* grapples with a familiar, controversial subject—the police. Wiseman shot the film during a six-week period in Kansas City. Many of the scenes involve routine situations: several family disputes, a stolen purse incident, an overcharging cab driver, a lost child. There are no demonstrations or riots, and the most violent moments take place during a couple of arrests, one of a prostitute and the other of a juvenile. As in *Titicut,* the police are an institution expected both to serve people in trouble and to act as an enforcement agency. The encounters between the police and the primarily ghetto-bound populace they deal with are a means to explore a range of problems on both sides of the institutional relationship.

   A difference between *Titicut Follies* and *Law and Order,* and always a concern in cinema verite, is the degree to which an audience infers a generalized examination of a subject, as opposed to considering the film as a report of specific conditions at a particular point in time. Every cinema-verite film establishes certain strong limitations in time and/or space, which affect possibilities for generalization. In most films discussed so far, the limitations have been a function of the decision to focus on an individual, in which case the film is structured by time; that is, someone is followed during a demarcated period, whether it is Dylan during one concert tour, Jane Fonda from the beginning of rehearsal until the close of a show, or Paul Brennan during a sales trip to Florida. In films about events, space expands through editing; many places are covered, as in the integration crises in *The Children Were Watching* and *Crisis: Behind a Presidential Commitment,* or the Altamont events in *Gimme Shelter.* In either case, however, structural limitations put restrictions on generalization. Most cinema-verite films, through the very way they are constructed, do not in themselves argue large questions. That is, we may see an event such as Altamont or a personality like Dylan as being representative of larger social forces or cultural phenomena, but nothing in the film itself suggests such a generalization. To this extent, then, cinema verite has been a medium for reporting; the films are presentations, we could say, of unanalyzed data.

Law and Order, and all subsequent Wiseman films, do seek through structure to lead an audience to more general evaluations. While Wiseman's films do have a structure, its limitations are of space and not of time. All scenes in a film are, of course, connected to the institution, but there are rarely sequential time connections. Sometimes one incident may be referred to at a later point (this happens with an arrest in *Law and Order*) but not often. Instead, each sequence, by being out of chronological time, relates to others only through the accumulation of information about the event itself, through thematic rather than dramatic connections. Taken out of time, the films become less journalistic. While one could argue, for instance, the relative merits of the Kansas City Police Department versus those of other cities, the nonchronological structure argues that *Law and Order* is a film about the police and not a film about the Kansas City Police. (A small point, but one that the films support, is Wiseman's use of generalized titles.)

Another element involved in the way Wiseman's films are structured as general arguments, one that distinguishes *Law and Order* (and films following) from *Titicut Follies,* has to do with the nature of the institution under investigation. It is quite possible to see *Titicut* as an indictment of this one specific mental hospital, although one could guess that perhaps (or even probably) these conditions are common. In the case of police, on the other hand, people do have certain pre-existing views that they will inevitably bring to the film. In other words, Wiseman concerns himself with subject matter already in the public consciousness.

Finally in this regard, and perhaps most importantly, the absence of personality orientation is a major element in extending the level of argument. A film about one policeman, in a crisis period or not, would remain a film about one policeman. This is not to argue that such a film would lack possibilities for generali-

zation but only to say that through withholding audience identification, Wiseman makes clear the broader nature of his concerns.
It should also be noted that so far we have discussed only a first
level of generalization, from individuals to the institution; later we
will consider reflection of issues beyond the institution itself.

In *Law and Order,* more than in any other Wiseman film, one
might feel on initial consideration that the presence of the camera
and tape recorder affected what was being filmed. This makes
it a simple matter to believe that events shown are too distorted
to be evaluated. How could anyone expect police to behave as
they "really" are, one might ask, when their every move is under
close scrutiny? In Wiseman's case, the question is complicated
by his not concentrating on certain people, so that the possibility
of a subject's growing acceptance of the camera in intimate situa-

Law and Order. Police officer mediates dispute between husband and wife and
landlady.

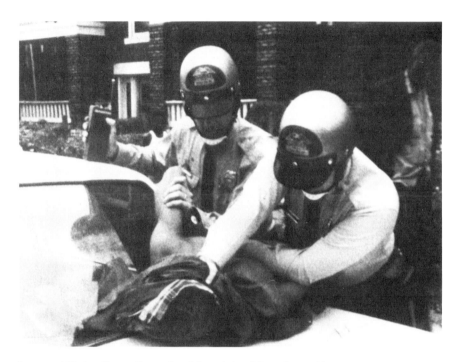

Law and Order. Two officers forcibly subdue hit-and-run driver.

tions is not a potential argument. Once again, however, the question of camera awareness is not this simple.

All activities in Wiseman's films suggest a tacit acceptance of the camera because the people being filmed believe themselves to be behaving within their proper roles. It is natural to assume that no one in a film, especially a public employee on the job, wants to commit acts that he feels will put him in a bad light. If we see a police officer choking a prostitute or strongly subduing a boy being arrested (both occur in *Law and Order*), then it is able to happen in front of the camera only because the policeman thinks he is fulfilling the requirements of his job. To expect a film to show a scene of a policeman harassing someone out of personal hatred or just for fun is naive. An individual's complicity in the act of being filmed precludes such activities.

Wiseman's films show people living within their normal routines.

One can imagine the possible excesses that surely occur in un-filmed situations, but this adds another dimension to our evalua-tion of the issues rather than detracting from the validity of what is there. Also, when we begin to realize that what looks very strange to us is, in fact, perfectly commonplace for the people involved, we begin to pass beyond third-person observation to become empathetic participants; bringing the audience into the film in this way is no mean feat given the lack of sustained character identification in Wiseman's films.

There are some lapses of sensibility in *Law and Order,* but they serve to underscore the tension of mixed feelings the rest of the film creates. When Wiseman shows a policeman buying candy for a lost child, he comes closest to a deliberate attempt to upset preconceived notions about the police. Although it may be true that police frequently buy candy for children (just as they also rough up prostitutes), the scene is one-dimensional, a play for a specific reaction. The expected ambiguity of possible re-sponses typical in Wiseman's work is lost, along with contextual complexity. As happens only rarely in his films, experience looks oversimplified.

A scene of two policemen talking about their salaries and the lure of better jobs in California presents further problems. It looks uncomfortably staged and awkwardly attempts to fill in facts in a narrative fashion. Verbal information, people talking about speci-fic problems rather than living them, has little place in Wiseman's films or in American cinema verite generally. In a scene like this, our thoughts jump to a different and inferior level; we know we are hearing one side of a debate. Anyone wishing to find out about police pay or other general issues can go read about them, but one could never find in print the participation in complex events provided by nearly all of *Law and Order.*

High School
High School, if it were to follow the pattern, would deal with a ghetto school in a terrible state of disrepair. Instead, Wiseman's

third film is an examination of a Philadelphia high school whose
student body is typically upper-middle class and predominantly
white. *High School,* unlike Wiseman's first two films, is about a
"successful" institution, and the question shifts from whether the
institution is equipped for the responsibilities society places upon
it to whether the institution is doing the job we want it to. Goals
and policies themselves, rather than the efficiency of their implementation, are to be questioned.

The film is a series of interactions between students and their
parents, teachers, and administrators. It is not a general study of
educational methods or the attitudes of youth. Its primary concern
is for those aspects of attending high school that have nothing to
do with classroom learning or the development of intellectual
capacities—issues like the development of sexual roles, competi-
tiveness, dress habits, relationships with authority figures. *High*

High School. Students are polled about attitudes toward black people.

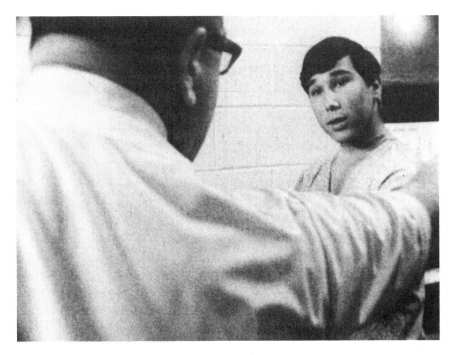

High School. Dean of discipline giving punishment to student.

School is a rigorously selective work whose fragmented structure is a result of Wiseman's sensing the parts of the high school experience that are relevant to his argument and his willingness to sacrifice dramatic continuity for a unity that does not become apparent until the film's conclusion. He sees the logical connections within his material and vests the film with the mathematical elegance of a neatly executed proof.

High School is a film of frustrating confrontations. A student is scolded by a vice-principal for talking back to a teacher, another for being in a hall during lunch without a pass, yet another for suggesting at a meeting that tuxedos might not be necessary for the school dance. The viewer begins to notice how rarely he hears the kids talking, and what the students are told in scene after scene is startlingly similar. "We're out to establish that you're a man and can take orders." "We're going to do in this school what the majority wants." "It's nice to be individualistic, but there are certain places to be individualistic." Wiseman constantly locates and selects situations that express institutional philosophies. Along with the verbal expressions of repression, *High School* has frequent scenes of students being forced to enact a variety of subservient, competitive roles. Girls hang from rings in a gym class as their teacher yells out "Tarzan" and "Super-Tarzan" when they reach appropriate levels of endurance, and in another gym class they perform exercises to a series of commands in a song called "Simon Says." In one of the film's longer and more spectacular scenes, three boys emerge from a mock-capsule in full astronaut regalia after having spent 193 hours in simulated space flight, part of a handsomely funded space project. There are also many scenes dealing with sexual attitudes, including separate lectures to segregated groups of boys and girls, and a number of curious instances of role reversals—among them one where football players in wigs and dresses perform as cheerleaders and girls in the band march with mock-rifles (in a scene strongly reminiscent of the variety show in *Titicut Follies*). The high school clearly has more than education on its mind, or rather, the educational process includes the inculcation of a broad spectrum of attitudes.

Classroom experiences do play a part, but not a promising one. A teacher subjects her class to a reading of "Casey at the Bat." Later, another teacher attempts to explore poetic devices through discussion of a Simon and Garfunkel song, "Sounds of Silence." The second scene (and its relationship to the first) is again evidence of the possibilities for multiple interpretation in cinema verite.[3] Some see the second teacher as a junior version of the first, noting her unawareness even of the irony behind the message of the song she has selected. An alternative but not totally contradictory view sees this teacher as a hopeful sign of progress within the school, someone who tries to select relevant and involving subject matter, but the students are so accustomed to being bored by the educational process that they can't distinguish between the two. In either case, it is important to note that Wiseman's mosaic structure allows for the comparison (that is, provides the evidence) but refuses to supply direct interpretation.

When one feels that meaning in a cinema-verite work is clear, it becomes a simple matter to speak of filmmaker intentions. However, because the events in cinema verite are uncontrolled and editing generally attempts to avoid the imposition of value judgments, filmmaker intent is not so easily defined. Wiseman is not saying that high schools are good or bad, and although one can guess what his own opinion might be, such a consideration is not germane. It is entirely possible to look approvingly upon the goals of the school, to see its values as ones that should be passed on to students. Indeed, some audiences do respond in such a manner.[4] While Wiseman's film is certainly subjective, this is not to say that he imposes a strict viewpoint upon the material. Once more, he explores conditions rather than proposing solutions. The investigation leaves the audience free not only to supply its own solutions but even to determine whether or not problems exist for which solutions must be sought.

The film's opening, however, is perhaps a bit overly suggestive. While we approach the school by car, very likely noting the factory-like appearance of its exterior, we hear a song called "Dock of the Bay." The song, as described by Wiseman in an interview, is about "the black experience in America . . . (and) the difference between the promise and what actually happened." Wiseman adds, "That seemed to me to be very relevant to the subject I was filming, so I put it in at the beginning of the film."[5] While very possibly relevant, music (and the verbal content within the song) employed in this fashion is akin to narration, and the direct expression of filmmaker attitude regarding his material by these means goes against the filming method. Above all, although the song may be thematically relevant (in Wiseman's opinion), it is structurally irrelevant. If one agrees that the song relates to other elements of the film, then one already sees "what actually happened" in this case, and there is no need to press it further through use of the song. If one does not see *High School* in these terms, then the song is not a means of persuasion. The general absence in cinema verite of music employed for point-making is in keeping with the intention of leaving the material sufficiently open for many shades of interpretation. When it is used, the filmmaker is in essence rejecting the complexity of his own material.

The beginning sequence in *High School* can be usefully contrasted to the last scene, which does indeed make a general statement (as the music attempts to do), but only by nature of the event itself. The principal of the school addresses a teacher assembly, and with tears in her eyes reads a letter written to her from a former student now in Vietnam. He is about to parachute into action, and he writes to thank his teachers and his school for all they have done for him. He expresses the wish that in the event of his death, his insurance money should go toward setting up a scholarship for a student at the school. "I know I am only a body doing a job," he writes. Almost emotionally overcome, the principal finishes the letter and says, "Now, when you get a letter like this, to me it means that we are very successful at Northeast High School. I think you will agree with me." From this statement, we can easily go backward and fit lots of things into place. The school's factory-like appearance, its repression of individuality, the military-like emphasis on authority, even the space program, lead to this aim—the production of "bodies" to "do a job." No external aids like music or narration are necessary to put the pieces together. The high school is doing the job it intends.

Hospital

From *Titicut Follies* to *Hospital,* we can see a development in Wiseman's shifting use of the institution to explore larger social issues. *Titicut Follies* is the most specifically concerned (of the four) with the particular problems within the institution itself. The major implied issue is simply the question of why society permits Bridgewater to exist. In *Law and Order,* issues are broadened to the extent that we ask questions about the role of police in society, but Wiseman to a large extent remains rooted in a close examination of the institution itself (as in discussion of police salaries, evidence of verbal abuse police must suffer, etc.). *High School* explores attitudes that society values through examining cultural indoctrination within the educational process. Once on this broader plane, Wiseman stayed there, and *Hospital* might be described as a return to *Law and Order* territory but with the added sophistication of argument found in *High School*. The hospital is a battleground for a wealth of social problems, to the point where the institution itself is primarily a mirror for other, larger concerns.

Hospital is nearly free of enclosed information; that is, most sequences have overt external ramifications. An added element is the frequency of cases where people within the institution try to deal with other institutions, always unsuccessfully. In *Law and Order,* there are some comments about the inefficiency of legal procedures and problems with juvenile courts, but *Hospital* provides a running critique on the inadequacy of other institutions. By extension we come to realize that the problems of other institutions and their resources to meet them are probably little different from Metropolitan Hospital's, though this is not explicitly stated.

Two telephone calls by doctors to other agencies neglecting their responsibilities point up the interdependency of the institutions and the way people can be caught between bureaucracies. The first complains about a patient who was transferred from a private hospital to a public one without benefit of anyone's notifying a doctor at the receiving end of the seriousness of her condition. The doctor's combined tone of anger and resignation is echoed subsequently by an ambulance driver who had to drive a patient around for several hours before finding a hospital that would admit her. The second call, later in the film, is made by a psychiatrist on behalf of a young homosexual, as he tries to extract a commitment from a social worker with the improbable

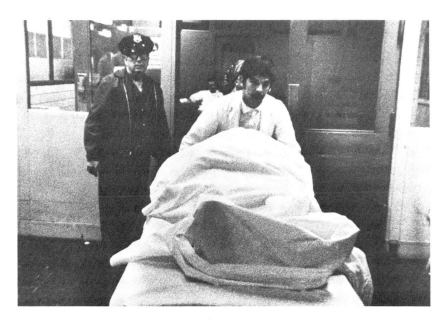

Hospital

name of Miss Hightower that her agency will help the boy. The camera stays on the doctor in unwavering close-up for nearly four minutes while his pleas are evaded by buck-passing and instructions to put his request in writing. The conclusion of the scene is the only moment in a Wiseman film when someone acknowledges the presence of a camera, as the doctor looks up unbelievingly and says that she hung up on him. Throughout *Hospital* there are frequent indications of institutions exerting pressures on each other, compounding inefficiencies and increasing the likelihood that stopgap means will be employed to combat long-term problems.

Both doctors, and all the staff people in *Hospital,* do show a good deal of concern for the patients. In contrast to *Titicut,* the audience is not permitted the easy escape of seeing a solution in the hiring of better personnel. In fact, Wiseman's later films frequently resolve situations in a manner that suggests his advancing sensibility in regard to the nature of institutional problems.

One particularly sensitive scene (which again includes unsatisfactory contact with a social worker) involves a young boy brought to the hospital who, while left alone with his alcoholic grandmother, has fallen out a fifteen-foot-high window. Somehow he has not been injured and should be released. A nurse hears the facts in the case and struggles to find a way to keep the boy for a day so that neglect forms can be filled out. Calling to another ward ("I know the old goat is listening, so just answer yes or no. . . . Do you have a bed for a little boy? . . . I'll do anything"), talking to a social worker (who asks, "Are there any other siblings in the home?"), she is finally ready to take the boy to her own house. In tears, not knowing what to do and warned about overinvolvement, she asks if she can get the boy something to eat before his release, resigned to not being able to do any more than this. Wiseman knows when to stop, for the next part of the episode could have lapsed into the sentimentality of the *Law and Order* candy scene. This incident is of the sort that has been so debased by women's magazine fiction and television soap opera that a good part of *Hospital's* impact derives from being brought back to direct experience, coming to realize again that these desperate struggles involve real people.

Hospital re-echoes *Titicut Follies* in a scene that again demonstrates the degree of refinement in Wiseman's later work. In an encounter that recalls the interview between the psychiatrist and the sex offender in *Titicut,* a woman doctor has to examine an old man and ask him about sores on his genitals and the condition of his urine. He is embarrassed to talk to a woman but at the same time near crying in fear that he's dying of cancer. She gently prods the information from him as she assures him, "You shouldn't be ashamed. . . . We want to fix you up. I have to know all these things." We feel closer to them both than to the two in *Titicut,* where the doctor was obnoxious and the patient far from sympathetic. In *Hospital,* both the necessity for people dealing with institutions to sacrifice a degree of privacy and the accompanying respect required toward those who seek assistance are evident. The film has many such scenes, doctor-patient encounters that depict one person trying to make another's life a little more bearable.

Wiseman's films usually contain some material whose sole purpose is "atmosphere." Especially in *High School* and *Hospital,* one feels an attempt to communicate the oppressiveness of the institutional environment. Long traveling shots down halls and frequent views of people waiting compensate for the tight close-up shooting in most scenes. A by-product of Wiseman's concern for one-to-one encounters is that a sense of place is secondary. While this is useful in imparting a generality to the conditions examined—his institutions could be anywhere—the buildings themselves serve to express the institution's philosophy. Therefore, we get the factory-like shots at the beginning of *High School* or views of crowded, noisy waiting rooms in *Hospital.* Even a trivial activity like janitors walking down halls cleaning up are repeated in both films (and similarly in his later *Essene*), again to supply a feeling for the physical plant. This visual shorthand becomes something of a convention, so that in *Hospital* transitions between scenes are facilitated by returns to the waiting room. As a convention, a simple means to put sequences together, such shots are perhaps useful. In themselves, however, they are not too convincing because their intent is obvious. Atmosphere is not a factor that can be manipulated.

Wiseman uses his preference for close shooting to advantage at the end of *Hospital,* when he finally pulls back. As a group of patients in a church service sing "Ave Maria," Wiseman cuts to outside the hospital. The sound of the singing begins to decrease while the camera slowly zooms out. The hospital recedes until it is far in the background as the shot becomes filled with the sight and sound of cars speeding along a highway. When last seen, the hospital is an indistinguishable building behind a steady stream of people moving by, oblivious to what's going on inside.

Basic Training

Basic Training is the first Wiseman film to follow at least a near-chronological sequence. Recruits are seen alighting from buses and undergoing the initial battery of regulatory procedures: uniform issuing, haircuts, fingerprinting. Drilling scenes at several points in the film are a progressive frame of reference to the soldiers' growing proficiency at following orders. While there are occasional moments of personality and discipline problems, the general force of the film asserts the overall efficiency of the training process in developing soldiers with a sense of Army pride. The film ends with "graduation," as the now polished troops pass in review before officers and an admiring civilian crowd.

While the film is open to individual analysis apart from Wiseman's other work, the filmmaker's selection of material bears a clear relationship to concerns in his other films. The most certain connections in this case are between *Basic Training* and *High School,* although a more complex web of connections among all the films can be explored (dealing with such things as the function of the church services in both *Basic Training* and *Hospital*). Wiseman is sensitive not only to the similarities between institutions but also to the neat matrix of inverse influences—the ways institutions take on the functions and appearances of each other. In *High School* Wiseman repeatedly points up militaristic aspects of the high school experience; in *Basic Training* he emphasizes the high-school-like aspects of the training process. It is important to note that he is not only implicitly arguing that high school and basic training are alike in some respects; he shows how the two institutions draw on the techniques of each other to the point where neither has an independent identity. Instead, they come to be seen as two steps in much broader processes of molding and regulating citizens in nonvoluntary situations.

In *High School* the military connection is made explicit in the final scene, the reading of the letter from the former student now in Vietnam, thus suggesting the easy, practically inevitable transition from high school student to soldier. The connections in the film to the military also include previously mentioned scenes of Army-like endurance tests and the exercises in unison to recorded commands in girls' gym classes, as well as the astronaut sequence, again pointing up the school's encouragement of yet another primarily military function. (A corresponding endurance test in *Basic Training* is a grueling forced exposure to tear gas.) There is an official military rhetoric in *High School,* which has precise counterparts in *Basic Training,* lines like "We're out to establish you're a man and can take orders." There are even marching bands in both films. And, of course, the overall pervading atmosphere of boredom in *High School* is not without a military analogue. The sum total of this evidence (still, though, only one dimension of the film) is sufficient to conclude that the selection process is deliberate, that Wiseman is making a conscious argument about military aspects of the high school experience.

In *Basic Training,* to reverse the direction of the comparison, the high school connections are equally pronounced. The graduation, already mentioned, has a ceremony complete with valedictorian's speech. Just as *High School* out-Armies *Basic Training* in some respects, this film goes beyond *High School,* as no graduation scene appeared in Wiseman's earlier film. Wiseman avoids the typical, the expected (like showing a graduation ceremony in *High School*), when those experiences are part of common knowledge. (It is only in *Law and Order* and *Hospital* that the typical is stressed, presumably because Wiseman feels the public loses sight of the daily activities of these institutions.) He prefers to seek out defining moments, situations that either reveal institutional philosophy or (by their possibly seeming out of place) facilitate the kind of institutional connections we are talking about. Basic training is, after all, a kind of educational process and perhaps a more efficient, concentrated learning experience than high school. The film is full of assembly lectures, not the doctors' sex talks in *High School,* but now indoctrination lessons about Why We Are in Vietnam and the importance of the "winning" tradition in the Army. Where *High School's* teachers drilled bored students on literature, *Basic Training's* instructors "teach" about rifles, bayonets, land mines, and the like, to a far more rapt audience. (There are many scenes of "classes.") Combat practice, pairs of men hitting each other with clubs, looks like part of a high school physical education program. The Army even employs audiovisual aids in its instruction, as shown in a humorous scene of an instructor teaching recruits how to brush their teeth properly by asking them to follow an animated musical demonstration on TV sets. The inevitable discipline problems (like a soldier failing to make reveille formation) certainly recall the vice-principal scenes in *High School,* with the same kinds of remarks about not getting out of line by the same sort of petty bureaucrat, although punishment here is a lot stiffer than an hour's detention. Again, the accumulation of evidence makes the military-high school connections very difficult to ignore.

Basic Training. Drilling of recruits.

Basic Training

Basic Training. Two Army "regulars" watch the progress of a new unit.

A curious connection between the two films, strange because the scenes in question do not seem of crucial importance within either film by itself, becomes apparent in the repeated situations involving parents of the students and soldiers. Their use suggests, in part, Wiseman's attempt to demonstrate that the institutions function not only *in loco parentis,* but in accordance with parents', that is, society's, wishes. In both films, the parents cooperate fully with the institution, either acquiescing to its philosophy or expressly favoring it. In *High School,* parental complicity is clear in scenes such as the castigation of a student for failing to respect authority or another in which a parent comes to complain about a student's grade and ends by agreeing with the philosophy behind it. The instances in *Basic Training* are even more blatant. A mother present at her son's promotion beams admiringly as she says, "I think he's found his niche in the world." During a family visit, one recruit proudly shows off his rifle. His father advises him "to do what you're supposed to at all times," while his mother warns, "If you don't come out of here a true man, you'll never be a man." Such scenes are points of contact with the outside world, emphasizing the institution as an extension and reflection of broader social values.

Basic Training complements *High School* in the nature of its argument. Because the Army is a more distinct subculture, Wiseman emphasizes its points of commonality. "It turns out there is nothing that puts professional soldiers at a distance from the rest of us. That's infinitely more depressing than showing that drill sergeants are a bunch of animals."[6] Wiseman's feeling is evident throughout the film; there are no instances of truly unusual or shocking behavior. During a rifle demonstration, a recruit innocently inquires whether the specific weapon being exhibited has been used to kill people. The instructor's answer is a measured, rational discussion defending the use of weapons as a means of self-preservation in war; it is not the gung-ho, let's-kill-'em sort of harangue we might expect. Basic training is presented as a survival course, necessary instruction to keep these nice, normal kids from getting killed.

A difference between the two films is evident in their respective final sequences. *High School's* last scene deliberately reaches out beyond the institution itself. *Basic Training* has no such transcendent moment, nor is one necessary. When one of the recruits at "graduation" says, "We came here from different places with different backgrounds. . . . We are now emerging as trained fighting men in the United States Army," he only reiterates an ideology that is already evident. The question, common to all of Wiseman's films, is whether the institution functions in our best interest. His studies of public, tax-supported institutions take us into places we might never venture for ourselves (or places we have been, without ever considering their function as institutions) and has us ask whether they indeed represent our true values and priorities.

Essene

Essene is the first Wiseman film to deal with an institution that is neither public nor tax-supported—a monastery. Instead of institutional cross-connections and issues of public concern, Wiseman seems to be exploring personal, human qualities, so that *Essene* is both his most specific and his most universal work. *Essene* is not so much about an institution as about a community.

The absence of personality orientation in Wiseman's previous films, the tendency to see people in terms of their function within the institution and as vehicles to express institutional philosophy, encourage a detached, analytical attitude. To quote him (in an interview after *Hospital*): "I think the star of each film is the institution. I don't want you to come out feeling, for instance, that Dr. Schwartz in *Hospital* is a charming, personable fellow. I want you to come out with a feeling of what a big city hospital is like, or a high school, a prison, a police department. I want you to switch your level of identification from a person . . . to Metropolitan Hos-

pital. That's really what I'm after."[7] In *Essene,* Wiseman does give
a sense of the institution, but he does so through emphasis upon
individuals to a far greater extent.

For the first time in a Wiseman film, we identify people by name
and have at least some sense of individuals apart from their institutional identities. Even those in authority appear to be speaking
as much for themselves as for the positions they hold. While strata
within the community exist, there is a good deal more communication at the same level than in previous Wiseman films. In *Essene,* this leads to more frequent questioning of the role of the
institution itself. Again, this is part of an evolution in Wiseman's
work. *High School* has one scene of students speaking out, the
only time in that film where they seem to be more than just bodies being moved around. *Hospital* has a number of instances
where people go beyond their customary roles, such as the scene
where a nurse tries to defy authority in hope of helping a mis-
treated boy. In *Basic Training,* there is a greater proportion of
discussions questioning the institution's validity, usually by groups
of recruits debating Army policies. *Essene* is about an institution
constantly examining itself. Wiseman's films show an increasing
tendency toward situations where people within the institution
criticize it; as a consequence, they become more than just func-
tionaries or victims. *Essene* is a long way from the marked, unquestioned division of institutional roles in *Titicut Follies, Law and
Order,* and even *High School.*

A situation characteristic in Wiseman films, and most marked in
the last two, is the case of a "misfit," someone who does not ad-
just to the discipline of the institution. The connection between
reoccurrences of this kind of situation is in the basic condition
that any institution exercising authority must develop means to
respond to those who will not (or cannot) submit willingly. In
the process, the nature of authority is revealed, in regard both to
what the institution deems an infraction and to the manner of its
response.

In *High School,* there are three separate instances of boys brought before the vice-principal for discipline. In one, a boy is accused of disrespect for his teacher, and he is punished despite his protestations of innocence. (This is where the institutional philosophy of "we're out to establish you're a man and can take orders" comes out.) Another case involves a hefty student who has slugged a smaller classmate, and he's dealt with harshly. While we might be more sympathetic to discipline in this case, one point of the repeated episodes involving infractions of rules is the uniformity of response by authority, with little regard for nuances between offenses. Anyone out of line for whatever reason gets put back in by whatever means necessary. The assembly line keeps rolling.

While there are minor discipline problems of the same order in *Basic Training,* a more interesting and well-developed case involves a recruit who is literally and figuratively "out of step," who just can't do anything right. After repeated problems, he attempts suicide, and his first sergeant asks the base chaplain to see him. Their meeting has the customary Wiseman ambiguity; the boy needs help, though maybe not the kind he gets, and all he might really need is just to be released from the institution. The chaplain lectures him with lines like "All of life is really about ups and downs" and does not appear to be of much assistance. At one point in their talk he glances furtively at his watch; he seems to consider the "problem" rather routine. But the recruit is treated kindly, and the institution is prepared to bend to some extent to accommodate him. Ironically, the boy is later seen during a demonstration of strangling and other killing techniques as the volunteer "victim," a strange role for someone who had earlier tried to kill himself. Despite a certain institutional insensitivity and occasional harshness of language, the Army seems an even more benign institution than the high school. Their reasons for disciplinary action are at least explained, though we can still question the need for it.

These issues are most fully explored in *Essene.* The opening scene is a discussion of authority, and the point is made that "everything is done with the approval of the Abbot." The tension throughout is established by the next scene, where "egocentric habits" are considered. The constant conflict in *Essene* is between individuality (usually called "ego") and the need for submission to the group. A revealing scene in this regard is a discussion in which one monk asks for "a theological rationale for discipline" and is answered by an argument for the tradition of asceticism in the Church. "If you don't have discipline, you have chaos," he is told, and he is further instructed to consider the monastery discipline as a form of preparation to receive God's graces. The next scene continues on this point; the Abbot lectures to a class about the need for law and "the tension between the spirit and the law." That Wiseman considers these questions paramount is evident in his final "summing up" scene, a long sermon by the Abbot about "Martha and Mary complexes," the possessive and contemplative qualities of the human personality. *Essene* is structured upon this duality.

The possessive quality is most apparent in the film's "misfit" case, which constitutes practically a subplot in an otherwise typically nonnarrative structure. Brother Wilfred is first seen talking to the Abbot, and his stubborn individuality is quite apparent from their discussion. He talks about his dislike for the use of first names, feeling that the custom is unnecessarily familiar. The Abbot's reply is expected, a defense of their use as a result of living together in a community, the familiarity a natural product of shared experience. Wilfred wants none of it, believing that he has the right to decide who can be familiar and who can't. In the only scene shot outside the monastery, Wilfred is followed into town on a shopping trip. The clerk at one of the stores, apparently aware of Wilfred's idiosyncrasies, kids him about whether he missed roll call this morning and asks if they line up in formation standing at attention (a slight but helpful link to *Basic Training*). The issue comes to a head in a meeting led by the Abbot, who states his conclusion that Wilfred indicates no desire to reform, to give himself to the group. The monastery, the most humanistic of institutions, seems ultimately the most inflexible toward those who are out of step.

The contemplative quality, the willingness to submerge oneself within the spirit of the institution, is explored through scenes of religious observance and communal expressions of faith that are close to group therapy. The connection is acknowledged during one discussion when a monk talks about the "extremely thera-peutic" nature of their meetings and the "emphasis on healing" in their life. In a long, remarkable scene, one monk tells an ex-tended parable about finding God. At the end, he kneels on the floor, while the whole group gathers around him and sings "Heal him, Jesus." They all embrace, just as they do after one of their services. In that scene, Wiseman follows the procession of hugs through at least a dozen people in a single shot, thus emphasiz-ing the sense of community.

Essene, like all of Wiseman's films, is generally shot in tight close-up. This stylistic tendency has frequently been criticized, espec-ially in *High School,* where the use of close-ups has been called "grotesque" and a means of "ridicule."[8] Discussion of this char-acteristic has been deferred until now because *Essene* disproves the argument that this method of shooting invites ridicule. A shoot-ing preference for close-ups, when constantly employed (and it is in Wiseman's films), is a strictly neutral device. There is no one made ridiculous in *Essene* because the camera stays close; if anything, the continual expressions of emotion are that much more moving as a result.

A distinction must be made between the content of a shot and possible intention expressed by framing and camera movement. If a teacher in *High School* looks grotesque (though even that judgment is certainly open to dispute), this is a viewer's inter-pretation rather than a filmmaker's. Otherwise, why are some close-ups seen as grotesque and others as sympathetic? A more rigorous rationale is needed to assert filmmaker intention behind a framing decision. Wiseman's close-ups are for us to see what's going on, and no more.

This is not to argue that camera style cannot express a film-maker's response to what he films. But there are more varieties of filmmaker intention that communicating "good" or "bad" evaluations through framing. Consistent use of close-ups does say something about Wiseman's level of involvement, just as long shots would say something else. Intention can also be expressed through stylistic shifts, such as choosing to shoot one person close and another at a distance. If Wiseman zooms in on the vice-principal in *High School* when he glares at a student, intention is expressed, but it is the movement that is expressive, and not the close-up itself. The point then becomes whether the altered framing choice contradicts the activity being shown, but that

Essene. Father Anthony with the Abbot at Mass.

Essene. The Abbot.

is another matter entirely. Selection, the choice of what to film, is not automatically equivalent to a point of view. A close-up is a close-up, and not a philosophy of life. Wiseman's visual style does not vary from film to film, but one cannot conclude that he considers each institution and the people in them as equivalent. However much his point of view is disputed, the overriding issues continue to revolve around content. While filmmaker personality is not entirely hidden, there are other things to talk about than who might look grotesque and who doesn't.

  Essene, through its apparent differences in subject matter from earlier Wiseman films, clarifies our understanding of institutions. Where Wiseman's institutions are themselves microcosms of society, the monastery can be seen as a microcosm of the other institutions. We can divide the institutions in his earlier films into two groups: those that deal with people society deems in need of assistance *(Titicut Follies, Law and Order, Hospital)* and those that serve society by asserting its values through "education" *(High School, Basic Training). Essene* combines these two functions. The monastery seeks to help people (recall the emphasis on "healing") and also enforces institutional values (and therefore must maintain discipline). A monastery, seemingly the most specialized and superfluous of the Wiseman institutions, is the most universal.

  Considering all of Wiseman's institutions, some generalizations can be made. Institutions are conservative in both philosophy and approach. They reflect the status quo and do not sponsor innovation. Those dealing with the poor are not equipped to handle the complex problems placed on their doorstep and tend to blame other institutions for the failure to meet the needs of the poor. The institutions can effectively realize their intentions when they have a specific job to do and are properly funded. Part of the point in drawing these "messages" from the films is to show that these are not really "message films" at all. They are a bridge to experience; while arguments can be inferred through structure, it is exposure to the events themselves in all their complexity that makes this inference possible. Wiseman's films do not "illustrate" specific problems; they present material from which a variety of inferences on a number of levels can be drawn.

Wiseman's films might not appear to meet certain necessary conditions of a cinema-verite approach, especially regarding structure. The way the films are put together, not in a continuous chronology and with some degree of intellectual distance, would suggest that he is closer perhaps to more propagandistic documentary forms or at least to documentary traditions more concerned with persuasion and social reform. While Wiseman's relationship to cinema verite is irrelevant in terms of the films' importance, he is not a serious distance from the mainstream.

Wiseman's films show identical commitments to the key cinema-verite notions of uncontrolled shooting and "open" editing. While Wiseman's films are not personality oriented, his units of construction, or "scenes," still show complete, spontaneous situations. Scenes play themselves out with all the ambiguity characteristic of good cinema verite; while the films are mosaic in structure, the pieces are independently complete. Episodes are often quite long, as long as any in the films discussed previously. Wiseman never seems to take situations "out of context"; that is, the structural position of an episode does not in itself press a certain argument. While sequence is important in films structured more closely on fictional forms, Wiseman scenes (except for final "summing up" shots) look as if they could be switched around in a variety of permutations without altering possible meanings. As we have noted, in a film like *On the Pole* or *Salesman,* the meaning of a shot is often dependent upon our trust in "honest" editing, our faith that film chronology approximates actual chronology. Wiseman's films make no such demands.

Wiseman's structure can be seen as a development from the structure of repetition noted in the Maysles' films. (Once more, this is not to argue relative superiority.) If *Salesman* were played out, theoretically, within a defined area and with a variety of people instead of a few main characters, the result could be very close to a Wiseman film in structure. Structure develops in Wiseman's films from thematic repetitions, variations (for the most part) of his basic situation, the institutional employee and his "client." As is the case in most Maysles films, a greater number of scenes in a Wiseman film would not "tell us more"; there is no story that could be continued. One could carry over the argument that we learn no more from *High School* by the end than after the first ten minutes, but again that's part of the point. The institution is constantly defining itself. Also, we learn a great deal from the varieties of repetition, arguably more than if situations were more diverse. Wiseman even extends the possibilities in structural repetition by the cumulative effect of all the films and the variations from one to another.

Wiseman's "summing up" scenes are an important structural element, but while they give cause for re-evaluating all we've seen to that point, they do not argue for a perception of the institution at variance with the rest of the film (in the way that a dramatic climax might change our view of the characters). When a man at the end of *Law and Order* runs off out of frustration at the policeman's inability to solve his complex family problem, we do not alter our view of the police. We may see a final manifestation of conditions noted previously, but the nonsequential ordering of scenes prevents us from drawing tighter retrospective connections.

Wiseman demonstrates a faith in the complexity of uncontrolled events that his editing serves to magnify rather than restrict. His highly personal, subjective view of the world is committed to communicating that complexity. The subtexture of sophisticated argument does not obscure the films' sense of spontaneity and immediacy. He shows that cinema-verite filmmaking, with its refusal to intervene directly in the events under observation, does not imply social irresponsibility. A distanced filmmaker can still be a committed filmmaker.

Conclusion

The primary cinema-verite issues relate to the question of controlled forms for uncontrolled shooting. Given that no film can
ever break down completely the barrier between the real world
and the screen world, cinema verite knowingly reaches for un-
attainable goals. It is the necessary awareness of the relationship
between uncontrolled shooting and its possible structures that
makes cinema verite so disciplined and difficult an approach.
Cinema verite is not random filming.

If all that mattered in cinema verite was capturing "life as it is,"
there would be no reason to distinguish between Richard Leacock and any news cameraman, just as in photography Cartier-
Bresson would be equivalent to most amateurs. Cinema verite,
like all film forms, communicates meaning through selection.
Therefore, we cannot justify uncontrolled documentaries merely
by saying they appear more "real," nor can we pretend that these
films just happen.

If there has been one underlying goal in this study, it has been
to explore the tension within cinema verite regarding personal
style. While these filmmakers rarely invest meaning in controlled
images (through specific camera placement, cuts within sequences
for emphasis, and the like), their respective films do display certain measures of control that have to be considered as elements
of style. Cinema verite of the kind discussed here is a personal
cinema in a very literal sense, and we do not respond out of in-
stant recognition of unmodified truth. Instead, we react to seeing
events that, while presented within a meaningful structure, have
a force of their own, a force independent of questions of style.
Uncontrolled documentaries carry with them a sense of life going
on beyond the camera, of the filmmaker as only one aspect of a
larger reality. This is not a sense expressed through visual metaphor or expressive camera technique but a result of refusing to
make events subordinate to filming by means of direct control.

Out of its commitment to uncontrolled shooting, cinema verite
tends to personalities and events that in themselves are visibly
complex. The challenge seen in dealing with complex, uncon-

trolled events without reduction is a major element behind this filming approach, and consequently there are few cinema-verite films about passive, introspective people or about events free of ambiguity or at least of multiple components. Uncontrolled documentary does not seek to provide the "key" to an event, to break a situation down into its essential parts. Instead, it risks structural irrelevancy by allowing events to develop of their own accord.

Cinema verite extends its forfeiture of control to its relationship with an audience. The belief in the complexity of reality (though selection of events is crucial) has led to more than the seeking out of fresh material. Subjectivity does not express itself in terms of the filmmaker's passing judgment on his subject. It is impossible to know, and quite irrelevant, whether Leacock likes John Kennedy or the Ku Klux Klan, how the Maysles feel about Marlon Brando, or if Wiseman approves of monasteries. We should not be so burdened with a sense of inevitable expression of filmmaker point of view that we lose sight of the essentially open nature of the events in these films. Subjectivity expressed through subject matter preferences and structural tendencies is not equivalent to providing direct interpretation for an audience.

If there are fundamental differences among the filmmakers discussed here, they are expressed most strongly in structure and, through structure, content. The development of American cinema verite can best be seen as a search for new structures. The first films were strongly dependent upon fictional devices, although the primary commitment to uncontrolled shooting became evident as soon as the equipment made the realization of that goal possible. The preference for drama as expressed through crisis structures went hand-in-hand with a strong personality orientation, which depended on personalities of a particular type. When that type was missing *(Nehru, Petey and Johnny),* faults in structure were most evident.

As cinema verite moved away from recognizable dramatic structure, subject matter changes appeared as well. While Joe Levine might have been the subject of a "Living Camera" film, it is dif-

ficult to imagine later Maysles personalities treated within that
form. But the Maysles films are still very much about specific people, even more rigorously than the Drew films, which did on occasion seek to explore events of a complex nature, if always in
personal terms. The later Leacock and Pennebaker films represent further explorations in possible forms and varieties of subject
matter. *Happy Mother's Day* seems to glory (and rightly so) in the
challenge of its material and the approach taken to it, just as
Don't Look Back purposefully avoids providing expected kinds of
information. But in all these cases, structural and subject choices
can be seen as growing out of prior cinema-verite concerns.

   While Frederick Wiseman's films are markedly different, in an
overview some similarities are apparent. From *Meet Marlon Brando* and *Salesman* to Wiseman's films is not so much a grand
structural leap as a difference of interest; in both cases, there is
some common interest in structures dependent to an extent
upon repetition. Wiseman is not as free of influence from earlier
American cinema verite as might be thought. The institutional
orientation and common subject matter of *Football* mark it as a
clear precursor to *High School,* just as the salvation through
group therapy and close personal relationships in *David* anticipate *Essene.* The increasing tendency in Wiseman's films to
scenes of longer duration and the leaning in *Essene* toward a
greater degree of personality orientation (although neither is a
pronounced development) at least indicate a continuing concern
with structural approaches.

   The filmmakers discussed here are too few in number and the
time since their first films too brief to attempt any general assessment of cinema-verite possibilities. At this point, we can only hope
in the most tentative fashion to get a sense of the questions
involved in uncontrolled documentaries and some idea of the
purpose behind the approach. And as further explorations in uncontrolled documentary continue, we ought to be as free of pre-
conception as, ideally, the films are.

Notes

Cinema Verite: Definitions and Background

1. See, for example, Louis Marcorelles, "Le cinéma direct nord americain," *Image et Son,* No. 183 (April 1965): 47.

2. N. P. Abramov, *Dziga Vertov* (Lyon: Premier Plan, 1965), p. 15.

3. Georges Sadoul, "Dziga Vertov," *Artsept,* No. 2 (April/June 1963): 18.

4. Dziga Vertov, "Textes et Manifestes," *Cahiers du Cinéma,* No. 220–221 (May–June 1970): 7.

5. Dziga Vertov, "Kinoks-Revolution," *Cahiers du Cinéma* **24** (June 1963): 32.

6. Dziga Vertov, "The Writings of Dziga Vertov," *Film Culture,* No. 25 (Summer 1962): 55.

7. Ibid.

8. Vertov, "Textes et Manifestes," p. ll.

9. Vertov, "Writings," p. 58.

10. Ibid.

11. Sergei Tretyakov, quoted in Jay Leyda, *Kino* (London: George Allen and Unwin, 1960), p. 177.

12. For a discussion of category distinctions, see Georges Sadoul, "Actualité de Dziga Vertov," *Cahiers du Cinéma* **24** (June 1963): 23–31.

13. Vertov, "Textes et Manifestes," p. 15.

14. Ibid., p. 11.

15. Sadoul, "Actualité de Dziga Vertov," p. 30.

16. Vertov, "Textes et Manifestes," p. 15.

17. Vertov, "Writings," p. 57.

18. Ibid.

19. Ibid.

20. Ibid., p. 60.

21. Sadoul, "Actualité de Dziga Vertov," p. 26.

22. Ibid.

23. Vertov, "Writings," p. 58.

24. Sadoul, "Actualité de Dziga Vertov," p. 27.

25. Ibid., p. 28.

26. Citations in this paragraph are taken from *The Odyssey of a Film-maker* because it is in English, but a better-organized account strictly on Flaherty's technique can be found in "La Méthode de Robert Flaherty," a translation of a lecture given by Mrs. Flaherty in 1964, in *Image et Son,* No. 183 (April 1965), pp. 25–32.

27. Frances Flaherty, *The Odyssey of a Film-maker* (Urbana, Illinois: Beta Phi Mu, 1960), p. 11.

28. Ibid.

29. Ibid.

30. Quoted in Siegfried Kracauer, *Theory of Film: The Redemption of Physical Reality* (New York: Oxford University Press, 1965), p. 247.

31. Quoted in ibid., p. 260.

32. Edmund Carpenter, "Notes on Eskimo Art Film," in Arthur Calder-Marshall, *The Innocent Eye: The Life of Robert J. Flaherty* (New York: Harcourt, Brace and World, 1963), pp. 69–72.

33. Calder-Marshall, *The Innocent Eye,* p. 72.

34. Notes of Helen van Dongen in Karel Reisz and Gavin Millar, *The Technique of Film Editing,* 2nd ed. (New York: Hastings House, 1968), p. 136.

35. Calder-Marshall, *The Innocent Eye,* p. 222.

36. Ibid., p. 87.

37. Richard Griffith, *The World of Robert Flaherty* (New York: Duell, Sloan, and Pearce, 1953), pp. 164–165.

38. Robert Flaherty, "Robert Flaherty Talking," in *The Cinema 1950* (London: Pelican, 1950), p. 11.

39. Calder-Marshall, *The Innocent Eye,* p. 197.

40. Ibid., p. 193.

41. See photos of Flaherty and Leacock in Calder-Marshall, *The Innocent Eye,* between pp. 216 and 217.

42. Ibid., p. 220.

43. Gideon Bachmann, "The Frontiers of Realist Cinema: The Work of Ricky Leacock," *Film Culture,* No. 22–23 (Summer 1961): 14.

44. Ulrich Gregor, "Leacock Oder Das Kino Der Physiker," *Film* (Munich) **4** (January 1966): 15; Louis Marcorelles and André S. Labarthe, "Entretien avec Robert Drew et Richard Leacock," *Cahiers du Cinéma* **24** (February 1963): 18.

45. Cesare Zavattini, "Some Ideas on the Cinema," *Sight and Sound* **23** (July–September 1953): 64–70.

46. Ibid., p. 64.

47. Ibid., p. 65.

48. Cited in Eric Rhode, "Why Neo-realism Failed," *Sight and Sound* **30** (Winter 1960/61): 27.

49. Kracauer, *Theory of Film,* pp. 63–64.

50. Zavattini, "Some Ideas on the Cinema," p. 68.

51. Ibid.

52. Ibid.

53. Ibid., pp. 68-69.

54. Ibid., p. 69.

55. A. William Bluem, *Documentary in American Television* (New York: Hastings House, 1965), pp. 125–126.

56. Flaherty, "Robert Flaherty Talking," p. 12.

57. Bluem, *Documentary in American Television,* p. 126.

58. James Agee, *Agee on Film: Reviews and Comments* (New York: Grosset and Dunlap, 1967), p. 297.

59. Ibid.

60. Ibid., p. 298.

61. André Bazin, "Cinema and Television: Interview with Jean Renoir and Roberto Rossellini," *Sight and Sound* **23** (Winter 1958–59): 26–30.

62. Marcorelles and Labarthe, "Entretien avec Drew et Leacock," p. 27.

63. Bazin, "Cinema and Television," pp. 26–27. A nearly identical quote is used

at the beginning of the chapter on cinema verite in Reisz and Millar, *Technique of Film Editing,* p. 297.

64. Bazin, "Cinema and Television," p. 27.

65. Kracauer, *Theory of Film,* p. ix.

66. Ibid., p. 60.

67. Ibid., p. 212.

68. Ibid., p. 213.

69. Ibid., pp. 245–246.

70. Ibid., pp. 247–248.

71. Paul Rotha, *Documentary Film* (London: Faber and Faber, 1952), p. 106. Cited in Kracauer, *Theory of Film,* p. 247.

72. Kracauer, *Theory of Film,* p. 248.

Drew Associates

1. "Television's School of Storm and Stress," *Broadcasting* **60** (March 6, 1961): 83.

2. Louis Marcorelles and Andre S. Labarthe, "Entretien avec Robert Drew et Richard Leacock," *Cahiers du Cinéma* **24** (February 1963): 1'9.

3. Author's interview with Robert Drew. See page 127 for more on word and picture logic.

4. Marcorelles and Labarthe, "Entretien avec Drew et Leacock," p. 19.

5. Information in this paragraph has been taken from three sources: Ulrich Gregor, "Leacock Oder Das Kino Der Physiker," *Film* (Munich) **4** (January 1966): 14–15; Richard Leacock, "To Far Places With Camera and Soundtrack," *Films in Review* **1** (March 1950): 3; Robert Christgau, "Leacock Pennebaker: The MGM of the Underground?" *Show,* n.s. **1** (January 1970): 92.

6. Leacock, "To Far Places," p. 7.

7. Louis Marcorelles, "The Deep Well," *Contrast* **3** (Autumn 1964): 248.

8. Author's interview with Richard Leacock.

9. Gregor, "Leacock," p. 15.

10. James Blue, "One Man's Truth: An Interview with Richard Leacock," *Film Comment* **3** (Spring 1965): 20.

11. Author's interview with Richard Leacock.

12. Information in this paragraph has been taken from two sources: Ian Cameron and Mark Shivas, "Interview with Richard Leacock," *Movie,* No. 8 (April 1963): 16; Gregor, "Leacock," p. 15.

13. Marcorelles and Labarthe, "Entretien avec Drew et Leacock," p. 19.

14. Information from author's interviews with Robert Drew and Richard Leacock; "Television's School of Storm and Stress," p. 83.

15. James C. Lipscomb, "Cinéma-Vérité," *Film Quarterly* **17** (Winter 1964): 63.

16. Louis Marcorelles, "Le cinéma direct nord américain," *Image et Son,* No. 183 (April 1963): 52.

17. Christgau, "Leacock Pennebaker," p. 92.

18. Cameron and Shivas, "Interview with Leacook," p. 16.

19. Author's interview with Robert Drew.

20. Marcorelles and Labarthe, "Entretien avec Drew et Leacock," pp. 20–21.

21. Sarah Jennings, "An Interview with Terence Macartney-Filgate," in *Terence Macartney-Filgate: The Candid Eye,* ed. Charlotte Gobeil, Canadian Filmography Series, No. 4 (Ottowa, 1966), p. 6.

22. Author's interview with Richard Leacock; Gregor, "Leacock," p. 16.

23. George Bluestone, "The Intimate Documentary," *Television Quarterly* **4** (Spring 1965): 52.

24. Marcorelles and Labarthe, "Entretien avec Drew et Leacock," p. 21.

25. Author's interview with Richard Leacock.

26. Author's interview with Albert Maysles.

27. Author's interview with Richard Leacock.

28. Claude Julien, "Un homme dans la foule," *Artsept,* No. 2 (April/June 1963): 46.

29. Jean-Luc Godard, "Richard Leacock," in "Dictionaire de 121 Metteurs en Scène," *Cahiers du Cinéma* **25** (December 1963–January 1964): 140.

30. "Television's School of Storm and Stress," p. 83.

31. Author's interview with Robert Drew.

32. Robert Lewis Shayon, "The Fuse in the Documentary," *Saturday Review* **43** (December 17, 1960): 29.

33. Cesare Zavattini, "Some Ideas on the Cinema," *Sight and Sound* **23** (July–September 1953): 67.

34. A. William Bluem, *Documentary in American Television* (New York: Hastings House, 1965), pp. 128–130.

35. Ibid., p. 130.

36. Ibid., p. 134.

37. "Television's School of Storm and Stress," p. 84.

38. Paul-Louis Thirard, "Drew, Leacock and Co.," *Artsept,* No. 2 (April/June 1963): 43.

39. Louis Marcorelles, "L'Expérience Leacock," *Cahiers du Cinéma* **24** (February 1963): 17.

40. Gregor, "Leacock," p. 18.

41. Marcorelles and Labarthe, "Entretien avec Drew et Leacock," p. 26.

42. Louis Marcorelles, "American Diary," *Sight and Sound* **32** (Winter 1962--63): 5.

43. "Living Camera," *New York Herald Tribune,* August 11, 1964.

44. Bluem, *Documentary in American Television,* p. 195.

45. A good photo of the two-man crew filming on the train appears in ibid., p. 96.

46. Marcorelles and Labarthe, "Entretien avec Drew et Leacock," p. 26.

47. Colin Young, "Cinema of Common Sense," *Film Quarterly* **17** (Summer 1964): 27.

48. Ibid.

49. Marcorelles and Labarthe, "Entretien avec Drew et Leacock," p. 24.

50. Gerard Alcan, "Experimental Film-makers Who Make News," *Film World* **2** (1965–66): 168–169.

51. Henry Breitrose, "On the Search for the Real Nitty-Gritty: Problems and Possibilities in *Cinéma-Vérité,"'Film Quarterly* **17** (Summer 1964): 38.

52. Marcorelles and Labarthe, "Entretien avec Drew et Leacock," p. 25.

53. Breitrose, "The Real Nitty-Gritty," p. 38.

54. Marcorelles, "Le cinéma direct," p. 52.

55. Ibid.

56. Author's interview with D. A. Pennebaker.

57. Patricia Jaffe, "Editing Cinéma Vérité," *Film Comment* **3** (Summer 1965): 46.

58. Young, "Cinema of Common Sense," p. 28.

59. Marcorelles, "L'Experiénce Leacock," p. 15.

60. Cameron and Shivas, "Interview with Leacock," p. 18.

61. Young, "Cinema of Common Sense," p. 28.

62. Breitrose, "The Real Nitty-Gritty," p. 39.

63. Lipscomb, "Cinéma-Vérité," p. 63.

64. Gregor, "Leacock," p. 17.

65. Cameron and Shivas, "Interview with Leacock," p. 17.

66. Author's interview with Robert Drew.

67. Author's interview with Richard Leacock.

68. Jean-Claude Bringuier, "Libres propos sur le cinéma-vérité," *Cahiers du Cinema* **25** (July 1963): 16–17.

69. Cameron and Shivas, "Interview with Leacock," p. 18.

70. Young, "Cinema of Common Sense," p. 28.

71. Jane Fonda, "Jane," *Cahiers du Cinéma* **25** (December 1963–January 1964): 187.

72. Hal Seldes, "D. A. Pennebaker: The Truth at 24 Frames per Second," *Avant-Garde,* No. 7 (March 1969): 48.

73. Louis Marcorelles, "Nothing But the Truth," *Sight and Sound* **32** (Summer 1963): 116.

74. Ibid.

75. Author's interview with D. A. Pennebaker.

76. For a good illustrated synopsis see "The Chair," *Show* **4** (April 1964): 5l–55.

77. Marcorelles, "Nothing But the Truth," p. 115.

78. Louis Marcorelles, "La foire aux vérités," *Cahiers du Cinéma* **24** (May 1963): 30.

79. Robert Vas, "Meditation at 24 F.P.S.," *Sight and Sound* **35** (Summer 1966): 121.

80. Godard, "Richard Leacock," p. 140.

81. Cameron and Shivas, "Interview with Leacock," pp. 17–18.

82. Blue, "One Man's Truth," p. 19.

83. Ibid.

84. Antony Jay, "Actuality," *The Journal of the Society of Film and Television Arts,* No. 15 (Spring 1964): 6.

85. Val Adams, "TV Filmed Kennedys in Alabama Crisis," *New York Times,* July 25, 1963, p. 49.

86. "Not Macy's Window," *New York Times,* July 27, 1963, p. 16.

87. *New York Times,* August 7, 1963, p. 32.

88. Gregor, "Leacock," p. 16.

89. Information in this paragraph is from: John Horn, "Documentaries Score," *New York Herald Tribune,* October 22, 1963; Bluem, *Documentary in American Television,* pp. 131, 133, 249.

90. *New York Herald Tribune,* October 24, 1963.

91. Jack Gould, "TV: Too Many Cameras," *New York Times,* October 22, 1963, p. 75; and "Behind Closed Doors," *New York Times,* October 27, 1963, p. 3.

92. "Government on Camera," *New York Times,* October 23, 1963, p. 40.

93. Gould, "Behind Closed Doors," p. 3.

94. Gould, "TV: Too Many Cameras," p. 75.

95. "Documentarists on Documentary" in Bluem, *Documentary in American Television,* pp. 264–265.

Direct Cinema and the Crisis Structure

1. Louis Marcorelles and André S. Labarthe, "Entretien avec Robert Drew et Richard Leacock," *Cahiers du Cinéma* **24** (February 1963): 19.

2. Author's interview with Robert Drew.

3. Gideon Bachmann, "The Frontiers of Realist Cinema: The Work of Ricky Leacock," *Film Culture,* No. 22–23 (Summer 1961): 18.

4. Marcorelles and Labarthe, "Entretien avec Drew et Leacock," p. 24.

5. Ibid.

6. Author's interview with Robert Drew.

7. Patricia Jaffee, "Editing Cinéma Vérité," *Film Comment* **3** (Summer 1965): 44–45.

8. Louis Marcorelles, "Le cinéma direct nord américain," *Image et Son,* No. 183 (April 1965): 52.

9. "Documentarists on Documentary" in Bluem, *Documentary in American Television* (New York: Hastings House, 1965), p. 259.

10. Ibid.

11. Andrew Sarris, "Digging Dylan," in *Film 67/68,* ed. Richard Schickel et al. (New York: Simon and Schuster, 1968), p. 252.

12. Jean-Claude Bringuier, "Libres propos sur le cinéma-vérité," *Cahiers du Cinéma* **25** (July 1963): 16.

13. Author's interview with Robert Drew.

14. Ibid.

The Maysles Brothers

1. "Maysles Brothers," *Film Culture,* No. 42 (Fall 1966): 114.

2. Antony Jay, "Actuality," *The Journal of the Society of Film and Television Arts,* No. 15 (Spring 1964): 5.

3. A. William Bluem, *Documentary in American Television* (New York: Hastings House, 1965), p. 128.

4. See, for example: Gary Crowdus, "BeatleMANIA . . . and Cinema Verite," *The Seventh Art* **2** (Summer 1964): 29.

5. Louis Marcorelles, "Le cinéma direct nord américain," *Image et Son,* No. 183 (April 1965): 52–53. Patricia Jaffe makes a similar response to this scene in her "Editing Cinéma Vérité," *Film Comment* **3** (Summer 1965): 47.

6. Colin Young, "Cinema of Common Sense," *Film Quarterly* **17** (Summer 1964): 40.

7. Robert Steele, "Meet Marlon Brando," *Film Heritage* **2** (Fall 1966): 4.

8. Ibid., p. 2.

9. See page 131.

10. Steele, "Meet Marlon Brando," p. 4.

11. See Zwerin interview in Alan Rosenthal, *The New Documentary in Action: A Casebook in Film-Making* (Berkeley: University of California Press, 197I), pp. 86–91.

12. Rosenthal, *The New Documentary,* p. 81.

13. See, for example, James Blue, "Thoughts on Cinema Verite and a Discussion with the Maysles Brothers," *Film Comment* **2** (Fall 1964): 29; "Maysles Brothers," p. 114.

14. Joseph Gelmis, "A Drama Unfolds on the Road," *Newsday,* May 9, 1969, p. 48A.

15. Author's interview with David Maysles.

16. Albert and David Maysles, "Gimme Shelter: Production Notes," *Filmmaker's Newsletter* **5** (December 1971): 29.

D. A. Pennebaker

1. Pennebaker edited some of the material shot with Godard into a film called *One P.M.* Al Maysles also worked with Godard, as his cameraman for one episode of the fiction film *Paris vu par. . . .*

2. G. Roy Levin, *Documentary Explorations: 15 Interviews with Film-Makers* (Garden City, N.Y.: Doubleday, 1971), p. 230.

3. Alan Rosenthal, *The New Documentary in Action: A Casebook in Film-Making* (Berkeley: University of California Press, 197I), p. 192.

4. Levin, *Documentary Explorations,* p. 240.

5. Ibid., p. 260.

6. Ibid.

7. Ibid.

8. See, for example, the selection of review excerpts in D. A. Pennebaker, *Don't Look Back* (New York: Ballantine, 1963), pp. 156–l59.

9. *Keep On Rockin'* was originally titled *Sweet Toronto.* The name was changed

after the final segment, a performance by John Lennon, was cut from the film because of contractual problems.

Richard Leacock

1. Ulrich Gregor, "Leacock Oder Das Kino Der Physiker," *Film* (Munich) **4** (January 1966): 16.

2. Patricia Jaffe, "Editing Cinéma Vérité," *Film Comment* **3** (Summer 1965): 46.

3. Louis Marcorelles: "Le cinéma direct nord americain," *Image et Son,* No. 183 (April 1965): 54.

4. James Blue, "One Man's Truth: An Interview with Richard Leacock," *Film Comment* **3** (Spring 1965): p. 18.

5. Louis Marcorelles, "The Deep Well," *Contrast* **3** (Autumn 1964): 264.

6. Blue, "One Man's Truth," p. I7.

7. Author's interview with Richard Leacock.

8. Ibid.

9. Jaffe, "Editing Cinéma Vérité," p. 46.

10. Marcorelles, "The Deep Well," pp. 246–247.

11. Author's interview with Richard Leacock.

12. See, for example, comments on this film and *Chiefs* by Ed Pincus in G. Roy Levin, *Documentary Explorations: 15 Interviews with Film-Makers* (Garden City, N.Y.: Doubleday, 197I), p. 368.

13. Author's interview with Richard Leacock.

14. Blue, "One Man's Truth," p. 17.

15. Author's interview with Richard Leacock.

16. Ibid.

Frederick Wiseman

1. Beatrice Berg, "'I Was Fed Up With Hollywood Fantasies,'" *New York Times,* February 1, 1970, II, p. 25.

2. Author's interview with Frederick Wiseman.

3. The variety of responses to this one scene can be found in: Harvey G. Cox, "High School," *Tempo* **1** (June 15, 1969): 12; Charles E. Fager, "Sweet Revenge: High School," *Christian Century* **86** (September 3, 1969): 1142; Joseph Featherstone, "High School," *New Republic* **160** (June 21, 1969): 30; Pauline Kael, "High School," *New Yorker* **45** (October 18, 1969): 202–203.

4. Fred M. Hechinger, "A Look at Irrelevant Values," *New York Times,* March 23, 1969, p. 11; James Cass, "Don't You Talk—Just Listen!" *Saturday Review* **52** (April 19, 1969): 57.

5. Alan Rosenthal, *The New Documentary in Action: A Casebook in Film-Making* (Berkeley: University of California Press, 1971), p. 73.

6. "Public Documents," *Newsweék* **78** (October 4, 1971): 99.

7. Quoted in Stephen Mamber, "The New Documentaries of Frederick Wiseman," *Cinema* (Beverly Hills) **6** No. 1: p. 39.

8. William Paul, "Documentary Follies," *Village Voice,* October 8, 1970, p. 65; G. Roy Levin, *Documentary Explorations: 15 Interviews with Film-Makers* (Garden City, N.Y.: Doubleday, 1971), p. 322.

Filmographies

Drew Associates

This listing is based upon information supplied by Robert Drew, verified for the most part (with some additions and corrections) against credits as they appear in the films. Credits were written, according to Drew, on the basis of the group's "own code of meanings." To help clarify that code, explanations of the key credit terms, adapted from material supplied to the author by Robert Drew, follow.

Executive Producer: Editor-in-chief, assigns film ideas, oversees the shooting, and manages the editing

Filmmaker: Photographer or correspondent, who also partici-pates in planning and editing of the film

Correspondent: Journalist, organizer, sound-man during shoot-ing, who often also plans and participates in the editing of the film.

The breakdown of films by series refers to the initial American television showings, but the indicated date for each film is the year of completion (since some films were not publicly screened until well after they were made). In the absence of detailed in-formation, no films prior to *Primary* are included, although there is some discussion of the earlier films in the text.

Primary, 1960
Produced by Time-Life Broadcast. Executive Producer: Robert Drew. Filmmakers: Richard Leacock, D. A. Pennebaker, Terence Macartney-Filgate, Albert Maysles. Correspondent: Robert Drew. Editor: Robert Farren.

On the Pole, 1960
Coproduced by Time Inc. and Drew Associates. Executive Producer: Robert Drew. Filmmakers: Richard Leacock, D. A. Pennebaker, William Ray, Abbot Mills, Albert Maysles. Correspon-dents: James Lipscomb, Gregory Shuker. Editors: Larry Moyer, Robert Farren, Anita Posner.

"Close-Up!" (Films shown as part of ABC series of that name)

Yanki No!, 1960
Produced by Time-Life Broadcast. Executive Producer: Robert
Drew. Filmmaker: Richard Leacock, with Albert Maysles, D. A.
Pennebaker. Narrator: Joseph Julian. Translator: Patricia Powell.
Reporters: William Worthy, Quinera King. Editors: Robert Farren,
Stephen Schmidt, Zina Voynow.

X-Pilot, 1960
Coproduced by Time Inc., ABC-TV, and Drew Associates. Execu-
tive Producer: Robert Drew. Associate Producer: Howard
Sochurek. Filmmakers: Terence Macartney-Filgate, Albert
Maysles. Reporter: Gregory Shuker. Narrator: Joseph Julian.

The Children Were Watching, 1960
 Coproduced by Time Inc., ABC-TV, and Drew Associates. Exec-
utive Producer: Robert Drew. Filmmaker-Producer: Richard Lea-
cock. Photographer: Kenneth Snelson. Correspondents: Lee
Hall, Gregory Shuker. Editors: Zina Voynow, Stephen Schmidt.
Narrator: Joseph Julian.

Adventures on the New Frontier, 1961
Coproduced by Time Inc. and Drew Associates. Executive Pro-
ducer: Robert Drew. Filmmakers: Richard Leacock, D. A.
Pennebaker, Albert Maysles, Kenneth Snelson. Correspondents:
Lee Hall, Gregory Shuker, David Maysles. Reporters: Gerald
Feil, Jean Snow. Narrator: Joseph Julian. Editors: Robert
Farren, Anita Posner, Stephen Schmidt, Peggy Lawson, Larry
Moyer, George Johnson, Irwin Denis. Inaugural music courtesy
of U.S. Marine Band.

Kenya, Africa, 1961 (ABC Special)
Coproduced by Time Inc., ABC News, and Drew Associates.
Executive Producer: Robert Drew. Filmmaker-Producer: Richard
Leacock. Filmmaker: Albert Maysles. Correspondent: Gregory
Shuker. Technical Supervisor: Gerald Feil. Narrator: Joseph
Julian. Editors: Robert Farren, Larry Moyer, Robert Guenette.

On the Road to Button Bay, 1962 (CBS Special)
Coproduced by Time-Life Broadcast and Drew Associates. Executive Producer: Robert Drew. Filmmakers: Stanley Flink, Abbot Mills, Hope Ryden, James Lipscomb, Richard Leacock, D. A. Pennebaker. Assistants: Peter Eco, Alfred Wertheimer, Editors: Leon Prochnik, Saul Lanoa, Mike Jackson, Nancy Sen. Assistant Editors: Mara Janson, Tom Bywaters. Narrator: Garry Moore.

"Living Camera"

Eddie, 1961
Coproduced by Time-Life Broadcast and Drew Associates. Executive Producer: Robert Drew. Filmmakers: Richard Leacock, D. A. Pennebaker. Photographers: Albert Maysles, Abbot Mills, William Ray. Correspondents: Robert Drew, Gregory Shuker, James Lipscomb. Editors: Anita Posner, Robert Farren. Narrator: Joseph Julian.

David, 1961
Coproduced by Time-Life Broadcast and Drew Associates. Executive Producer: Robert Drew. Filmmakers: Gregory Shuker, D. A. Pennebaker, William Ray. Correspondent: Nell Cox. Editors: Hope Ryden, Betsy Taylor, Mike Jackson. Narrator: Joseph Julian.

Petey and Johnny, 1961
Coproduced by Time-Life Broadcast and Drew Associates. Executive Producer: Robert Drew. Producer: Richard Leacock. Filmmakers: James Lipscomb, Abbot Mills, William Ray. Assistants: Patricia Isaacs, Peter Powell. Editors: Patricia Jaffe, Patricia Powell. Narrator: Piri Thomas.

Football (Mooney vs. Fowle), 1961
Coproduced by Time-Life Broadcast and Drew Associates. Executive Producer: Robert Drew. Filmmaker: James Lipscomb. Photography of Coach Fowle: William Ray. Photography of Coach Mooney: Abbot Mills. Photography of Activities: Richard

Leacock, D. A. Pennebaker, Claude Fournier. Correspondents: Hope Ryden, Peter Powell. Editors: Leon Prochnik, Rosemary Hickson, Mike Jackson, Jerry Gold, Sol Landa, Bruce Torbet. Narrator: Joseph Julian.

Blackie, 1962
Coproduced by Time-Life Broadcast and Drew Associates. Executive Producer: Robert Drew. Filmmakers: William Ray, D. A. Pennebaker. Correspondents: Gregory Shuker, Peter Powell. Editors: Luke Bennett, Joyce Chopra. Narrator: Joseph Julian.

Susan Starr, 1962
Coproduced by Time-Life Broadcast and Drew Associates. Executive Producer: Robert Drew. Producers: Hope Ryden, Gregory Shuker. Filmmakers: Hope Ryden, D. A. Pennebaker. Photographers: D. A. Pennebaker, Claude Fournier, Peter Eco, James Eco, James Lipscomb, Abbot Mills, Richard Leacock, Correspondents: Hope Ryden, Patricia Isaacs, James Lencina, Sam Adams. Narrator: Joseph Julian.

Nehru, 1962
Coproduced by Time-Life Broadcast and Drew Associates. Executive Producer: Robert Drew. Filmmakers: Gregory Shuker, Richard Leacock. Editors: Joyce Chopra, Morten Lund, Gary Youngman.

The Aga Khan, 1962
Coproduced by Time-Life Broadcast and Drew Associates. Executive Producer: Robert Drew. Filmmakers: Gregory Shuker, D. A. Pennebaker, James Lipscomb. Editors: Ellen Huxley, Patricia Powell, Leon Prochnik, Nicholas Proferes, Harry Chapin.

Jane, 1962
Coproduced by Time-Life Broadcast and Drew Associates. Executive Producer: Robert Drew. Producer: Hope Ryden. Filmmakers: D. A. Pennebaker, Richard Leacock, Hope Ryden, Gregory Shuker, Abbot Mills. Editors: Nell Cox, Nancy Sen,

Eileen Nosworthy. Additional photography: James Lipscomb, Alfred Wertheimer.

The Chair, 1962
Coproduced by Time-Life Broadcast and Drew Associates. Executive Producer: Robert Drew. Filmmakers: Gregory Shuker, Richard Leacock, D. A. Pennebaker. Correspondents: Gregory Shuker, Robert Drew, John MacDonald, Sam Adams. Editors: Ellen Huxley, Joyce Chopra, Patricia Powell, Richard Leacock. Assistants: Gary Youngman, Sylvia Gilmour, Nick Proferes. Narrator: James Lipscomb.

Crisis: Behind a Presidential Commitment, 1963 (ABC Special)
Produced by ABC News. Executive Producer: Robert Drew. Producer: Gregory Shuker. Filmmakers: Richard Leacock, James Lipscomb, D. A. Pennebaker, Hope Ryden. Narrator: James Lipscomb. Editing Assistants: Nicholas Proferes, Eileen Nosworthy.

The Maysles Brothers
Information is based upon material provided the author by David Maysles but covers only those films discussed at length in the text. For fuller listing see Albert and David Maysles and Charlotte Zwerin, *Salesman,* pp. 127–128.

Showman, 1962
Produced by Albert and David Maysles. Filmmakers: Albert and David Maysles. Film Editors: Daniel Williams, with Tom Bywaters, Nancy Powell. Narration: Norman Rosten.

What's Happening! The Beatles in the U.S.A., 1964
A film by Albert and David Maysles.

Meet Marlon Brando, 1965
Produced by Maysles Films, Inc. A film by Albert and David Maysles. Edited by Charlotte Zwerin.

Salesman, 1969
A Maysles Films, Inc. Production. A film by the Maysles Brothers
and Charlotte Zwerin. Contributing Film Editor: Ellen Giffard.
Assistant Editor: Barbara Jarvis. Sound Mixer: Dick Vorisek.

Gimme Shelter, 1970
A Cinema V Release. Directed by David Maysles, Albert Maysles,
and Charlotte Zwerin. Camera: Albert Maysles and 22 others.
Sound: David Maysles and 14 others. Film Editors: Ellen Giffard,
Robert Farren, Joanne Burke, Kent McKinney.

D.A. Pennebaker

For a filmography of his own work compiled by the filmmaker,
see his contribution to G. Roy Levin, *Documentary Explorations,*
pp. 225–233.

Elizabeth and Mary, 1965
A film by Arthur E. Gillman, M.D., and D. A. Pennebaker.

Don't Look Back, 1966
Produced by Albert Grossman, John Cort, and Leacock Penne-
baker Inc. A film by D. A. Pennebaker, with Howard and Jones
Alk.

Monterey Pop, 1968
A Foundation Leacock Pennebaker Production. Directed and
Conceived by D. A. Pennebaker. Photography: James Desmond,
Barry Feinstein, Richard Leacock, Albert Maysles, Roger Mur-
phey, D. A. Pennebaker, Nick Proferes. Editor: Nina Schulman.

Original Cast Album: Company!, 1970
Produced by Talent Associates. A film by D. A. Pennebaker.
Photography: James Desmond, Richard Leacock, D. A. Penne-
baker.

Keep On Rockin', 1970
A film by D. A. Pennebaker. Photography: D. A. Pennebaker,
James Desmond, Richard Leiterman, Richard Leacock, Roger
Murphey, Barry Bergthorsen, Randy Franklin, Bob Neuwirth,
D. A. Pennebaker.

The Children's Theater of John Donahue, 1972
A film by D. A. Pennebaker. Photography: D. A. Pennebaker,
James Desmond. Sound: Kate Desmond.

Richard Leacock
For a filmography of his own work compiled by the filmmaker,
see his contribution to G. Roy Levin, *Documentary Explorations,*
pp. 195-199.

Happy Mother's Day, 1963
Made by Richard Leacock and Joyce Chopra, with Nancy Sen.
Narration: Ed McCurdy.

A Stravinsky Portrait, 1964
Photographer and Editor: Richard Leacock. Sound: Sarah Hudson. Producer: Rolf Liebermann for Norddeutscher Rundfunk.

Campaign Manager (Republicans — The New Breed), 1964
Filmmakers: Noel Parmentel, Richard Leacock, Nick Proferes.

Ku Klux Klan — The Invisible Empire, 1965
CBS Reports. Producer and Writer: David Lowe. Photography:
Richard Leacock. Sound: Noel Parmentel.

Chiefs, 1969
A film by Richard Leacock with Noel Parmentel.

Frederick Wiseman

Titicut Follies, 1967
Produced, Directed, and Edited by Frederick Wiseman. Codirected and Photographed by John Marshall.

Law and Order, 1969
Produced, Directed, and Edited by Frederick Wiseman. Photographed by William Brayne.

High School, 1969
Produced, Directed, and Edited by Frederick Wiseman. Photographed by Richard Leiterman.

Hospital, 1970
Produced, Directed, and Edited by Frederick Wiseman. Photographed by William Brayne.

Basic Training, 1971
Produced, Directed, and Edited by Frederick Wiseman. Photographed by William Brayne.

Essene, 1972
Produced, Directed, and Edited by Frederick Wiseman. Photographed by William Brayne.

Film Rental Sources

Drew Associates
The following films are available from Time-Life Films, 43 West 16th Street, New York, New York 10011:
Primary
Yanki, No!
The Children Were Watching
Adventures on the New Frontier
Kenya, Africa
Eddie
David
Petey and Johnny
Football (Mooney vs. Fowle)
Susan Starr
Nehru
Jane
The Chair
Crisis: Behind a Presidential Commitment
On the Road to Button Bay may be rented from Girl Scouts of the U.S.A., 830 Third Avenue, New York, New York 10022.

The Maysles Brothers
For all films through *Salesman* listed in the Filmography, write to Maysles Films, Inc., 1697 Broadway, New York, New York 10019. *Gimme Shelter* is available from Cinema V, 595 Madison Avenue, New York, New York 10022.

D.A. Pennebaker and Richard Leacock
Nearly all the films discussed in these chapters are available from Pennebaker Inc., 56 West 45th Street, New York, New York 10036.

Frederick Wiseman
Titicut Follies is rented by Grove Press Film Division, 214 Mercer Street, New York, New York 10011.
    All subsequent Wiseman films are available from Zipporah Films, 54 Lewis Wharf, Boston, Massachusetts 02110.

A Suggested Course Schedule

This twelve-program sequence is included as a possible guide to film educators and film societies. Films within each unit have been grouped to allow for direct connections and consequently to facilitate discussion. Each program runs approximately two hours. Selections have been made on the basis of availability and representativeness and with a desire to present material that raises a range of issues. Anyone planning a course or series along these lines is encouraged to consult the bibliography of this volume for supplementary material.

Primary
The Children Were Watching

Eddie
Football

Petey and Johnny
Nehru

Yanki, No!
Kenya, Africa

The Chair
Crisis: Behind a Presidential Commitment

Showman
What's Happening! The Beatles in the U.S.A.

Meet Marlon Brando
Salesman

David
Jane

Elizabeth and Mary
Don't Look Back

Happy Mother's Day
A Stravinsky Portrait
Campaign Manager

Chiefs
Law and Order

High School
Basic Training

Bibliography

Abramov, N. P. *Dziga Vertov*. Lyon: Premier Plan, 1965.

Adams, Val. "TV Filmed Kennedys in Alabama Crisis," *New York Times*, July 25, 1963, p. 1.

Agee, James. *Agee on Film: Reviews and Comments*. New York: Grosset and Dunlap, 1967.

Alcan, Gerard. "Experimental Film-makers Who Make News." *Film World* **2** (1965–66): 167–170.

Atkins, Thomas R. "Frederick Wiseman Documents the Dilemmas of Our Institutions." *Film News* **28** (October 1971): 14.

Bachmann, Gideon. "The Frontiers of Realist Cinema: The Work of Ricky Leacock." *Film Culture*, No. 22–23 (Summer 1961): 12–23.

Barnouw, Erik. *A History of Broadcasting in the United States: The Image Empire*, vol. III (1953–70). New York: Oxford University Press, 1970.

Barron, Arthur. "Network Television and the Personal Documentary." *Film Comment* **6** (Spring 1970): 16–19.

——. "Towards New Goals in Documentaries." *Film Library Quarterly* **2** (Winter 1968–69): 19–24.

Bazin, André. "Cinema and Television: Interview with Jean Renoir and Roberto Rossellini." *Sight and Sound* **28** (Winter 1958–59): 26–30.

Benayoun, Robert. "Où commence le témoignage?" *Positif*, No. 49 (December 1962): 23–28.

Berg, Beatrice. "'I Was Fed Up With Hollywood Fantasies.'" *New York Times*, February 1, 1970, pp. 25–26.

Blue, James. "Direct Cinema." *Film Comment* **4** (Fall/Winter 1967): 80–81.

——. "One Man's Truth: An Interview with Richard Leacock." *Film Comment* **3** (Spring 1965): 15–23.

——. "Thoughts on Cinéma Vérité and a Discussion with the Maysles Brothers." *Film Comment* **2** (Fall 1964): 22–30.

Bluem, A. William. *Documentary in American Television*. New York: Hastings House, 1965.

Bluestone, George. "The Intimate Documentary." *Television Quarterly* **4** (Spring 1965): 49–54.

Borov, Abbe. "Shooting Cinema Verite." *Filmmaker's Newsletter* **3** (January 1970): 4.

Bradlow, Paul. "Two . . . But Not of a Kind: A Comparison of Two Controversial Documentaries about Mental Illness, *Warrendale* and *Titicut Follies.*" *Film Comment* **5** (Fall 1969): 60–61.

Breitrose, Henry. "On the Search for the Real Nitty-Gritty: Problems and Possibilities in *Cinéma-Vérité.*" *Film Quarterly* **17** (Summer 1964): 36–40.

Bringuier, Jean-Claude. "Libres propos sur le cinéma-vérité." *Cahiers du Cinéma* **25** (July 1963): 14–17.

Calder-Marshall, Arthur. *The Innocent Eye: The Life of Robert J. Flaherty.* New York: Harcourt, Brace and World, 1963.

Callenbach, Ernest. "Acting, Being, and the Death of the Movie Aesthetic." *New American Review,* No. 8 (1970): 94–112.

———. "Going Out to the Subject: II." *Film Quarterly* **14** (Spring 1961): 38–40.

Cameron, Ian, and Shivas, Mark. "*Cinema-Vérité:* A Survey Including Interviews with Richard Leacock, Albert and David Maysles, William Klein, Jean Rouch, and Jacques Rozier." *Movie,* No. 8 (April 1963): 12–27.

Cass, James. "Don't You Talk—Just Listen!" *Saturday Review* **52** (April 19, 1969): 57.

"The Chair," *Show* **4** (April 1964): 51–55.

Christgau, Robert. "Leacock Pennebaker: The MGM of the Underground?" *Show,* n.s. **1** (January 1970), p. 34.

Coles, Robert. "Stripped Bare at the Follies." *New Republic* **158** (January 20, 1968): 18.

Cox, Harvey G. "High School." *Tempo* **1** (June 15, 1969): 12.

Craddock, John. "If . . . High School." *Film Society Review* **5** (September 1969): 30–38.

———. "Salesman." *Film Library Quarterly* **2** (Summer 1969): 8–12.

Crowdus, Gary. "BeatleMANIA . . and Cinema Verite." *The Seventh Art* **2** (Summer 1964): p. 15.

"Débat à propos de la punition et Showman." *Artsept,* No. 2 (April/June 1963): 101–104.

Denby, David. "Documenting America." *Atlantic* **225** (March 1970): 139–142.

Dowd, Nancy Ellen. "Popular Conventions." *Film Quarterly* **22** (Spring 1969): 26–31.

Fager, Charles E. "Sweet Revenge: High School." *Christian Century* **86** (September 3, 1969): 1141–1142.

Featherstone, Joseph. "High School." *New Republic* **160** (June 21, 1969): 28–30.

Flaherty, Frances. "La Méthode de Robert Flaherty." *Image et Son,* No. 183 (April 1965): 25–32.

———. *The Odyssey of a Film-Maker.* Urbana, Illinois: Beta Phi Mu, 1960.

Flaherty, Robert. "Robert Flaherty Talking" in *The Cinema 1950.* ed. Roger Manvell. London: Penguin, 1950, pp. 11–29.

Fonda, Jane. "Jane." *Cahiers du Cinéma* **25** (December 1963–January 1964): 182–190.

Friedenberg, Edgar Z. "Ship of Fools: The Films of Frederick Wiseman." *New York Review of Books* **17** (October 21, 1971): 19–22.

Gardner, Paul. "TV Series Joins Search for Truth." *New York Times,* October 5, 1964.

Gelmis, Joseph. "Camera Is Candid, as Is the Result." *Newsday,* May 8, 1969, p. 24A.

———. "A Drama Unfolds on the Road." *Newsday,* May 9, 1969, p. 48A.

Gerard, Edmund Bert. "The Truth About Cinema Verite." *American Cinematographer* **50** (May 1969): 474.

Gobeil, Charlotte, ed. *Terence Macartney-Filgate: The Candid Eye.* Ottawa: Canadian Filmography Series, 1966.

Godard, Jean-Luc. "Richard Leacock" in "Dictionnaire de 121 Metteurs en Scene." *Cahiers du Cinéma* **25** (December 1963–January 1964): 139–140.

Gould, Jack. "Behind Closed Doors." *New York Times,* October 27, 1963, p. 3.

———. "TV: A.B.C. Goes to Latin America." *New York Times,* December 8, 1960.

———. "TV: Too Many Cameras." *New York Times,* October 22, 1963, p. 75.

"Government on Camera." *New York Times,* October 23, 1963, p. 40.

Graham, John. "There Are No Simple Answers: Frederick Wiseman on Viewing Film." *The Film Journal* **1** (Spring 1971): 38–47.

Graham, Peter. "*Cinéma-Vérité* in France." *Film Quarterly* **17** (Summer 1964): 30–36.

Gregor, Ulrich. "Leacock Oder Das Kino Der Physiker," *Film* (Munich) **4** (January 1966): 14–19.

Griffith, Richard. *The World of Robert Flaherty*. New York: Duell, Sloan, and Pearce, 1953.

Haleff, Maxine. "The Maysles Brothers and 'Direct Cinema.'" *Film Comment* **2** (Spring 1964): 19–22.

Handleman, Janet. "An Interview with Frederick Wiseman." *Film Library Quarterly* **3** (Summer 1970): 5.

Hechinger, Fred M. "A Look at Irrelevant Values." *New York Times,* March 23, 1969, p. 11.

Hitchens, Gordon. "Half a Dozen Avant-Gardes." *Film Society Review,* May 1968, p. 35.

Horn, John. "A Criticism of 'Crisis' Program's Critics." *New York Herald Tribune,* October 25, 1963.

———. "Documentaries Score." *New York Herald Tribune,* October, 22, 1963.

———. "'The Living Camera' Turns Out a Disappointment." *New York Herald Tribune,* October 8, 1964.

"How do teachers react to *High School?*" *American Teacher* **54** (February 1970): 13.

Jacobs, Lewis. *The Documentary Tradition: From Nanook to Woodstock*. New York: Hopkinson and Blake, 1971.

Jaffe, Patricia. "Editing Cinéma Vérité." *Film Comment* **3** (Summer 1965): 43–47.

Jay, Antony. "Actuality." *The Journal of the Society of Film and Television Arts,* No. 15 (Spring 1964): 5–7.

Jersey, William. "Some Observations on Cinema Verite." *Motive* **27** (November 1966): 11–12.

———. "Some Thoughts on Film Technique." *Film Comment* **2** (Winter 1964): 15–16.

Julien, Claude. "Un homme dans la foule." *Artsept,* No. 2 (April/June 1963): 45–48.

Kael, Pauline. "High School," *New Yorker* **45** (October 18, 1969): 199–204.

Kolker, Robert P. "Circumstantial Evidence: An Interview wiith Albert and David Maysles." *Sight and Sound* **40** (Autumn 1971): 183–191.

Kracauer, Siegfried. *Theory of Film: The Redemption of Physical Reality.* New York: Oxford University Press, 1965.

Leacock, Richard. "La Caméra Passe-Partout." *Cahiers du Cinéma* **16** (April 1959): 37–38.

———. "For an Uncontrolled Cinema." *Film Culture,* No. 22–23 (Summer 1961): 23–25.

———. "Mixed Media, Film, and Opera." *Theatre Crafts* **2** (March/April 1968): 29–35.

———. "Ricky Leacock on 'Stravinsky' Film." *Film Culture* No. 42 (Fall 1966): 113.

———. "To Far Places With Camera and Sound-track." *Films in Review* **1** (March 1950): 3–7.

Levin, G. Roy. *Documentary Explorations: 15 Interviews with Film-Makers.* Garden City, N.Y.: Doubleday, 1971.

Lipscomb, James C. "Cinéma-Vérité," *Film Quarterly,* 17 (Winter 1964), pp. 62–63.

McLean, Deckle. "The Man Who Made *Titicut Follies.*" *Boston Sunday Globe,* July 17, 1969, p. 10.

McWilliams, Donald E. "Frederick Wiseman." Film Quarterly **24** (Fall 1970): 17–30.

Mamber, Stephen. "High School." *Film Quarterly* **23** (Spring 1970): 48–51.

———. "The New Documentaries of Frederick Wiseman." *Cinema* (Beverly Hills) **6** (No. 1): 33–40.

Marcorelles, Louis. "American Diary." *Sight and Sound* **32** (Winter 1962–63): 4–8.

———. "Le cinéma direct nord américain." *Image et Son,* No. 183 (April 1965): 47–54.

———. "The Deep Well." *Contrast* **3** (Autumn 1964): 246–249.

———. *Direct Cinema, Aesthetic of Reality.* Paris: UNESCO, 1964.

———. *Eléments pour un nouveau cinéma.* Paris, UNESCO, 1970.

———. "L'Expérience Leacock." *Cahiers du Cinéma* **24** (February 1963): 11–17.

———. "La foire aux vérités." *Cahiers du Cinéma* **24** (May 1963): 26–34.

———. "Nothing But the Truth." *Sight and Sound* **32** (Summer 1963): 114–117.

———, and Labarthe, André S. "Entretien avec Robert Drew et Richard Leacock." *Cahiers du Cinéma* **24** (February 1963): 18–27.

Maysles, Albert and David. "Gimme Shelter: Production Notes." *Filmmaker's Newsletter* **5** (December 1971): 28–31.

———, and Zwerin, Charlotte. *Salesman.* New York: Signet, 1969.

"Maysles Brothers." *Film Culture,* No. 42 (Fall 1966): 114.

Mekas, Jonas. "Movie Journal: Short Conversation with Ricky Leacock." *Village Voice* **17** (February 10, 1972): 59.

———. "Notes on the New American Cinema." *Film Culture,* No. 24 (Spring 1962): 6–16.

"No Business in Show Business." *New York Herald Tribune,* October 24, 1963.

"Not Macy's Window." *New York Times,* July 27, 1963, p. 16.

"Open Program at N.Y. Fest Draws Acclaim; Wiseman's Views on Films." *Variety* **256** (October 8, 1969): 6.

Paul, William. "Documentary Follies." *Village Voice,* October 8, 1970, p. 54.

Pennebaker, D. A. *Don't Look Back.* New York: Ballantine, 1968.

"Public Documents." *Newsweek* **78** (October 4, 1971): 99.

Reisz, Karel, and Millar, Gavin. *The Technique of Film Editing.* 2nd ed. New York: Hastings House, 1968.

Rhode, Eric. "Why Neo-realism Failed." *Sight and Sound* **30** (Winter 1960/61): 26–32.

Rosenthal, Alan. *The New Documentary in Action: A Casebook in Film-Making.* Berkeley: University of California Press, 1971.

Rotha, Paul. Documentary Film. London: Faber and Faber, 1952.

Ruspoli, Mario. *The Light-Weight Synchronized Cinematographic Unit.* Paris: UNESCO, 1964.

Sadoul, Georges. "Actualité de Dziga Vertov." *Cahiers du Cinéma* **24** (June 1963): 23–31.

———. "Dziga Vertov." *Artsept,* No. 2 (April/June 1963): 18–19.

———. "Dziga Vertov." *Image et Son,* No. 183 (April 1965): 8–18.

———. *Dziga Vertov*. Paris: Editions Champs Libre, 1971.

Sarris, Andrew. "Digging Dylan" in *Film 67/68*, eds. Richard Schickel and John Simon. New York: Simon and Schuster, 1968, pp. 248–253.

———. "Film: The Illusion of Naturalism." *TDR: The Drama Review* **13** (Winter 1968): 108–112.

———. "The Independent Cinema." *Motive* **27** (November 1966): 28–31.

Seldes, Hal. "D. A. Pennebaker: The Truth at 24 Frames per Second." *Avant-Garde*, No. 7 (March 1969): 46–49.

Shayon, Robert Lewis. "The Fuse in the Documentary." *Saturday Review* **43** (December 17, 1960): 29.

Sitton, Bob. "An Interview with Albert and David Maysles." *Film Library Quarterly* **2** (Summer 1969): 13–19.

Steele, Robert. "Meet Marlon Brando." *Film Heritage* **2** (Fall 1966): 2–5.

Swallow, Norman. *Factual Television*. New York: Hastings House, 1966.

"Television's School of Storm and Stress." *Broadcasting* **60** (March 6, 1961): 82–84.

"Tempest in a Snakepit." *Newsweek* **70** (December 4, 1967): 109.

Thirard, Paul-Louis. "Drew, Leacock, and C°." *Artsept*, No. 2 (April/June 1963): 41–44.

Thomson, David. *Movie Man*. New York: Stein and Day, 1967.

Vas, Robert. "Meditation at 24 F.P.S." *Sight and Sound* **35** (Summer 1966): 119–124.

Vertov, Dziga. "Kinoks-Revolution." *Cahiers du Cinéma* **24** (June 1963): 32–34; **25** (August 1963): 18–20.

———. "Textes et Manifestes." *Cahiers du Cinéma*, No. 220–221 (May–June 1970): 7–16.

———. "The Writings of Dziga Vertov," *Film Culture*, No. 25 (Summer 1962): 50.

Waddell, Mike. "*Cinema Verite* and the Documentary Film." *American Cinematographer* **49** (October 1968): 754.

Wakefield, Dan. "American Close-ups." *Atlantic* **223** (May 1969): 107–108.

Weyergans, Francis. "Le fins [sic] et le moyen." *Cahiers du Cinema* **22** (June 1962): 34–40.

Yglesias, Jose. "Whose Truth?" *The Nation,* October 23, 1967, pp. 410–412.

Young, Colin. "Cinema of Common Sense." *Film Quarterly* **17** (Summer 1964): 26.

———. "Film and Social Change." *The Journal of Aesthetic Education* **3** (July 1969): 21–27.

Zavattini, Cesare. "Some Ideas on the Cinema." *Sight and Sound* **23** (July–September 1953): 64–70.

Zimmerman, Paul D. "Shooting It Like It Is." *Newsweek* **73** (March 17, 1969): 134–135.

Index